IN SEARCH OF THE AWESOME MYSTERY

Seán Ó Duinn OSB

In Search of the
Awesome Mystery

LORE OF MEGALITHIC, CELTIC AND
CHRISTIAN IRELAND

the columba press

First edition, 2011, published by
the columba press
55A Spruce Avenue, Stillorgan Industrial Park,
Blackrock, Co Dublin

Cover by Bill Bolger
Origination by The Columba Press
Printed in Ireland by Gemini International Ltd

ISBN 978 1 85607 745 3

Contents

CHAPTER ONE

God, the Awesome

The rabbit emerged from the dark hedge to cross the road. His long ears picked up the sound of some tremendous force rushing towards him. The lights of the oncoming car fascinated him so that, dazzled, he crouched down unable to move, rooted to the spot. The car mowed him down. He died instantly confronting an awesome force over which he had no control.

The two words used here, 'fascinated' and 'tremendous', are significant. '*Tremendum et Fascinans*' is the phrase used by the great theologian Rudolf Otto in his treatment of the subject of worship and the confrontation of the human with the divine. God, the divine, is both awesome and fascinating and very, very dangerous. We find that we cannot turn away from him completely and yet we are overcome by his power and magnificence. This results in the cry 'Come, let us worship' for worship, bowing down in awe before the majesty of God, is the natural reaction to the human's confrontation with the divine.

Chapter 19 of the Book of Exodus describes the Theophany or 'God-revealing' on Mount Sinai where God reveals himself to Moses and the people of Israel through terrifying eruptions of natural forces: '... there were peals of thunder and flashes of lightening, dense cloud on the mountain and a very loud trumpet blast; and in the camp, all the people trembled. Then Moses led the people out of the camp to meet God; and they took their stand at the bottom of the mountain. Mount Sinai was entirely wrapped in smoke, because Yahweh had descended on it in the form of fire. The smoke rose like smoke from a furnace and the whole mountain shook violently.' (16-18).

'Experiencing all this, the people were all terrified and kept their distance' (Ex 20:18).

Similarly, a biblical account (2 Sam 6:1-11) describes King

David and a vast crowd bringing the great and holy treasure, the Ark of the Covenant, to Jerusalem, with tremendous rejoicing. The Ark rests on a cart pulled by oxen and at one point where the ground is uneven the oxen stumble. A man called Uzzah put his hand on the Ark to steady it, 'and God smote him there because he put forth his hand to the Ark and he died there beside the Ark of God ... And David was afraid of the Lord that day.'

Another well-known account of the appearance of God to a human being is the biblical story of the Burning Bush. In the story Moses sees a bush which is on fire and yet it is not being burned. He draws near to examine this phenomenon more closely. Then 'God called to him from the middle of the bush. "Moses, Moses", he said. "Here I am", he answered. "Come no nearer", he said. "Take off your sandals, for the place where your are standing is holy ground. I am the God of your ancestors", he said, "the God of Abraham, the God of Isaac and the God of Jacob". At this Moses covered his face, for he was afraid to look at God' (Ex 3:4-6).

In this case, then, the human being, when confronted by the mystery of God, covered his face and took off his shoes. It seems that this was a natural, instinctive reaction – the man wanted to hide himself and place a barrier, however inadequate, a veil, between himself and the divine. By taking off his shoes he put himself into immediate contact with the earth as if hiding in it and becoming one with it as a frightened child flees to his mother. We will encounter again these two phenomena – the veil and the removal of shoes in the context the ancient liturgies of the Oriental churches.

Turning, then, from the Bible to the native tradition of Ireland, we find a colourful account of the worship of the god Crom Cróich in the Rennes *Dindsenchas* (*Rev Celt,XVI* (1895), No 85) associated with Maigh Sléacht near Ballymagauran, Co Cavan.

The Dinnseanchas begins in the ordinary way: 'Magh Slécht, canas roainmniged?' 'Ní ansa' – 'Maigh Sléacht, how is it so named?' 'Not difficult'. 'There was there the king-idol of Ireland, namely the Crom Cróich, and around him were twelve idols made of stones; but he was of gold. Until Patrick's coming, he was the god of every folk that colonised Ireland. To him they used to offer the firstlings of every issue and the firstborn of every clan. It is to him that Ireland's king, Tigernmas son of Follach, came at Samhain (Halloween), together with the men and women of Ireland, in order to adore him. And they all prostrated before him, so that the tops of their foreheads and the gristle of their noses and the caps of their knees and the ends of their elbows broke, and three fourths of the men of Ireland perished at those prostrations. Whence 'Maigh Sléacht' – the Plain of Prostrations.'

In quite a remarkable piece of research, John P. Dalton on 'Cromm Cruaich of Magh Sléacht' (*PRIA*, 1922, Sect C, 23-67) identified the site of Crom Cruaich's extensive sanctuary in Maigh Sléacht near the village of Ballymagauran in Co Cavan and the site of the statue of the god along with 'his sub-gods twelve' at Darraugh Rath – a very large high-banked lios on an elevated site overlooking the lake-dotted plain of Maigh Sléacht below.

Today, this well-preserved rath is enormously impressive and, although no signs of the idols are visible, one can easily imagine Crom Cruaich looking down with disdain on his worshippers on the plain below from his exalted position on the hill. He occupied an elevated position separated by height and space from the plain below which was the domain of the populace – a situation not un-like the layout of a traditional Christian church in which the sanct-uary, reserved to the priests and their assistants, occupies an ele-vated position separated from the lower nave, which is the place of the congregation. A further comparison may be remarked in the custom of many churches in having the offerings of bread and wine placed in the middle of the nave. Likewise, it was on the level plain below that the worshippers of Crom Cruaich deposited their offerings. If the offerings consisted of corn, cattle and children this would have occupied a large space, which in fact Maigh Sléacht is. A considerable distance, then, would have separated the worship-pers from the god, expressing vividly the idea that the people were not anxious to approach Crom Cruaich too closely while at the same time making sure to pay their respects – an attitude not unlike the traditional Irishman who kneels at the back of the church during Mass and obstinately refuses to budge from there. Strangely enough, Christ commends the tax-collector who came to the temple but 'stood some distance away, not daring even to raise his eyes to heaven; but he beat his breast and said "God, be merciful to me, a sinner"'. (Lk 18:13).

If the level area at the foot of the hill-sanctuary served as the space in which the people brought offerings of very considerable bulk, such as sheaves of corn, bags of oats and barley as well as livestock, there must have been a highly organised system of dealing with this and storing the produce. It would have involved officials to serve as 'sacristans' who may have lived in local forts such as Rath Sléacht giving access to the Plain of Prostrations.

But, on the other hand, we may ask if the grain and other offerings were stored in buildings of some kind to be consumed gradually, who actually consumed them? Perhaps the local officials in charge of the cult of Crom Cróich were given a part of the offerings for their own use as would be expected. This would account for some of the produce offered to the god. These thatched wooden buildings would have disappeared with the passing of the centuries and the advent of the new religion of Christianity. But what of Crom Cróich's own portion?

Presumably Crom was a supernatural being, a divine entity, and would not eat the corn offered him as a human being would. But he might be considered as consuming the vital essence of the corn, the unseen core or spiritual centre suitable for a supernatural being while the outward part might be left to decay in special offertory trenches built for the purpose. In Psalm 50 (49) the Hebrew God says to the people: 'Do I eat the flesh of bulls, or drink the blood of goats? Offer to God a sacrifice of thanksgiving and pay your vows to the Most High.' What God wanted in this case was the inner dispositions of the people's heart – their feelings of thanksgiving to him for favours received and their admission of dependence on him. The two ideas are not exclusive and the outword sacrifice of cattle and grain was to be an outward expression of the inward submission of mind and heart.

It is doubtful if Crom Cróich was quite so spiritually minded as to concern himself with the dispositions of his worshippers, but the consumption of the vital essence of the offerings by the god while leaving their outward substance is an idea found expressed in a different context among the funeral rites of the Todas of the hills of southern India.

The funeral rites are celebrated within a stone circle and the ashes from the cremated body are finally buried at the entrance to a ring of stones. The body is first laid on a bier and set down near the funeral pyre which burns very slowly. The body is wrapped in a cloak furnished with a large pocket and into this the mourners put their funeral offerings such as money, ornaments and various small luxuries as they pay their respects. The body is swung over the fire three times and then set down again. As the bier swings over the fire it is believed that the soul of the deceased takes flight to the other world taking with it the offerings which the people have contributed. But it is the inner essence of the offerings which go with the dead man to the other world. The outward substance still remains. This being so, the contributors put their hands in the pocket of the deceased's cloak and recover what they have given. Naturally, the people consider this to be a very satisfactory operation – as well they might. The dead man has received desireable gifts from his friends which he will use in the other world while the contributors have suffered no loss by this transaction – a highly satisfactory arrangement all round based on a very clear distinction between the inner essence of the offerings and the external substance (cf Vulliamy, 1926, 131-133).

The account of the people's worship of Crom Cróich is continued by the Christian narrative of an episode in the life of St Patrick in which the saint comes into contact with the god. The 'Quarta Vita' (Colgan, 'Triadis Thaumaturgae', Acta Lovanii 1647, cap. liii) tells the story:

There was a certain idol (in Mag) Slécht adorned with gold and silver, and twelve gods made of copper placed on this side and on that facing the idol. Now the king and the whole people used to adore this idol, in which lurked a very bad demon who used to give answers to the people, wherefore they worshipped him as a god. St Patrick, moreover, when preaching all around, came to the plain in which the idol was situated and, lifting his right hand threatened to overthrow the idol with the 'Staff of Jesus' which he held in his hand. But the demon, who was in the idol, fearing St Patrick, turned the stone towards its right side, and the mark of the staff still remains in its left side; and yet the staff did not leave the saint's hand. Moreover, the earth swallowed the twelve other images up to their heads, which alone remain to be seen in memory of the miracle. The demon, indeed who (had) lurked for a long time in the idol and deluded men, came forth at St Patrick's command.When the peoples with their king, Loegaire, saw him they were afraid, and asked St Patrick to command the horrible monster to leave their presence. St Patrick ordered him to depart into the abyss. Then all the peoples gave thanks to Almighty God who deigned to deliver them through St Patrick from the power of darkness.

This Latin text of the 8th or 9th century takes the tradition of Crom Cróich quite seriously and interprets it in a typical Christian fashion and mentions a significant item not recorded in the Dinnseanchas, that is, that this 'very bad demon used to give answers to the people' (*in quo daemon pessimus latitabat; qui responsa populis dare solebat*). In other words, this was an oracular deity/demon and Maigh Sléacht a sanctuary in which oracles took place like the great oracular temple of Apollo at Delphi. In the texts we have seen so far, two kings are mentioned – Laoghaire and Tigernmas – both of them associated with Tara. If Maigh Sléacht were an oracular site it is to be expected that kings would undertake the journey from their own kingdoms to consult the oracle on matters of state. From Greece comes the story of the reinstitution of the Olympic Games by King Iphitos of Elis, a shadowy figure of the 9th century BC. He is said to have re-established the Games on the advice he had received from the Delphic Oracle. The king had asked the Oracle how to end the civil wars and pestilence which was gradually destroying the land of Greece. The priestess advised him to restore the Olympic Games and declare a truce for their duration (Swaddling, 2004, 10).

With regard to oracles being a feature of the sanctuary of Maigh Sléacht, a curious piece of information is provided by Maire MacNéill in her great work *The Festival of Lughnasa* (Dublin 1982, Vol 1, 177-179). Not far to the north of Darraugh Fort, the presumed sanctuary of Crom Cróich, lies the hill of Benaghlin (*Binn Eachlainn* or *Binn Eachlabhra*) in Co Fermanagh. From its peak can be seen the ancient patrimony of the Maguires (*Maguidhir*).

This hill was a venue for the celebration of the Festival of Lughnasa on *Domhnach Chrom Duibh* the last Sunday in July. On this Sunday large crowds of people gathered on Binn Eachlabhra to admire the view, pick *fraocháin* (bilberries) and visit the caves of which there are many in the limestone highlands of southern Fermanagh, and generally entertain themselves with dancing, fiddling and wrestling as at other Lughnasa sites. The Binn Eachlabhra gatherings continued until the 1940s. Only four miles away at Cill Naile is another Lughnasa sight and within a 20 mile radius there are several others including significantly The Black Rocks or Maguire's Chair from where Darraugh Fort – the supposed site of Crom Cróich – is visible. Some held that in pagan times there was a connection between the two sites.

Both The Black Rocks and Binn Eachlabhra are dominated by the Cuilcagh mountains. There is a tradition of runaway marriages in connection with the Lughnasa gatherings in this area as at the Tailtean Weddings in Co Meath. The area is richly endowed with antiquities from the Bronze Age and at one time may have been thickly populated.

Binn Eachlabhra is considered to be a particularly numinous place inhabited by Donn na Binne MagUidhir, the first prince of Fermanagh and now deified as belonging to the Irish Pantheon, the Tuatha Dé Danann – the goddesses and gods of Ireland. The Maguires were often assisted in battle by Donn na Binne, their deified ancestor.

An extract from a local tale explains the practices associated with this particular site:

Do chuir (Tromcheo Draoídheachta) a litreacha agus a theachta uadh d'iarraidh cuidigh ... go Donn Binn Eachlabhra ris a ráidhtear Binn Eachlúna anois, as coigeadh Uladh; agus is uime dearthar Binn Eachlabhra ris an mbinn sin .i. a dtráthaibh na Samhna do thigeadh each sleamhain slíocaidh móruathbhásach as an mbinn amach go nuige a lár agus do labhradh do ghuth daonda fria cách agus do bhéaradh fios foirfe fíreolgach do gach neach dá n-iarrrfadh sgéala air fá gach ní dá n-éireochadh dhó go ceann bliadhna uadh an tSamhuin sin agus dfhaigfidís pronntaidh agus tíodhlacthaidh móra aice ann sin .i. aig an mbinn agus do ghéillidís na puible go haimsir Phádruig agus na naomhchléire dhi (MacNeill,1982,1, 178).

(Tromcheo Draoédheachta sent letters and messages from Ulster to Donn Binn Eachlabhra – Donn of the Speaking-Horse Mountain seeking help. It is called Binn Eachlúna now. And the reason it is called that is that at Samhaintide (1st November) a slippery, sleek, great-horror horse used to come out of the mountain up to his middle and used to talk to everybody in a human voice and he used to give accurate truly-enlightened knowledge to anybody who asked him for information regarding all that would happen to him from that Samhain to the end of the year. And they would leave food and large offerings to it – at the mountain, and the people submitted to it (*dhi* – her – the mountain) until the time of Patrick and the holy clerics.)

(It is clear from the original Irish that the horse was male while the mountain (*Binn*) is a feminine noun.)

Here the oracular tradition of the two sites – Binn Eachlabhra, sacred to Donn and Darraugh Fort, sacred to Crom Cróich is clearly centred on the Feast of Samhain. This is to be expected because in Irish tradition Samhain (Halloween) is the beginning of the dark half of the year – from Samhain to Bealtaine (1st May). The bright half is from Bealtaine to Samhain. Then, since the Celts calculated the day as beginning with sunset on the previous night in a movement from darkness to light, so the year began with winter making Samhain New Year's Eve from our point of view. There is a vestige of this system in the Liturgy of the Catholic and Orthodox churches where on great Feasts First Vespers or Evening Prayer of the Feast is sung on the Eve – the evening before. For instance, the Feast of St John the Baptist is on 24 June. The celebration of the Feast, however, begins on the previous evening 23 June. In modern practice, many Catholics go to

Sunday Mass on Saturday evening on the grounds that Sunday begins at sunset on Saturday. This corresponds to the Celtic system though, of course, in the church it springs from Jewish sources.

Samhain, New Year's Eve, the beginning of the year is naturally the occasion for divination, for foretelling what is to happen to us during the coming year and a remnant of this is to be found in the traditional domestic celebration of Samhain where four plates are placed on a table. One contains water, another earth, another a ring and the fourth salt. The person who wants to know his destiny for the coming year is blindfolded and touches a plate. Water means emmigration; earth death; the ring marriage and salt prosperity. This is fundamentally the same idea of prognostication, or foretelling the future for the coming year, as that practised at Maigh Sléacht and Binn Eachlabhra but on a reduced scale.

Nor is this idea of Samhain divination limited to the sacred cultic area of north-west Cavan. In the ancient story *Airne Fíngein*, the *Bean Sí* Rothniamh emerges from Sí Chliach on Cnoc Áine, the sanctuary of the goddess Áine near the village of Hospital (*Ospidéal Áine*) in Co Limerick, on the night of Samhain, to inform Fínghein, the local king, of the political events to take place during the coming year.

In this case, it is not a magical horse who gives the information but Roth Niamh (shining wheel – sun / moon) a *Bean Sí* or member of the Tuatha Dé Danann from the sacred hill-sanctuary (Sí) of Áine, the local fertility goddess. In all three cases a uniform pattern is evident – a supernatural being gives information regarding events of the coming year at Samhain and this takes place at a sacred site or sanctuary of the Celtic deities.

A Welsh text based on the *Historia Regum* of Geoffrey of Monmouth says: 'In the islands there are sixty cliffs and an eagle's nest on each cliff; and once a year the eagles come together and by their cries they announce such events as will occur in the kingdom from this to the end of the year' (Vendryes, J., 1953,xix).

It will be noted that the divination tradition belongs to the Feast of Samhain both in Binn Eachlabhra, over the border from Cavan, and in Maigh Sléacht itself.

As is clear from the Dinnseanchas it was at Samhain also that the offerings were brought to Crom Cróich. This is the natural time for such offerings, as the harvest has just been completed. There was an abundance of corn and farmers sometimes killed off cattle that they may not have been able to feed during the long months of winter. This was the period when agricultural produce was at its most abundant. So this was the time for people to pay their taxes to Crom Cróich, the harvest God, for having given them an abundant harvest. If they contributed generously there was the hope that he would give them another prosperous harvest next year. Again, a remnant of this may be discerned in the rites of Samhain today. Young people in extravagant dress, masked and carrying the 'aghaidh fidil' or turnip-lantern go from house to house collecting money or goods. The belief is that if the householder treats them generously he will have a prosperous year but if they are treated badly misfortune will invade the house for the coming year. If the 'Geamairí' or mummers represent the Tuatha Dé Danann, or ancient gods who control the fertility of the land, they are in the position of being supernatural tax collectors for Crom.

So, the key to the interpretation of the Maigh Sléacht accounts in the Dinnseanchas and the Patrician documents may be found in the Samhain rites of the present day, if it is remembered that what is a small domesticised and mostly children's performance today was once a major public celebration involving a lot of people, cattle, foodstuffs, and extending over an extensive land area.

We get a clearer view of the supernatural tax-collecting, reward-punishment ensemble (what the Americans call 'trick or treat') from the way in which the Rite of Samhain was performed in parts of Gaelic Scotland.

The masked Geamairí went from house to house collecting, but in this case they were grown-up men, not children and what they wanted was whiskey.

In many Scottish houses the fire was in the centre of the room – not against the wall. This arrangement was convenient for ritual movements. If the householder was very generous and treated the Geamairí well they lined up one after another and walked around the fire proceeding '*deiseal*' – keeping the fire at their right hand.   This is the well-known Celtic ritual movement – the '*Cor deiseal*' or sunwise movement around a sacred object often seen at Holy Wells. The performers follow the course of the sun – a propitious movement to establish the householders in the order of the cosmos. This will bring good luck to the family for the coming year.

If, on the other hand, it proves to be a stingy household and they are treated badly, the Geamairí go around the fire proceeding '*tuathal*' – going against the sun (anticlockwise). This ritual will bring bad luck to the house as it is not in accordance with cosmic order.

It is evident that the Rite of Samhain was a serious matter, having repercussions for the family and wider community. What is remarkable, however, is that the Samhain bonfire, which forms so important a part of the traditional celebration, is not mentioned in the writings on Maigh Sléacht.

Micheál Ó Duigeannáin, in a rather critical approach to Maigh Sléacht (*On the Medieval Sources for the Legend of Cenn (Crom) Cróich of Mag Slícht*, 1940/1995) concludes that 'whatever claims Mag Slécht may have as the local centre of some widespread cult, it certainly was not what O'Curry, in a moment of fervour, called it: "the Delphos of our Gadelian ancestors".'

Ó Duigeannáin (*Féil-Scríbhinn Eoin Mhic Néill*, 1940/1995) conveniently gathers together in one place the relevant sources regarding the worship of Crom Cróich at Maigh Sléacht from *Leabhar Gabhála Éireann*, the *Metrical Dinnseanchas*, the *Prose Dinnseanchas*, the Patrician Sources – Colgan's '*Quarta Vita*', Colgan's '*Tertia Vita*' and the '*Vita Tripartita*'.

He admits, however, that the folklore of *Domhnach Chrom Dubh* or Garland Sunday would have to be taken into account in any discussion of Maigh Sléacht as a great religious site of the pagan past. Here, he seems to equate Crom Cróich of Maigh Sléacht with the widely venerated harvest god Crom Dubh, and indeed, this equation would be widely accepted. He was of course writing over forty years previous to Maire MacNéill's research on the cult of Crom Dubh in her great masterpiece *The Festival of Lughnasa*

(Oxford 1962).

By putting the various documents together we can arrive at a comprehensive view of the data on Crom Cróich of Maigh Sléacht:

1 The king idol of Ireland (*rig-hidhal Hérenn*) was in Maigh Sléacht (*LG*)
2 He caused every 'tuath' to be without peace (*Met D*)
3 The idol was of stone and it was decorated with gold and silver (*V 4*)
4 12 gods made of copper were here and there facing Crom (*V4*)
5 Four times three idols of stone in rows (*Na srethaib – trí hídail chloch fo chethair*) (*Met D*)
6 Twelve other idols covered with copper were around him (*dá ídal déac aili cumdachta ó umai imme*) (*V Tri*)
7 The people used to ask him for milk and corn (*Met D*)
8 From the kingship of Eremon to St Patrick worship had been paid to stones (*Met D*)
9 Crom Cróich was the god of every group that took Ireland until the coming of Patrick (*Pro D*)
10 A demon lurked in the idol
11 He used to answer the peoples' questions and so they worshipped him as a god (*V4*)
12 The idol faced the south (south-east?) towards Tara

Features of the worship of Crom

13 The Gaeil used to adore him (*Met D*)
14 They used to offer the first-born of every stock to Crom (*Pro D*)
15 They used to offer the first-born of every family to Crom (*Met D*), (*Pro D*)
16 The King of Ireland, Tigernmas Mac Follaich, came to Maigh Sléacht with the men and women of Ireland to adore Crom (*Pro D*), (*Met D*), (*LG*)
17 This occurred at Samhain (*Pro D*), (*Met D*), (*LG*)
18 King Laoghaire also used to adore Crom at Maigh Sléacht (*V3*)
19 The crowds used to prostrate around Crom, the name cleaves to the great plain (the Plain of Prostrations) (*Met D*)
20 Tigernmas, with three fourths of the Men of Ireland around him,

21 died at the great assembly (*Immórdáil Maige Slécht*) worshipping Crom Cróich (*LG*), (*Pro D*)

22 4000 fell at the prostrations (*Pro D*)

23 They all prostrated before Crom until their foreheads, and the soft part of their noses, and the caps of their knees, and the points of their elbows broke; so that three fourths of the Men of Ireland died at these prostrations. Hence the name Maigh Sléacht (*Pro D*)

24 This is the reason why Maigh Seanaigh (the original name) is now called Maigh Sléacht (*Met D*)

St Patrick's confrontation with Crom Cróich

25 Patrick used a sledge-hammer on Crom from head to foot. He removed with rough usage the weak monster that was there (*Met D*)

26 St Patrick came to the plain where the idol was situated and threatened to overthrow the idol with the 'Staff of Jesus' which he held in his hand (*V4*)

27 The demon, fearing Patrick, turned the stone towards its right side and on the left hand side of the stone the mark of the crozier still remains (*V4*)

28 Yet, the crozier did not leave the saint's hand (*V4*)

29 The earth swallowed the other twelve idols up to their heads (*V4*)

30 Only these heads remain in memory of the miracle (*V4*)

31 At St Patrick's command the demon emerged from the stone (*V4*)

32 King Laoghaire and his people were afraid and asked Patrick to banish the horrible monster (*V4*)

33 St Patrick ordered the demon to depart into the abyss (*V4*)

34 Then all the people gave thanks to Almighty God who deigned to deliver them through St Patrick from the powers of darkness (*V4*)

35 And at St Patrick's prayer the image which the peoples adored was broken up and reduced to ashes (*V3*)

36 Patrick founded a church in that place – Domhnach Maighe Sléacht – and put his relative Mabran in charge of it (*V*

Tripartita)

37 Patrick's Well is there also in which he baptised many (*V Tripartita*)

While the details of the story vary slightly, it is a remarkably clear account of the worship of the god Crom Cróich at Maigh Sléacht so that he would give his people an abundance of food – *blicht agus ith* – milk and corn – and answer their questions regarding the future.

Crom is seen here as a god with a widespread cult with Maigh Sléacht as an important central shrine to which the kings of Tara with their numerous followers came on pilgrimage.

Patrick may have seen it as a serious rival to the Christian centre he wanted to establish in Armagh, and O'Curry's idea of Maigh Sléacht as a kind of Irish Delphi may have been a real insight rather than a product of a 'moment of fervour'.

According to the *Vita Tripartita* Patrick first saw the idol from the water called *Guth Ard*. This, undoubtedly is Garadice Lake (*Guth Ard Theas* – South Guth Ard). In the *Metrical Dinnseanchas* King Tigernmas and his crowd of pilgrims from Tara approached Maigh Sléacht with considerable misgivings: 'They beat palms, they bruised bodies, wailing to the demon who had enslaved them' – the lamentations (*ac coi ri demun rosdaer*) may have given the name to the lake – *Guth Ard Theas* – South Loud Voice.

Dalton opines that a direct path led from Tara to Maigh Sléacht and that this was taken by the royal pilgrims Tigernmas and Laoghaire and by St Patrick himself. Passing through Granard, they would have arrived at Tuam Sheanchaidh and sailed across Lough Garradice to the entrance to the sanctuary of Crom Cróich.

Dalton points out that near Carrigallen are two Tobair Phádraig which may recall Patrick's activity. Obviously, the motives of the various visitors to Maigh Sléacht were different – the pagan pilgrims came as worshippers of Crom Cróich while Patrick came as a fervent missionary of a new religion bent on overthrowing him.

From the Maigh Réin, or Newtowngore side of Lake Garadice 'the eye is instantly arrested by the graceful outlines of Darraugh, as well as by the venerable aspect of the quaint rath-frontlet' (Dalton, op cit, 29) If the whole account were not a fantasy, here was Maigh Sléacht, the site of Crom's sanctuary.

This sanctuary extended over a landscape of hills, woods, level land and lakes. This is a site where earth and water meet – a 'threshold area' evocative of the meeting of the divine and the human.

At the top of the wonderfully detailed map produced by Dalton, the mountains of Cuilcagh and Sliabh Rossan and Binn Eachlabhra delineate the ritual area to the north, while in the south a line may be drawn from Killeshandra to Fenagh Abbey. Within this area of about 15 miles by 12 lie a great number of ancient sites of various types to testify to its sanctity.

From the north-west the Blackwater makes its way windingly into Garadice Lake and on the other side is the river Gráinne. In the triangle formed by the meeting of these two rivers in the extensive lake area, Darraugh Rath is situated on a high level, and this, according to Dalton, is the site of the holy place of Crom Cróich/ Cruaich or Cenn (Ceann) Cruaich – the head of the hill. The name Darraugh is probably connected with '*Dair, darach, doire*' – a place associated with oak trees and 2000 years ago the area may have been more densely wooded than it is today. Moreover, Dalton maintains that the water area may have been more extensive also so that it extended partially around the foot of the hill on which the rath is situated. This phenomenon of isolating the *Neimheadh* or sanctuary and making it somewhat inaccessible is a feature of another sacred site associated with the *Fomhóraigh* or dark gods on the coast of Sligo of which we will see further later. At any rate, the partial isolation of the sacred place, the separation of the sacred from the profane would be in accordance with the worship-traditions of many races. There is the biblical tradition of the Holy of Holies which only the High Priest entered and that only once a year. A continuation of this feature is plainly seen in churches of the Byzantine, Syrian and Coptic Rites where a screen with curtains separates the sanctuary from the nave.

Close to Darraugh Rath is the 'fair green' of Ballymagauran where from time immemorial fairs have been held at the two pivotal points of the Celtic year – Samhain and Bealtaine (1 November and 1 May).

The church – Domhnach Maighe Sléacht – in the area was

founded by St Patrick and a rath once enclosed the building and the graveyard. Only a part of the enclosing rampart now survives in Kilnavart. St Patrick's Well was near and a tradition states that the saint performed a pilgrimage on his knees from the well to the church. There are church ruins on Garadice Lake, and on Mogue Island on Templeport Lake there are the remains of the church of St MoAodhÓg.

Another Tobar Phádraig is placed to the north-west near Brackley Lake and still another near a bend in the Blackwater not far south of Bunerky Lake. Again, a Tobar Phádraig is found in the Crimlin townland of Maigh Réin in Co Leitrim about two miles south of the Cavan border. Could this possibly be 'Cromlinn'? – Crom's pool?

Southwards from this is St Caillin's monastery and holy well – Fenagh Abbey. His feastday is on 13 November – the significant date of Samhain.

Such a profusion of early ecclesiastical sites in a small area dotted with remains of an earlier race would indicate that the early Christian missionaries considered it important to establish the church there in a very definite way and, as it were, invading the enemy camp.

We have seen that two annual fairs were held at Samhain and Bealtaine at the fair green of Ballymagauran (*Baile Mhic Shamhradháin*) and that Samhain was the feast associated with Crom Cróich himself. This leads to the idea of the possibility of a ritual calendar – not a calendar hanging on the wall – but a calendar laid out on the landscape for pilgrimage purposes so that a specific shrine could be visited by the worshippers on a specific day or period in the course of a yearly cycle.

The calendar in daily use today is of course based fundamentally on the 'Four Stations of the Sun'. At four times in the course of the year the sun seems to behave in a peculiar way which can be observed and noted by the people of the earth, and this enables them to pinpoint certain key periods of the cycle.

On 21 December we have the shortest day of the year – the Winter Solstice. For the past six months the sun has been weakening – it has been rising each day a little further to the south with the result that the days have become shorter and shorter until the Winter Solstice when the sun recovers, as it were, and begins to rise a little further to the north each morning so that the day is becoming longer and this increase in sunlight continues until the sun reaches its most northerly rising point at the Summer Solstic (21 June) and from that time on it begins to decline again. The beam of light from the rising sun entering the megalithic monument at Brú na Bóinne (Newgrange) at the Winter Solstice is a remarkable calendrical marker which has been functioning for 5000 years. If, for instance, in the simplest possible way, one were to put up a stone for each day beginning on the day after the sun entered Newgrange, by the time you had collected 365 stones you were back at the Winter Solstice again. The Winter Solstice is emphatically marked in Ireland by the Newgrange phenomenon, the Feast of Christmas and the ancient rite of the 'Dreoilín' – 'Hunting the Wren'.

On the other pivot of the year – the Summer Solstice – bonfires blaze to encourage the declining sun to keep up its strength to ripen the corn and to honour St John the Baptist whose birthday it is. The church took over this calendar by putting the Birth of Christ (the Light of the world) at the Winter Solstice when the light is increasing and the Birth of St John the Baptist who was six months older than Our Lord at the Summer Solstice when the light was decreasing. This corresponds to the Baptist's saying regarding Christ: 'He must increase and I must decrease' (John 3:30).

The other two 'Stations of the Sun' are the Equinoxes, the Spring Equinox (21 March) and the Autumn Equinox (21 September). At these points the sun rises exactly in the east so that night and day are of equal length. Upon these 'Four Stations of the Sun' our calendar is based.

The insular Celts of Ireland and Wales, however, introduced four other feasts into this basic solar calendar. These are the well-known Feasts of Samhain (1 November), Imbolg (Féile Bríde) (1 February), Bealtaine (1 May) and Lughnasa (1 August). These introduce the four seasons and it will be noticed that each of them falls exactly half way between the solar feasts. For instance, Samhain occurs half way between the Autumn Equinox and the Winter Solstice while Bealtaine occurs half way between the

Spring Equinox and the Summer Solstice.

The reason for the introduction of these festivals is not entirely clear but they seem to be linked up with major points of the agricultural year as would be expected from a people whose civilisation was rural rather than urban.

The custom of the '*Buaile*' persisted until comparatively modern times. At Bealtaine with the arrival of summer the cows were taken up to the hills for summer grazing. Younger people accompanied them to do the milking, butter and cheese-making. They lived in makeshift huts for the duration, and at Samhain as the weather turned cold, the cows were brought down to the low sheltered fields near the farmhouse.

It is surmised that the constellation of the *Pleides* (The 7 Sisters) played a part in this and that the cows remained below from Samhain to Bealtaine while the Pleides were high in the night sky. Then at Bealtaine, Maya the principal sister, is supposed to perform a little farewell dance and lead the others down below the horizon. This is the signal for the cows to the taken up to the hills. So in this charming legend there is a kind of see-saw action between the affairs of earth and sky – when the cows go up the 7 Sisters come down and when the cows come down the 7 Sisters go up. In Irish the word for Pleides is *An Treidín* – the little herd – giving again the idea of a heavenly and an earthly herd.

The numerous Tobair Phádraig or St Patrick's Wells in this area, with the 'Pattern' or '*Turas*' – pilgrimage – to them on St Patrick's Day (17 March) – is a significant date – the Spring Equinox, the beginning of the year . 'Lady Day' – 25 March, the Feast of the Annunciation of the Blessed Virgin Mary – was the official start of the year in Britain until the British belatedly adopted Pope Gregory's Calendar in 1752 (Danaher, 1972, 67). For much of Europe, the Spring Equinox was associated with Easter – the first Sunday after the first full moon after the Spring Equinox – with new growth of vegetation, the increase of herds, all spoke of rejuvenation and new beginnings. In accord with this, St Patrick's Feast occurs at this time to emphasise that this is a new beginning, the introduction of a new religion and a new mentality.

A short distance west of the Lughnasa site Binn Eachlabhra

with its talking horse is another Lughnasa site – at Cill Náile – the Church of Náile – a saint also venerated at Inver in Donegal. His Feast is on 27 January, coinciding with the Celtic Feast of Imbolc. At Magauran Fair, then, Samhain and Bealtaine were celebrated at the same site and similarly at Cill Náile Imbolc and Lughnasa were celebrated. At these two sites one could celebrate the full complement of the four Celtic Feasts of the year by visiting them on the appropriate dates and performing the appropriate ritual.

Again, the ruins of St Mogue's (MoAodhÓg) church are in St Mogue's Island in Templeport Lake close to Darraugh Rath. While belonging to Breifne, he became Bishop of Ferns and was a dominant figure in the ecclesiastical life of the south-east. His feast-day is on 31 January coinciding with Imbolc.

Dalton's map lists several Lughnasa sites: Binn Eachlabhra, Cill Náile, one near a bend on the Blackwater River, one near a bend on the Claddagh River and one at Scararoo.

The feastday of St Caillín of Fenagh Abbey is again on a strikingly significant date – 13 November – a Samhain date.

Dotted around this labyrintine landscape of lakes, islands, mountains, hills, woods are sites to which pilgrimages were made and at which rituals were performed at the four feasts of the Celtic Calendar embracing the cycle of the year. In terms of extent this is a small area of about 15 miles square but it contains numerous ritual sites. This may be due to the presence of Crom Cróich's ritual centre sending its influence outwards towards the whole of Maigh Sléacht with the other lesser sites concentrating on the celebration of Lughnasa while the central site emphasised Samhain. This may not be the case, however, if it is taken into account that Lughnasa may be a later introduction and due to the defeat of Balor of the Evil Eye (probably Crom Cróich in another guise) by Lugh Lámhfhada at the Battle of Maigh Tuireadh.

Flowing near Darraugh Rath is the river Gráinne (Woodford River) which divided the ancient territory of Breifne into West Breifne ruled by Ó Ruairc and East Breifne ruled by Ó Raghlaigh, the two great dynastic families of that region. The County Coat of Arms shows two circles of wavy lines, symbolising the watery lake-filled terrain, surrounded by three lions. The two rampant lions are from the arms of Ó Raghlaigh while the lion passant is from the arms of Ó Ruairc. The motto '*Feardhacht is Fírinne*' (Manliness and Truth) is associated with Ó Raghlaigh.

The definitive location of Crom Cróich, however, is difficult to ascertain due to the number of megalithic remains in this area of Killycluggin, Kilnavert and Lissanover near Ballymaguaran but near Kilnavert there is a hill called 'Crom Cruaich', so that, at any rate, we are in the vicinity of the sanctuary.

The recent writer Cary Meehan, in her magnificent book *The Traveller's Guide to Sacred Ireland* (Gothic Image 2002), lays much stress on the Killycluggin Stone now in the County Museum in Ballyjamesduff and suggests that this may have been Crom Cróich himself. The injury to the top of the stone might correspond to the tradition of St Patrick hitting him on the head with his crozier.

This stone is a rounded boulder probably originally about five feet tall. It is elaborately decorated with spirals interconnected with La Tene style patterns, and resembles the Turoe Stone in Galway and the Castlestrange Stone in Roscommon. It stood at one time outside the Stone Circle in Killycluggin as a kind of outlier. The circle still exists though some of the stones have fallen, and trees grow around it making it a very impressive and mysterious site. A replica of the Killycluggin Stone stands at the side of the road so that it is readily accessible to visitors. Killycluggin is of Christian derivation being '*Cill a' Chlogáin*' – the church of the little bell.

What is called in English the Woodford River flows past these sites associated with Crom Cróich. In the original Irish it bears the significant name of '*Gráinne*' – a name familiar from the romance '*Toraíocht Dhiarmada agus Ghráinne*' in which Gráinne escapes from her intended husband Fionn Mac Cumhaill and elopes with the hero Diarmaid Ó Duibhne. The medieval romance, however, may hint that Gráinne, with her predilection for alternating husbands, was originally a goddess. The name is possibly associated with grain (*grán*) or ugliness (*gránnacht*). Its significance in this cultic context is that Gráinne the river is, like nearly all rivers in Ireland, feminine. Now, presumably like other gods such as An

Daghdha's marriage to the MórRíoghan at the River Uinnius as described in 'Cath Maighe Tuireadh' and likewise Lugh's marriage to Baoi after his great victory over Balar of the Evil Eye (Crom Cróich in another guise) in the same battle, (cf Tochmarc Emire) it is reasonable to suppose that Crom the corn god also married a goddess.

This marriage could be expressed in different ways. The most obvious one is the custom of the 'Cailleach' or last sheaf of the harvest. This is a well-known usage in Ireland, England and Scotland and involved special attention to the very last sheaf in the last cornfield of the farm to be reaped. It was felt that this was the grain goddess who was being evicted from her own domain so that a certain degree of reluctance accompanied the cutting of the last piece of corn in which she had been forced to take refuge. In some places the last piece of standing corn was bound in the middle and the mowers stood back and threw their sickles at it as if to avoid as far as possible personal responsibility for killing the goddess. The 'Cailleach' (old hag) was brought home and hung up in the house or sometimes buried in the land or sometimes the grains were taken off the straw and mixed with the seed-grain for next year's harvest. In other words, the Cailleach joined the corn-god in marriage to ensure next year's harvest.

In some places the last sheaf was called the 'Bride'/'Oats Bride'/'Wheat Bride' and in parts of Germany the corn-spirit was personified in double form as an Oats-Bridegroom and an Oats-Bride, both swathed in straw like the 'Strawboys' in Ireland. They danced together at the harvest festival.

At the great Stone Circle at Grange, Co Limerick, within the Lough Gur megalithic complex stands a huge stone, much bigger than all the others, to the righthand side of the entrance passage. This was known as Rannach Chruim Dhuibh, otherwise 'Ronadh Crom Dubh' (MacNéill, 1982, 346; 594) The exact meaning of Rannach is unknown but in view of its connection with Crom Dubh/Crom Cruaich/Crom Cróich and the harvest, one wonders if it is connected with 'rann' – a part, a division, a portion – referring in this context to Crom's Portion – of the offering of sheaves of corn or other goods to Crom at Samhain or Lughnasa.

This immense stone could be the Offertory Table at which the people laid their sheaves of corn as an offering to Crom. Local tradition of the Lough Gur area associate it with Lughnasa celebrations, horse racing, and Crom Dubh or 'Black Stoop', bent (*crom*) down under the weight of corn he carried on his back. This echoes Cary Meehan's description of the marriage of the harvest god with the corn-maiden in her discussion of the Killycluggin Stone at Maigh Sléacht:

> This stone stood at one time outside the stone circle in Killycluggin and was decorated all over with gold. It repre-sented the god Crom Cruach, or Crom Dubh who is the dark god, the 'bent one' who receives the 'first fruits' at Lughnasa or harvest in the form of the corn maiden, and carries her on his back down into his underground kingdom. This ritual or 'sac-rifice' ensured the continuing fertility of the earth. The 11 stones of the nearby circle formed his court' (2002, 75).

It may be remarked that the great father-god An Daghdha carries the goddesss daughter of Indech of the Fomhóraigh on his back in the scurrilous account in *Cath Maighe Tuireadh* (Grey, 1982, Sect 93).

In the matter of the worship of Crom Cróich / Crom Dubh we can distinguish two separate Feasts – Lughnasa itself – *Domhnach Chrom Dubh* (c.1 August) or the last Sunday in July or the first Sunday of August. Perhaps the most spectacular expression of the Festival of Lughnasa remaining today is 'Puck Fair' in Killorglin, Co Kerry, lasting for three days at the beginning of August where a great white Puck Goat from the Kerry Mountains presides over the fair from a high platform. He represents Crom Dubh for this is the time of the first fruits of the harvest. The first of the corn is ripe and the rest will follow in due course. The festival atmosphere of the fair reminds Crom Dubh, as Lord of the Harvest, to continue the good work of ripening the rest of the corn. The Festival of Lughnasa serves as a first-fruits festival somewhat on the lines of the Jewish practice: 'The Lord spoke to Moses, saying: Speak to the children of Israel, and thou shalt say to them: When you shall have entered into the land which I will give you, and shall reap your corn, you shall bring sheaves of ears, the first fruits of your harvest, to the priest, who shall lift up the sheaf before the Lord' (Leviticus 22: 9-11). This tradition was preserved in the Pentecost Ember Days of the Tridentine *Missale Romanum* but, of course, the harvest in Italy would occurs nearly two months earlier than in Ireland, in May rather than in August.

The Feast of Samhain (1 November) came at the end of the harvest, when the corn had been reaped and brought into the barns. This was the time of plenty and this was the time that taxes had to be paid to Crom Cróich/Dubh. Some cattle would also be killed but this may have been a practical necessity due to insufficient fodder to bring them through the winter. While Lughnasa and Samhain were the two pivotal points, the mystique of the corn involved the whole year as is evident from *Cath Maighe Tuireadh*: 'Spring for ploughing and sowing, and the beginning of summer for maturing the strength of the grain, and the beginning of autumn for the full ripeness of the grain and for reaping it. Winter for consuming it' (Grey, 1982, 157). The four Celtic Festivals of Samhain, Imbolc, Bealtaine and Lughnasa marked the beginning of the seasons.

Following this system, it is at Samhain that the *Hieros Gamos* or sacred marriage between the corn god and the corn goddess would take place. Nine months later, at Lughnasa, the ripened sheaf of corn would be placed on the sacred Lughnasa Hill – the belly of the earth goddess, the Great Mother.

Bringing the sheaves of corn, representing the earth-goddess, to the 'Cromleac' – Crom's stone/flag – may have been symbolic of the sacred marriage of god and goddess. In Egypt, cultic images were often taken from their cloistered sanctuaries and carried in procession on portable boats for quite long journeys. The goddess Hathor of Dendera travelled over 100 miles each way to visit Horus of Edfu for the yearly consummation of their sacred marriage (Bell, 1998, 134).

Megalithic monuments often occupy a situation close to water whether a river, stream or lake. It is a phenomenon often remarked on by researchers, and local legends tell of stones going to the river or lake to bathe or drink at certain times. One wonders if here there is not a dim folk-memory of a megalith representing the god being taken to the local river or lake and doused in it as a symbolic mating of god and goddess of the harvest. Or, what is more likely to have happened, a bucket of water from the lake or river being thrown over the megalith – the meeting of stone and water symbolising the sacred marriage.

Frazer gives an account of the Egyptian custom of providing a 'Bride of the Nile'. The life of Egypt was bound up with the annual flooding of the Nile which guaranteed the growth of corn and crops by which the population lived. The cutting of the dams and admission of the rising river was a great occasion occurring around the beginning of August in the Cairo area. At one of the canals a dam was built and behind it a an earthen figure, in which a little corn was sown, was raised up. This was the 'Bride of the Nile'. The river rose steadily and then the dam burst. The Nile with one mighty sweep carried off his bride (1923, 370). He literally 'swept her off her feet'.

Tradition states that at an earlier stage a young woman, beautifully arrayed, was thrown into the river as a sacrifice to ensure a proper inundation. This still carried the character of the sacred marriage –the Nile being male, the victim female.

A similar tradition is associated with the Sullan River in the West Cork region of Cúil Aodha and Baile Bhóirne. The Sullan, contrary to the ordinary condition of rivers in Irish, is masculine. According to local belief, every seven years it can be heard murmuring: *Is mise an Sullán fuar fada fireann; anois an t-am, cá bhfuil mo dhuine?* (I am the cold, long masculine Sullan; now is the time, where is my victim?)

The Sullan expects someone to be drowned every seven years in exchange for all the fish he provides. Here it is unspecified if the victim is expected to be female.

In the other great megalithic complex of Lough Gur and Cnoc Áine in East Limerick, although a Lughnasa site in which horse-racing took place at Lughnasa, Crom is less prominent than Áine or Áine Chliach who dominates this area. She is associated with the lake in which, according to the local tradition, she has been seen standing combing her hair. While she was bathing in the lake Maurice Fitzgerald, the first Earl of Desmond, had sex with her

and the fruit of their union was Gearóid Iarla Mac Gearailt the celebrated magician who now lives under this enchanted lake until
Lá na Cinniúna, the day of destiny.

Every seven years, when the moon is full, he can be seen riding
his white horse around the lake. The white horse has silver shoes
and when these are worn out this will be the day of destiny. Then
Gearóid Iarla, along with his Norman Knights, will awake from
their enchanted sleep, rise up out of the lake and set Ireland free.
This piece of Gaelic eschatology resembles that of Arthur of Wales
– the once and future king –who will return again from the mystic
land of Avalon when his people have need of him.

This late medieval tradition may be an echo or a retelling of the
earlier recorded mating of Áine and Ailill Ólom son of Eoghan
Mór of the Eoghanacht dynasty of Munster. This was the *Bainis Rí*
– the sacred marriage of the king to the goddess of the territory to
ensure the fertility of the land and the legitimacy of their kingship.
This idea of legitimacy may have been in the minds of the
Normans as they moved into the area, and marriage to Áine
linked them to the most archaic traditions of the Celtic peoples.

The *Bainis Rí*, however, was the marriage of a human king to a
supernatural goddess. But we may push this further back and ask
if at an earlier time the union was between two supernaturals – between a god and a goddess as in the case of *An Daghdha* and the
MórRíon, Lugh and Baoi, Neachtan and Bóinn, Aonghus Óg and
Caer, Midhir and Éadaoin.

In the archaic tradition of the sacral kingship a human king
was symbolically married to the local goddess to ensure the fertility
of the land and the prosperity of the kingdom. This *Bainis Rí* –
wedding of the king – was not concerned with the queen – the
king's human wife –but with the otherworldly goddess – a *Bean Sí*
or woman of the supernatural hollow hills (*Cnoc na Sí*) of the
divine race of the Tuatha Dé Danann.

Thus, in the kingship the divine and human were united – the
human king was the consort of the divine goddess. On this union
of human and divine rested the prosperity of the land. The idea of
the goddess handing over the territory temporarily to the king
finds its expression in the story of the adventure of the five sons of

Eochaidh Muigmedóin (*Eachtra Mac Eachagh Muigmedóin*). In the story, the five sons are out hunting and at the end they are very thirsty. One son goes off in search of water and arrives at a well guarded by a *cailleach* or ugly old woman who demands a kiss in exchange for a bucket of water. He refuses and goes off empty-handed. The same occurs in the case of three others. The last, Niall, has no hesitation in kissing the old woman and immediately she is transformed into the most beautiful woman in the world. She gives him the water saying '*Mise an Fhlaith*' – 'I am the kingdom'. In giving him the water she was giving him herself – the sovereignty. It is thought that a pun or play on words is involved in this ritual of royal inauguration for *Laith* is 'liquid' – water, mead, wine – and *Flaith* is 'kingdom/sovereignty'. When the goddess handed over the '*Laith*' to the candidate for kingship she handed over the '*Flaith*' – the kingdom itself. This incredibly archaic rite may have its origins in Sumer (modern Iraq) between the two rivers where civilisation began. Here, the king mated with the goddess at the beginning of the new year. Travellers could have transported the rite to the Celts of the Danubian region who eventually brought it to Ireland.

In contrast to our secularised governments of today, depending on human wisdom and resources exclusively, this ancient system presents a mystique in which the human and divine are mingled and the earthly ruler seen as the cohort of a divine woman.

The hill of Shantemon, three miles north-east of Cavan town, is said to be the site of inauguration of the O'Reilly kings. And so the landscape speaks of gods and goddesses, of the spirits of the land, of ancestor cults, ancient dynasties and mystical modes of thought. This quiet uncluttered countryside of lakes, trees, hills, mountains and plains and monumental relics of the past invites us to enter into an alternative experience of reality.

The profusion of megalithic monuments in Breifne suggest that it had been populated by a numerous population from the earliest times, while invaders from Europe at a later era may have found the profusion of lakes convenient for the building of defensive *crannóga* or lake-dwellings with which they were familiar.

It is difficult to know if Crom Cróich was a Celtic god imported by the invaders, or if he, as it were, grew from the native soil. If Maigh Sléacht were indeed a place of pilgrimage for the kings of Tara, this would indeed give the area considerable prestige as a national shrine.

If Crom Cróich of Maigh Sléacht is the equivalent of Crom Dubh as is generally agreed, then we have, as it were, the original source of the great Festival of Lughnasa which Máire MacNéill has shown to be so widespread throughout the country. In forms such as Puck Fair, dancing on Cnoc Fírinne (near Croom, Co Limerick), various fairs, and Christian pilgrimages such as those to Croagh Patrick, Lough Dearg and Cnoc Bhréanainn, lasts on to our own day. However, the cult of Crom Cróich in its original form of prostrations and offerings to him at Samhain – the end of the agricultural year – may have been modified by the defeat of Crom Cróich, alias Crom Dubh, alias Breas, alias Balar of the Evil Eye by the great generous god Lugh Lámhfhada. It is likely that the two gods united in their responsibility for the production of the corn, it being recognised that Crom/Balar/Breas and the dark underworld gods of the Fomhóraigh had a greater competence in agricultural matters than Lugh and the gods of light – the Tuatha Dé Danann. After his defeat by Lugh, the stingy god Crom/ Breas/Balar, who demanded exorbitant taxes in grain and live-stock, was still left in charge of the harvest though he was under the supervision of the generous Lugh and the Tuatha Dé Danann. It is probably Crom, who in the form of King Puck, still presides over the great harvest fair of Killorglin. At Cappawhite in Co Tipperary, it was a white horse draped in white that, from a fort, presided over the fair of Lughnasa (MacNéill, 1982, 292). Traditions speak of a head on a hill, and it may be, that at least in some places, a stone head representing Crom was taken from its place of storage and placed on top of the Lughnasa Hill for the duration of the festival, looking out propitiously on the ripen-ing corn in the surrounding fields. In a local church in Cloughane, Co Kerry, a stone head said to represent Crom Dubh was pre-served and kissed to cure toothache. It was stolen some years ago and never recovered. One wonders if in former times this head presided over the Festival of Lughnasa which was a great occasion of games, dancing, singing, courting, faction fighting and feasting at Clochán (MacNéill, 1982, 104). The same might be surmised for the three-faced stone head of Corlech Hill in Cavan, now in the National Museum in Dublin with an excellent replica in the museum in Ballyjamesduff. Crom was connected, then, to two great festivals of the Celtic calendar – Lughnasa and Samhain – the beginning and end of the corn harvest, and when one considers the place corn holds in human sustenance one can readily understand the significance of what was said of Crom Croich in the Dinnseanchas: 'He was the god of every folk that colonised Ireland.' The complicated arrangement of two festivals commemorating the same god seems to lie in the fact of Lugh's intervention to defeat Crom Cróich under his alternative guise as Balar of the Evil Eye at the Battle of Maigh Tuireadh. At a later stage, during the process of Christianisation, St Patrick takes the place of Lugh and in a series of encounters defeats the pagan Crom and in some accounts actually succeeds in converting him to Christianity. This explains the system by which some Lughnasa sites became sites of Christian pilgrimage.

We might reflect for a moment on the nature of the two religions which occupied successively the same sites on certain cases such as Croagh Patrick, Mount Brandon, St Brigid's Well, Liscannor, Co Clare and many others – a pattern well-known from the number of Protestant Cathedrals and churches which once belonged to Catholics.

Indeed, the instances of a later religion taking over the sacred sanctuaries of an earlier one is instanced in one of our most famous monuments, *Brú na Bóinne*, Newgrange, constructed about 3000 BC by the Megalithic People and later peopled by the much later Celtic deities, the Tuatha Dé Danann. In the ancient literature An Daghdha, Ealcmar, Aonghus Óg, Bóinn, Midhir, Éadaoin, Manannán Mac Lir, Eithne, Fionnbhar and Curcóg wander around Brú na Bóinne confidently as if the place had always been theirs.

The liturgy of Crom Cróich, according to the *Dinnseanchas*, was simple, consisting of prostrations and offerings even if these took on a very extreme form. The purpose of this was to obtain milk and corn (*Blicht is ith uaid nochuingitis for rith dar cend trin a sotha slain*). It was theologically recognised that Crom was a harvest god who had control over the produce of the earth and that without his goodwill the corn might not ripen and people would die of hunger. Even the Christians believed that the stone statue was inhabited by a demon. St Patrick expelled him and commanded him to descend into the abyss: 'The demon, indeed, who had lurked for a long time in the idol and deluded men, came forth at St Patrick's command. When the people saw him they were afraid, and asked St Patrick to command the horrible monster to leave their presence ... St Patrick ordered him to depart into the abyss. Then all the peoples gave thanks to Almighty God who deigned to deliver them through St Patrick from the power of darkness' (Colgan's *Quarta Vita*).

Here St Patrick is shown performing an exorcism in which he drives out a demon – not from a person but from a megalith. The idea of a stone taking on the form of a man is found in the fourteenth-century story *Forbhas Droma Dámhgháire* (The Siege of Knocklong) from the Book of Lismore, in which the warrior Colpa thinks he is attacking his opponent Ceann Mór and spilling his blood while all the time it is a stone he is striking. While all this is going on, the real Ceann Mór is safe and sound under the appearance of another stone. Similarly, at the end of the same story Mogh Roith, the great druid of Munster, turns the three druids of Cormac Mac Airt into stones: '*Maidir le Crotha, Céacht agus Cith Rua ón Maigh – draoithe de shíol Chonn Chéadchathaigh – rinne mé cruachlocha díobh i Maigh Roighne rua. Beidh na leaca sin ann go brách mar chuimhne ar an eachtra – cúis náire do Leath Choinn. Beidh an t-ainm Leaca Roighne orthu go deo na ndeor*' (Ó Duinn, 1992, 106) (As regards Crotha, Céacht and Cith Rua from Maigh – druids of the seed of Conn of the Hundred Battles – I made hard stones of them in red Maigh Roighne. The stones will be there for ever in memory of the event – a source of shame for the northern half of Ireland and they will be called 'Leaca Roighne' until the end of time.)

The distinction between these stones and a statue is quite clear. A statue of a famous soldier or statesman is carved to resemble that person but in no way is it believed that that person – who may be dead and gone for centuries – is actually inhabiting the statue. The statue is a reminder of the person who once was – even though it may inspire strong memories, as when Nelson's Pillar was blown up in Dublin.

The case of ritual megaliths, however, is quite different. In the ordinary stone circle the standing stones are not carved to resemble persons human or divine, though indeed, as seems to be the case in the great stone avenue in Avebury in England, gender was sometimes indicated – long stones alternating with diamond (lozenge) shaped stones to indicate male and female.

There is the folk-tradition of the stones going to a nearby lake or river on certain occasions to bathe or drink. Perhaps a variation of this idea was the custom in Navarre in times of drought of taking the statue of St Peter from the church and at the end of a great procession plunging him into a river three times as a reminder that rain was needed (Frazer,1923, 77).

Then there is the folkloric explanation of stone circles. The orthostats were young people turned into stone by an angry God for dancing on the Sabbath Day, and the outlying megalith outside the circle was the piper who played for them. While this 'explanation' is probably a product of Puritan England, behind it may lie an idea of 'inhabited stones' going back to a very remote period. Were the great Ancestors incarnated or 'instoned' in the megaliths at least on certain significant calendrical dates on which they made contact with the people? One can readily visualise a ritual meeting of the tribe at a stone circle at a specific sacred time to invoke the help and inspiration of the blessed ancestors who from their position of power in the Otherworld could assist the living by guaranteeing health and prosperity and the fertility of the land. Perhaps no scholar has described the part played by the Ancestors among ancient agricultural societies as vividly as the great Egyptologist, R. T. Rundle Clark:

> The early agricultural peoples combined fertility rites with the cult of the dead. They were, in fact, two aspects of one religion – expressions of the hopes and anxieties of the community. The world seemed full of power, everywhere would be found signs of the life-force, manifest in all living creatures, both ani-

mal and vegetable – in the heavens, in the waters and in the mysterious events of disease, death and decay. These forces could be temporarily localised in some person or place but ancient men were not sufficiently self-conscious to think of them as residing in individuals as such. The community was not merely composed of the living but of the ancestors as well. Life on earth was a temporary exile from the true undifferentiated group – life somewhere beyond. The ancestors, the custodians of the source of life, were the reservoir of power and vitality, the source whence flowed all the forces of vigour, sustenance and growth. Hence they were not only departed souls but still active, the keepers of life and fortune. Whatever happened, whether good or evil, ultimately derived from them. The sprouting of the corn, the increase of the herds, potency in men, success in hunting or war, were all manifestations of their power and approval. Hence the place where the ancestors dwelt was the most holy spot in the world. From it flowed the well-being of the group. Without the tomb or the cemetery, life on earth would be miserable, perhaps impossible.

The ancestors were not particularised. They were a collective concept without individual names. To the ancient Persians they were the *Fravashis*. The Romans had their *Manes*, the Chinese their *Tzu's*. The Egyptian knew them as 'the Souls', the 'Glorious Ones' or 'the Gods', but chiefly as 'the *Ka's'* (1959/1991, 119-120).

This powerful analysis of the basic tenets of ancient religion answers questions left unanswered by archeological excavations. The reports published by careful archeologists give details of the length, breath, height, circumference, date of an early monument with great detail and precision. On visits to important sites visitors are made aware of the period of construction, period of use, sources of the stones used, how many man-hours required to build the monument and so forth and this information, arrived at after much careful investigation demanding great patience and dedication, is of great importance and interest. This scholarly research is the basis from which universal principles can be established.

The average visitor to a sacred site such as a megalithic tomb or a stone circle will ask questions such as: 'What did the people do here?'; 'Why did they go to so much trouble dragging these huge stones here from a distance and lifting them without modern machinery?'

These are the difficult questions. It is easier to measure the diameter of a stone circle than to enter into the mind of prehistoric man. Since few artifacts such as pins, brooches, knives, pots are found at stone circles it is generally concluded that they were not used as domestic sites in which people lived and worked. They are often described as being of 'ritual use' or used for 'ritual purposes'. These phrases, however, are rather vague and leave the visitor unsatisfied.

Rundle Clark's religious analysis goes far beyond Egypt and it is quite extraordinary that so many of the same ideas and practices are found in parts of the ancient world separated by enormous time and space spans. This strange phenomenon gives rise to the persistent question if this is due to diffusion from a common centre or does it spring from a basic unity in the human psyche which reacts in the same way to fundamental drives and mindsets. Megaliths are found over vast areas of the world. 'In 1872, the British traveller Fergusson revealed that he had seen megaliths not only throughout Europe but also in Algeria, the Sudan, Ethiopia, Palestine, the Caucasus, Baluchistan, Kashmir, and India. After this came reports from almost all over the world, referring to every possible period. What could connect a megalithic tomb built in Ireland in 3000 (BC) with another from the eighteenth century (AD) in Madagascar?' (Mohen, 1990, 5).

Rundle Clark's analysis goes a long way towards explaining the purpose of these archaic megalithic monuments.

Even though some of them may contain graves they were not merely tombs – as a Cathedral may contain the graves of former bishops but is by no means merely an episcopal cemetery – they were above all sanctuaries or shrines where the living encountered the deified ancestors.

The ancestors had power to bring health, prosperity and fertility to the local community and these shrines were the places in which such help was sought. Here the tribe would gather and indeed pil-

grims from a considerable distance may have come, as King
Tigernmas and King Laoghaire are said to have come to Maigh
Sléacht from Tara – a considerable distance even today. The motives for undertaking a pilgrimage to such a sacred site would vary
with the needs of the pilgrim and probably differed little from
those of the modern Catholic pilgrim to Lourdes or to Santiago de
Compostela – they would include the basic things of life such as
health, security, prosperity. Máire MacNéill has argued that the religious importance of Croagh Patrick has its origins in the Celtic
festival of Lughnasa and the local tradition supports the
Lughnasa period (around beginning of August) as being the primary time to perform the pilgrimage, particularly on *Aoine Chrom
Dubh* (Crom Dubh's Friday) – probably the last Friday in July.

The Archeologist Chris Corlett, following on the footsteps of
Máire MacNéill, remarks on the highly impressive appearance of
Croagh Patrick –Ireland's most sacred mountain with its com-
manding view of the local landscape. It may, in prehistoric times
have been viewed as a great guardian presence – a *MáthairShliabh*
or mother-mountain as in the case of Sliabh Eibhlinne in Co
Tipperary, or as the twin hills *Dhá Chíoch Anann* (the Paps) on the
border of Cork and Kerry. Ana, according to the great 10th century
scholar Cormac Mac Cuilleannáin, was the mother of the gods of
Ireland. She gave her name to the Irish Pantheon the *Tuatha Dé
Danann* (Peoples of the goddess Ana).

Standing stones, mounds and rock art are found in the vicinity
of Croagh Patrick. At Killadangan the stone row is aligned to the
setting sun at the Winter Solstice, 21 December, the day on which
its beam reaches into the recesses of Newgrange at its rising.
Standing stones and local traditions suggest that the present
Tochar Phádraig – the pilgrim path to The Reek – is a continuation
of a pre-Christian pilgrim path ('Prehistoric Pilgrimage to Croach
Patrick', *Archeology Ireland* Vol 11, No 2, Summer 1997, 8-11). All of
this suggests that the present Christian pilgrimage to Croagh
Patrick at the Lughnasa period is a direct successor of a pre-
Christian pilgrimage to the same place at the same time, and what
a wonderful experience this is for the modern pilgrim to feel that
he is continuing a tradition going back countless ages and forming

a link with all those people who have climbed the sacred mountain throughout the centuries.

Now, apart from the question of time, place and the actual physical climbing of the mountain, is it possible to see any link with the pre-Christian pilgrimage in terms of ideas?

In general, the present-day Christian pilgrim to Croagh Patrick will have such motives as prayer for the success of his life, penance for his sins, compensation for past negligence, participation in an ancient religious tradition, a demonstration of a certain heroism demanded by such an exhausting and difficult exercise, and so forth. This extraordinarily difficult undertaking is certainly a challenge to the individual as in the case of other pilgrimages. On his return he will feel that he has accomplished a heroic and worthwhile undertaking. The shell which pilgrims to Santiago de Compostela brough back with them was often found in their graves, showing that they regarded the pilgrimage as a major event in their lives and wanted to bring it into the Otherworld with them.

According to Chris Corlett, local tradition speaks of a road leading from Tara and Cruachán, the royal seat of Connacht, to Croagh Patrick intimating that this was a pilgrimage place visited by royal patrons even in pre-Christian times.

Some hesitation is experienced when dealing with oral traditions of this kind. Nevertheless, it is well to remember the case of the entrance of the rising sun into Newgrange at the Winter Solstice. Before this extraordinary phenomenon was discovered by Professor O'Kelly, it was known to the local people that at some time of the year the sun entered the tomb. They didn't know when it was, but given the orientation of the monument it was easy to surmise that the tradition referred to the rising sun in the east at the Winter Solstice. And so it proved to be making Brú na Bóinne one of the most famous prehistoric sites in the world. To the credit of Professor O'Kelly he put the local oral tradition to the test. In her *Illustrated Guide to Newgrange*, his wife, Claire O'Kelly, has this to say: 'Witnessing this phenomenon for myself has caused me to remember that I dismissed as an "old wives' tale" a tradition current many years ago to the effect that at a certain time of the year the sun lit up the 3-spiral figure in the end-chamber' (1971, 94-95).

In the case of Croagh Patrick, then, the pointers are towards a great Lughnasa pilgrimage site in pre-Christian times, continued in Christianised form to modern times.

The question remains, however, as to why people undertook such a demanding exercise. One can understand a great and ambitious athlete setting out to perform a prodigious task and so acquire universal fame but in this case large numbers of ordinary people are involved today who do not consider themselves to be particularly heroic and in pre-Christian times it was probably no different. When the archeological facts are listed and itemised, the question always seems to remain – why?

Why is Cruach Phádraig a place of pilgrimage for pagans and Christians?

I think that the myth behind the ritual is the ancient story of the war of the gods, *Cath Maighe Tuireadh na bhFomhórach*, and that this story tells us why people climb the mountain at Lughnasa.

Maigh Tuireadh is an elevated plain north of Lough Arrow in Co Sligo, an area dotted with prehistoric monuments and is regarded as the setting for the celebrated battle between two groups of deities, the Tuatha Dé Danann, the bright gods of prosperity, and the Fomhóraigh, the dark gods of the ocean depths and the northern lands of the world. It must be remembered, of course, that this was a supernatural battle between two different groups of divinities, but a human geographical setting is chosen for the battle so that the story can be told in human categories.

According to the story, the Tuatha Dé Danann are being terrorised by the tyrannical and stingy Fomhóraigh who limit the food rations of the Tuatha Dé Danann chiefs and demand exorbitant taxes. Like Maigh Sléacht, the people have to leave their offerings of corn at Maigh nItha – the plain of corn. At one point the Fomhóraigh had planned to put a chain around the island of Ireland, attach a fleet of ships to the chain and drag Ireland northwards close to the Scandinavian lands where they could keep a closer watch on the Irish. In this, however, they never actually succeeded.

The god Breas had a Tuatha Dé Danann mother, Eri, and a Fomhórach father, Ealatha. It was hoped that by electing Breas King of the Tuatha Dé Danann that he would bring peace and reconciliation to the two parties. This, however, was not the case. The Fomhórach half of his nature asserted itself and he proved to be a tyrant and oppressor. The *file* (poet) Cairbre subjected him to satire on account of his stinginess. Visitors to the king's house came away without the smell of beer from their mouths nor the grease of meat on their knives. After this denunciation Breas appealed to the Fomhóraigh for help.

After due negotiations, the Fomhóraigh agreed to make war on the Tuatha Dé Danann and proceeded to assemble a massive army with a great fleet of ships. Their leader was to be the formidable *Balar Balchéimneach* or Balar of the Evil Eye. He had a destructive poisonous fiery eye which normally had to be kept covered for it destroyed whatever it looked upon. Folklore describes its setting fire to drying up pools of water and setting trees on fire. Balar had acquired this baleful eye through looking through a window while his father was preparing a magic brew. The venom from the brew entered his eye making it an instrument of mass-destruction.

While the Fomhóraigh are amassing their army, the Tuatha Dé Danann are also preparing for battle. The great god Lugh Lámhfhada is appointed war-leader. A year is spent in organising the battle. Lugh summons those experts who will play a major part in the battle and discusses the procedures to be followed. The druids of Ireland are summoned, with their physicians, charioteers, smiths, wealthy landowners and lawyers. The magician Mathgen agreed to shake the 12 great mountains of Ireland to inspire fear on the Fomhóraigh. The cupbearer announced that he would dry up the 12 great lakes of Ireland against the Fomhóraigh in their thirst. The druid Figol will cause three showers of fire to fall on the Fomhóraigh and An Daghdha says that he himself will do everything already mentioned by the others.

Finally all is ready and the two armies assemble for battle on Maigh Tuireadh at Samhain. It has been arranged beforehand that Goibniu, Luchta and Credne will repair the weapons of the Tuatha Dé Danann so that they are always sharp and effective. The physician Dian Cécht, his sons Ochtriúil and Miach and his daughter Airmedh have a magic well full of herbs called 'Tobar

Sláine'. They chant spells over this, and those of the Tuatha Dé Danann who have fallen in battle are submerged in the well and come out as good as new. Lugh urged on the Tuatha Dé Danann to battle fiercely as it was better for them to die than to be in bondage to the Fomhóraigh and subject to tribute. He chanted a spell going around the army on one foot with one eye closed.

The breaking point of the battle came when Balar of the Evil Eye arrived. The lid was lifted up so that the baleful eye was exposed. But Lugh was ready and waiting for this development. In his sling was a stone. He whirled the sling with a mighty power. With deadly accurate aim, the shot went through Balar's head carrying the baleful eye with it out the back of his head. The venom spread to Balar's own troops and this was the beginning of the end for the Fomhóraigh. They were driven back to the sea and their tyranny curbed for ever. The MórRíon in the form of the *Badhbh* or crow of battle flew around the country announcing the great victory of Lugh and the Tuatha Dé Danann over the Fomhóraigh. A new era of prosperity had begun with the triumph of the generous god Lugh over the stingy god Breas and the destructive Balar. Breas, however, was allowed to live as he had knowledge of the mysteries of agriculture. Breas may be seen as Balar under a different aspect along with Crom Cróich / Crom Dubh and all associated with corn.

A great victory march took place then, from the battlefield of Maigh Tuireadh to Tailteann (Sliabh na Caillí, in Co Meath) and there the *Bainis Rí* takes place – the wedding of the new king Lugh with Boi the goddess of the land. It is thought that Loughcrew – the great megalithic cemetery, Sliabh na Caillí – may be named after her – 'Loch Chnoc / Chroc Boi'.

The fruit of this sacred marriage is seen at Lughnasa, in August, as the corn turns golden as it ripens. A sheaf of ripened corn is brought by the farmer to the summit of the Lughnasa hill and left there as an offering to the harvest god Crom, and at the same time an acknowledgement to Lugh to the effect that Lugh is ultimately in charge and that Crom is not allowed to take liberties with the distribution of the harvest.

Lughnasa is a 'First-Fruits' festival, not a 'Harvest Thanksgiving' for this is the beginning of the harvest, not the end. The god is urged to keep the sun shining and the weather mild to ripen the remainder of the wheat, oats and barley.

And so, the Battle of Maigh Tuireadh, in which the Tuatha Dé Danann led by Lugh Lámhfhada, won a signal victory over the dark Fomhórach gods led by Balar of the Evil Eye (Crom) leaves its mark on the Irish countryside century after century as people take to the hills at Lughnasa to commemorate the great victory by which corn – the staff of life – becomes available to them through the benevolence of supernatural forces.

The myth of Lugh the sun/sky god subjugating Crom the earth/underworld god may have been expressed in some re-markable sculptures to be found in parts of Europe. According to Miranda Green: 'The most common form in which the Celtic sky-god appears as a warrior is on horseback. He is in the guise of a Roman general, driving his horse at a gallop over a hybrid creat-ure, half man, half serpent, with a human head and torso but whose legs are in the form of snakes' (1992, 124). The Jupiter-Giant column of Neschers shows the giant with his large head and snake legs crouching down as the horse's front legs rest on this head and shoulders as he is driven into the earth (Green, 1992, Fig 53, 127).

> The giant under the rider is iconographically very interesting: its snake-limbs endow the being with a chtonic, earth-linked imagery. The portrayal of an uncouth, earthbound strength is frequently suggested by the massive head and shoulders, braced against the sky-horseman's weight; and the strained, aghast expression of its face demonstrates how intolerable was its burden …. We can see this at Koln, on a third-century group, where the giant consists merely of a hunched head and two snakes' (Green, 1992, 128).

While the sculptures portray the dominance of the sky-god, nev-ertheless the earth/underworld god has a part to play, for his domain is the earth with its mysterious powers of fertility without which the human race would cease to be. The distinctive virtues of sky and earth must work together in harmony to achieve the welfare of mankind and this harmony was symbolised in Celtic terms by the justice of the reigning kind – the *Fír Flatha*. If the king observed the four conditions – observance of the *geasa* or taboos that bound him, freedom from any physical defect, *féile* or royal generosity and *fír flatha*, strict integrity, freedom from corruption, justice in all his ways – harmony would prevail and there would be peace and prosperity in the land. Thus the role of the king was to ensure cosmic harmony. Indeed, the king carried a monumental responsibility and it must have been a heavy burden for a frail human being with all the doubts, weaknesses and faults to which we are prone, to be the consort of a divine woman.

CHAPTER TWO

The Death and Re-Birth of the Corn

An interesting folklore account associated with Co Sligo shows
that Crom had a devoted following and that St Patrick's intervention wasn't quite as welcome as may be assumed from the
Patrician Documents:

> *Bhí druíodóir annseo thíos i gConndae Shligigh, agus bhí sé ina
> ard-dhruíodóir ar na druíodóirí eile ar fad, agus b'é an lá féasta a
> bíodh aige héin agus ar a chuid fear an Domhnach seo a dtugann siad
> 'Domhnach Chrom Dubh' air agus 'Domhnach na bhFear' – sin ainm
> eile a thugann siad air freisin.*
>
> *Bhí Naomh Páraic a'goil (ag gabháil) thart annsin go dtáinic sé
> go Sligeach gur casadh leis cuide go na Págánaigh a bhí i Sligeach,
> agus bhí Naomh Páraic ag iarrai orrabh athrú na chreid' héin, agus
> dúirt siad leis nach m'maith leofa athrú go dtagadh lá an féasta agus
> go mbeadh siad fré chéile iad héin agus Cormac Dubh, gurb é a
> mhúineanns díofa le bheith ag cur agus a' baint, agus nuair a bhíonns
> uair bhreá le teacht agus droch-uair, agus go mbíonn féasta mór
> annsin an Domhnach sin, agus go mbíonn siad a' baint cuide go'n
> (den) bharr a bhíonns acab go bharr an earraigh, agus an samhradh,
> agus go dtugann Cormac Dubh annsin tosach an bhidh ar fad go na
> fir oibre ag an dinnéar an lá féasta, agus gurb é an t-ainm a dtugann
> siad ar a' lá sin 'Domhnach na bhFear' agus thugadh na fir
> 'Domhnach Chrom Dubh' air in onóir go Chormac Dubh'*
> (MacNéill, 1982, 595 – from IFC 889, 539-42).
>
> *(There was a magician down here in Co Sligo, and he was the
> High Magician over all of the other the magicians and the feastday he
> used to have for himself and his men was this Sunday called
> 'Domhnach Chrom Dubh' and 'Domhnach na bhFear' (Sunday of
> the Men) is another name by which it is called.*
>
> *St Patrick was going around until he arrived at Sligo and he met
> some of the Pagans who were in Sligo, and St Patrick was trying to
> convert them to his own religion, and they said to him that they*

would not like to change over until the feastday came and that them-
selves and Cormac Dubh would be together with each other; that it is
he who instructs them when to sow and when to reap and when good
weather is on the way and when bad weather is coming; and that they
have a great feast then on that Sunday and that they reap some of the
spring and summer crop and that Cormac Dubh then gives the begin-
ning of all the food to the workmen on the feastday, and that the name
they call that day is 'Domhnach na bhFear' and that the men called it
'Domhnach Chrom Dubh' in honour of Cormac Dubh.)

This remarkable account was recorded in 1942 by Liam Ó
Coincheanainn, Rinn na h-Áirne (Corrandulla, Co Galway).

The god, here spoken of as a master magician (ard-dhruíodóir)
is called Cormac Dubh probably because Cormac as a common
personal name would be more familiar to the speaker than 'Crom'
but despite this the name of the festival retains its ordinary form
'Domhnach Chrom Dubh'

The idea from north-east Limerick that Crom Dubh was the
god who introduced corn into Ireland is found again here in Co
Sligo in even a more definite form, for he continues to instruct the
people as to when to sow and to reap and to expect good weather
and bad. This is probably the most definite way in which Crom exercises his role as oracular god at Carraig Eachlabhra, as weather
forecaster, announcing beforehand a suitable time for reaping the
corn. Moreover, Crom gives the first of the produce to the reapers.
Here Crom Dubh is portrayed in a very different way from that of
the Patrician accounts. He is a benign figure who assists the people
in producing food, and the working mens' reluctance to change
over to the religion of St Patrick is quite understandable. They had
to consider the lives of their wives and children and it was Crom
Dubh who put the bread and butter on the table.

This account presents the widespread mythological theme of
the 'Culture Hero'.

The theme is found in many areas widely separated from each
other and consists in the belief that long, long ago, a great super-
human figure from some distant land visited the area and brought
with him the knowledge of agriculture and other crafts which he
taught to the people.

The god Osiris brought civilisation to the Egyptians introducing laws and teaching them to worship the gods. His wife Isis discovered wheat and barley growing in a wild state and Osiris organised their cultivation, and so the Egyptians took to a diet of corn. Leaving the government of the country to Isis, Osiris travelled far and wide bringing the benefits of agriculture to many countries. In areas too cold for the cultivation of the vine he taught the inhabitants how to brew beer from barley (Frazer, 1923, 363).

The story of Osiris, however, does not end with his teaching of methods of agriculture. A much more mysterious role was destined for him in which he becomes identified with the corn.

The highly complex legends of Osiris describe his murder by his evil brother Seth and his subsequent revival in mummy form as Lord of the Dead. His funeral rites, performed by his son Horus and other gods, as well as the lamentations of Isis and Nephtys, brought about his resurrection – not as he had been in ordinary human life – but as alive in the Underworld and judge of the dead. Osiris was the hope of dead Egyptians, for their funeral rites were modelled on the funeral rites performed by the gods over the body of Osiris himself and were believed to have the same effect as they had on him – to transform the dead man into a living man but in the Underworld. This gave the Egyptians the promise of eternal life in an alternate world when their earthly life was over. They became identified with Osiris and his fate became theirs (Frazer, 1923, 366-367).

Abydos in Upper Egypt held the head of the murdered Osiris and so became the great shrine of the dead but living god. Those who could were buried near the shrine to participate in the living state of Osiris in the Otherworld and even those who could not afford such a privilege arranged that their mummified bodies be transported to Abydos temporarily to be brought into contact with the god and then taken back to their own area for burial (Frazer, 1923, 367-368).

But apart from Osiris' resurrection to life in the Otherworld of the Dead and the similar effect of this on his followers on their departure from their human life in this world, there remains the matter of the corn.

According to Egyptian belief, not only did Osiris endow the dead with life in the Underworld but he also gave life to the corn.

During the hard torrid summer Osiris is in a state of listlessness and, with his exhaustion, vegetation stagnates. At the time of the Summer Solstice (21 June) the Nile begins to rise and flood the parched land. Osiris is seen to gradually throw off his lethargy as the water is directed in channels on the soil, and with the recession of the flood, the sowing of the corn can begin around November.

There was the constant fear that the Nile flooding would not take place or that the water would be insufficient or too much. As Rundle Clark explains:

> The coming of the new waters was more than a change of season, it meant the end of fear and terror, the rebirth of life in the hearts of men. Osiris is not the inundation itself but the life-force in plants and the reproductive power in animals and human beings, which are stimulated when the waters come ... When the waters pour out over the earth they cause the seed to grow in the soil and this sprouting of the vegetation is the uprising of Osiris' soul. This is clearly seen in a relief from Philae (1959, 100).

This detailed relief shows a black irrigation channel into which a cow-headed, horned goddess is pouring water from the Nile from a kind of jug. This is the great mother goddess Isis/ Hathor/ Sothis. Sothis is the goddess in her form as the Dog Star (Sirius) whose rising in the east just before dawn after the Summer Solstice heralded the annual inundation of the Nile upon which the life of Egypt depended. From the irrigated soil, stalks of corn rise up in profusion. Above the growing corn is a bird with a human head. This is the 'soul-form' of Osiris. When Osiris rises in his 'soul-form' the plants begin to grow. In fact they are really the same thing.

The deceased Osiris, then, is found in two forms. In the Papyrus of Ani he is pictured in mummy-form as Lord of the Dead but alive and well to greet the recently deceased. His followers who have acquitted themselves well in this mortal life are identified with him and become 'an Osiris' so that they live an eternal life with him in the Land of the Dead.

Another picture of the same kind shows the god Anubis lead-ing Hunefer, the deceased, into the hall where his heart, that is his conscience, will be weighed against order, justice, truth symbol-ised by a feather. The monster known as 'Eater of the Dead' is pre-sent to deal with somebody who fails the test. The god Thoth records the result which shows that Hunefer has passed. Horus leads him to Osiris who sits on his throne holding his crook and flail and backed by his sisters, the goddesses Isis and Nephthys (Rossiter, 82-83).

This is Osiris, Lord of the Land of the Dead, dressed as a Mummy to show that from the point of view of the earth-dwellers he is 'dead' but in fact he is alive in the Underworld with a differ-ent type of life from that which he had while he lived on earth. The idea is not unlike the Christian belief that while the body lies dead in the grave the soul is alive in heaven.

In discussing all of this, what we have in mind is the question of the myth of Crom Cróich/Cruach/Dubh being in some way con-nected with the myth of the great Osiris of Egypt and being a local variation of an international theme bound up with religious ritual. While the story of the kings of Tara accompanied by a large num-ber of followers coming to Maigh Sléacht to worship Crom Cruach with offerings, prostrations and cries may appear rather rough and primitive, and not improved by St Patrick's actions, at the same time, ancient myths, including those of Osiris, dealing with the stark realities of death and life, are not noted for their delicacy.

For the moment, it is Osiris' first role we are interested in – his role as 'soul-bird' or life of the corn. This brings Osiris and Crom Dubh together as being closely associated with the growth of cere-als, with the mysterious internal power or life force which makes the seed sprout in the moist earth-mother, emerge above the ground, gradually grow stronger under the influence of sun, rain and wind, develop ears of grain – some for re-sowing, some for human and animal consumption – turning a golden colour, ripen-ing to full maturity and then being killed and dismembered by the work of reaper and thresher to be made into bread so that man might live. No wonder that this extraordinary cycle has fascinated mankind over untold periods of time.

In the great and secret Greek religion of Eleusis, Demeter the Earth-Mother mourns for her daughter Persephone (Kore) who has been abducted by Pluto and taken to the Underworld. During her absence the land becomes a barren wasteland and no crops grow. But then Persephone is released and returns from the Underworld and, with that, the desert blooms as she returns with the resurrection of the grain. The desert blooms as the wheat begins to sprout and makes its way above the ground.

At the celebration of the return of Persephone on the holy night, it is said that at the high point of the holy mysteries the Hierophant or Priest, in the sight of the congregation, in dead silence, held up an ear of corn. This was the great mystery – life had sprung from death. Jesus used the same image: 'I tell you, most solemnly, unless a wheat grain falls on the ground and dies, it remains only a single grain; but if it dies, it yields a rich harvest' (John 12:24) Joseph Campbell quotes the commentary of St Hippolytus – thought to be the composer of Eucharistic Prayer No 2 in the Roman Liturgy:

> 'That great and marvellous mystery of perfect revelation, a cut stalk of grain', as the early Christian Bishop Hippolytus described it – forgetting for the nonce, apparently, that the culminating revelation of his own holy Mass was a lifted wafer of bread made of the same grain' (1976, 185).

Campbell continues: 'What could have been the meaning of such a simple act as the lifting of a cut stalk of grain? What is the meaning of the elevated host of the Mass? As in the play-logic, or dream-logic, of any traditional religious pageant, the sacred object is to be identified, at least for the moment of the ceremony, with the god. The cut stalk is the returned Persephone, who was dead but now liveth, in the grain itself. A bronze gong was struck at this moment, a young priestess representing Kore (Persephone) herself appeared, and the pageant terminated with a paean of joy' (1976, 186).

Here in this last episode, the risen goddess appears in double form – primarily as an ear of corn and secondarily in human form. But it would appear that the priestess, who stood in for Persephone, was only of minor importance – the great spiritual truth was that the goddesss had returned from the Otherworld in the corn – she *was* the corn, the sustenance of men. With the return of the corn life would go on for another year.

One can see the power of the religion of the 'Elusinian Mysteries' in this concept of a life-force, a divine current of energy personified as the goddess, flowing through vegetation, filling the plants, the cereals, with exuberant life.

In the cycle of nature, vegetation in winter decays and dies but with the arrival of spring the '*Neart*' or life-giving energy asserts itself and the plants and animals arise from their winter sleep as the comatose Osiris rose up resurgently. Year after year, Celts and other peoples who lived close to nature experienced this yearly cycle of decay and growth until it became part of their psychic constitution. But it was not only a beautiful intellectual theory but a reality corresponding to the cycle of the seasons. At Bealtaine, (May Day) Irish youths went around with the 'May Bush' singing:

> *Babóg na Bealtaine, Maighdean an tSamhraidh,*
> *Thugamar féin an Samhradh linn,*
> *Samhradh buí faoi luí na gréine,*
> *Thugamar féin an Samhradh linn'*

(The young woman of May, maiden of Summer, we brought the Summer with us. Golden Summer under the spreading sun; we brought the Summer with us)

The idea of *Neart* or divine energy flowing through plants and living matter was once common to many parts of the world, like the Melanesian concept of 'Mana' and a similar idea in Hinduism. We find it expressed clearly also in a W-Indian text:

> From Wakan Tanka, the Great Spirit, came a great unifying life-force that flowed through all things, the flowers of the plains, blowing winds, trees, birds and animals, and was the same force that had been breathed into the first man. Thus all things were kindred and were all brought together by the one mystery (Luther Standing Bear, Laxoto, *A Natural Education*, Summerton 1944,14).

In the cult of St Brigid, for instance, there is no doubt that it was widely believed that Brigid returned from the Otherworld on the Holy Night – at Imbolc – the night before the first of February. People placed sheaves of corn, cakes and other things outside the door so that Brigid would put a blessing on them as she passed by. The Brídeog procession, in which an image of the child Brigid is carried around from house to house, is a ritualisation of the idea of Brigid's annual return – the rite behind the myth or the myth behind the rite. The idea of the return of Brigid is expressed very clearly in a folklore account from Ring, Co Waterford: *Tá aiteanna sa cheantar seo agus ní dhúntar doirse an oíche sin mar creidtear go mbíonn Naomh Bríd ag gabháil timpeall an oíche sin agus go ndéanfadh sí an rath agus beannacht ar an teach agus ar mhuintir an tí* (IFC 900, 234). (There are places in this district in which the doors are not closed on that night as it is believed that St Brigid goes around on that night and that she brings prosperity and blessings on the house and household.)

A similar tradition holds for the goddess Áine Chliach of Cnoc Áine and Lough Gur in Co Limerick. In Áine's case, the great feastday was the Summer Solstice, St John's Eve (23 June) when the bonfires blaze. 'One Saint John's Night, it happened that one of the neighbours lay dead, and on this account the usual "cliars" (torches) were not lit. Not lit, I should say, by the hands of living men, for that night such a procession of "cliars" marched around Cnoc Áine as never was seen before, and Áine was seen in the front, directing and ordering everything' (*Rev. Celt.*, 1V, 189-190).

On another midsummer night, Áine appeared on the sacred hill to a number of girls. She took off her ring and asked them to look through it. There they saw the hill crowded with supernatural beings – Áine's companions, the Tuatha Dé Danann.

However, while Áine uses the calendar of the Four Stations of the Sun, the Insular Celtic calender is favoured by Rothniamh of the same Sí Chliach – Cnoc Áine. Rothniamh emerges from the supernatural hill at Samhain (1 November) as an oracular goddess to predict the events of the coming year for Fíngen Mac Luchta, the local king. This event is recorded in detail in the story 'Áirne Fíngein'. As in the case of Carraig Eachlabhra in Cavan, it is obvious that prediction of events to come during the following year was of great importance to people and especially to kings. As we have seen, vestiges of this remain today in the modern celebration of Samhain where the person who finds the ring in the *bairín breac* will be married within the year. Naturally, the time for predictions is at Samhain when the year begins.

CHAPTER THREE

Lughnasa Rites of Wensleydale

It appears that in these cases of predicting the future, the *Neart* or mysterious life-force surging through nature and expressed in the growth of vegetation, animal, birds, fish and humans, takes on a more strictly intellectual form. It is not only a vital impersonal energy that is involved but an energy that is able, as it were, to turn back and reflect on itself in a way demanding and intellectual personality. The goddess Rothniamh in Cnoc Áine, Apollo in Delphi, the speaking horse in Binn Eachlabhra, Co Fermanagh, all predicted the direction a specific expression of *Neart* would take in the particular circumstances. The idea of prediction, then, is of importance as it shows the progression from an impersonal power to a personal and intellectual form.

The cult of Crom Dubh turns up some astonishing features. Until now we have been speaking of its expression in Ireland. But in the area of Wensleydale in Yorkshire, in the village of West Witton, a rite is performed annually which leaves little doubt as to whom it is essentially directed.

In his magnificent study of this phenomenon in his book, *The Giant of Penhill*, (Northern Lights, Dunnington, York, 1987), Ian Taylor uncovers a world of ancient legends, hill-figures, ley lines and ideas linking the human condition with the cosmos in this remote area once populated by Celts, Norse, Saxons, Normans – all of whom have made their specific colourful contribution to the pattern of life.

Parallel to the road on which the village of West Witton is situated with its church of St Bartholomew (Feast 24 August), the river Yore or Ure flows and this name, like York itself, may well be derived from the Celtic *Iubhar / Iubharach* – the place of yew trees. At any rate, a local hill – Penhill – and several other placenames in this area of Wensleydale in North Yorkshire, are associated in myth and ritual with the Giant of Penhill who, undoubtedly, is the Yorkshire form of the Irish Crom Dubh.

The story is that, long long ago, a giant lived in a great fortress on the summit of Penhill. He was a figure of fear and terror to all the local inhabitants and he kept a great and ferocious hound. He also kept a great herd of pigs and every morning the hound rounded them up in twos in front of the castle so that the giant could count them.

The giant regarded himself as a son the Norse god Thor and his great and ferocious hound was his only friend and ally.

One day as the giant walked down the valley of the Yore which flows through Wensleydale, he saw a flock of sheep grazing and a shepherdess minding them. For his own amusement, the giant turned the hound on the sheep, killing many of them. The distraught shepherdess appealed to the giant to call off the dog but he struck her with his club and killed her.

Shortly after this episode, when the pigs were rounded up one morning for counting, the giant discovered that one was missing. He ordered the surly hound to go in search of the missing pig which was eventually found dead with an arrow through its heart.

The giant was furious and ordered all the archers in Wensleydale to assemble on Penhill. Meanwhile, the hound had deserted him and when the giant found him sulking at the edge of the forest he shot him dead with an arrow cast. Now his only friend was gone.

The archers assembled on Penhill but nobody would admit to having killed the pig. The giant ordered the men to bring their youngest sons next day and if nobody owned up he would kill the children.

A local holy man, a hermit from the area, stood forth fearlessly and denounced the giant, telling him that if he shed a single drop of blood he would never enter his castle again. But the giant only laughed at him.

Towards sunset next day, the people assembled with their youngest sons. Again, the priest told them to have courage for all would be well. From the battlements of his castle the giant looked down with contempt on the assembly and prepared to confront them. His steward implored him to desist as he had had an ominous dream warning him of disaster. The giant struck the steward leaving him unconscious and strode out to wreak havoc on the children.

On his way he encountered more dead pigs and he went berserk with rage. The priest again confronted him boldly and denounced him.

While all of this was taking place, the steward had awakened in the castle. He gathered together a heap of straw and soon the castle was a sea of flame. The giant looked back and saw his castle on fire. Just then the ghost of the shepherdess appeared before him holding the ghostly hound by a leash. She released the hound who made for the giant's throat. The giant stepped back and crashed down the cliff behind him to an instant death.

As we will see later, the ritual associated with the Giant of Penhill and performed annually, is called 'The Burning of Bartle'. The name comes from the village church of St Bartholomew and the rite is performed in the village of West Witton on the Saturday nearest to the Feast of St Barthlomew on 24 August. As Ian Taylor remarks, it is most likely that this name is a Christian adaption of a Celtic god. This indeed is a very appropriate calendar date – the beginning of the corn harvest – in Biblical terms, the First Fruits of the harvest. This does not correspond to the traditional Anglican Harvest Festival. The Harvest Festival, so popular in the Church of England, comes later in the year when the harvest is over and the corn safely in the barns, so that this Christian Festival constitutes a service of thanksgiving to God for an abundant crop. The 'Bartle Festival' is different – this corresponds to the Irish Festival of Lughnasa in early August. This is the beginning of the corn harvest when some of the corn has ripened and the rest is still to come. In this great Festival of Lughnasa it was customary for farmers to take a sheaf of ripened corn and lay it on a sacred hill. The meaning was clear – as the god has graciously ripened the first part of the harvest so may he continue to act until the end of the harvest when all the cornfields have turned a golden colour. This is not so much a rite of thanksgiving as in the Anglican Festival but rather a rite of petition and stimulation of the god to bring his good work to a successful conclusion.

A festive meal from the newly ripened corn as well as the more modern new potato crop was common in Ireland along with the *Fraocháin* (whortleberries) so that Lughnasa involved the eating of both cultivated and wild fruits. A peculiarity of this meal was that in some places the sheaf of corn was burned and then the hardened grain separated from the burnt material and made into flour for the festival supper (Danaher, 1972, 167). It is remarkable that in the Bartle legend the steward set fire to straw to burn down the castle and the effigy of Bartle used in the rite is traditionally made of old clothes and straw.

As regards the date and name, a remarkable parallel is found in Ireland in the person of 'Parthanan' or 'Partholon' – the Gaelic version of Bartholomew. He is called *Parthanán an Fhómhair* – Parthanan of the Harvest – and is well-known in popular folklore:

Tagann Lá Pharthanáin gairid do dheireadh an Fhómhair agus bíonn gach éinne ag iarraidh a chuid arbhair a bheith bainte aige faoi dtiocfadh an lá san, mar deirtear go ngabhann sé timpeall (sé sin Parthanán) ag bualadh an arbhair, agus ná fágfadh sé gráinne síl ar aon arbhar ná beadh bainte' (*Béaloideas*, 1932, 284).

(The day of Parthanán comes near the end of the harvest and everyone is trying to have his corn cut for that day, as it is said that he goes around (that is Parthanán) striking the corn and that he would not leave a grain of seed on any corn that would not be harvested.)

Presumeably, Crom Dubh the Irish Harvest god, considered that uncut corn at this late stage belonged to him and that it was the farmer's own fault if he had been tardy.

A remarkable similarity exists between the story of the Giant of Penhill and a story from Co Mayo, 'Sgéala ar Naomh Phádhraic agus ar Chrom Dubh' (The story of St Patrick and Crom Dubh) published by Conradh na Gaeilge in *Lúb na Caillighe* (1910), 33-40. According to the story, Crom Dubh lived in Dún Briste (the broken fort) now a little islet outside Downpatrick Head but once joined to the mainland. He had two sons and two dogs and all were known for their savagery. The people would hide their faces in their breasts when Crom Dubh's name was mentioned. He came yearly to collect his rent and anybody who escaped his dogs were thrown into his fire on top of a cliff. However, the people thought that bad as he was they had nobody else in whom to trust, except Crom Dubh, for he brought them light of day, darkness of night and change of seasons.

Like the hermit in the Penhill account, St Patrick bravely approached Crom Dubh's fortress. As he advanced Crom Dubh released his two fiercest mastiffs at him. St Patrick, using his crozier or bishop's staff, drew a protective circle around himself on the ground as he chanted: *Glas ar d'ionga; glas ar d'fhiacail* (a lock on your claw, a lock on your tooth). At this the dogs became terrified of Patrick's power, froth came from their mouths and their hair stood on end. Crom Dubh's son recognised that this was the beginning of the end for his father. In a dramatic gesture he set the whole countryside on fire. To this day the area is known as *Gleann Lasaire* – the glen of the blaze.

The people gathered from near and far to honour St Patrick, though among them was a lingering regret that Crom Dubh was no more (Dalton, J.,' Cromm Cruaich of Magh Sléacht', *PRIA* 1922, 62-64)

Here, as in the Penhill story, the traditional power-holder is challenged and in the confrontation the new-comer is victorious.

In the Irish story, Crom Dubh is portrayed as a despotic figure, and yet he is necessary, as it is he who controls the established order of night and day and the progress of the seasons, so that it is understandable that the people, while wishing to throw off his tyranny, might be reluctant to part with a character of such power that he controlled the order of nature. This is reminiscent of the great Celtic god An Daghdha who plays in the seasons on his harp: 'Come summer, come winter' (Gray, 1982, 71) and Nicholas Poussin's painting 'The Dance of the Seasons'. Here, perhaps, we may distinguish the very different character of Crom Dubh's pagan religion with its emphasis on the fertility of the land and the ordered cycle of the year, from the more 'Otherworldly' character of St Patrick's Christian religion. In the conflict between Crom Dubh and St Patrick one can see the perennial struggle between this present world (*An Ceantar*) and the heavenly otherworld (*An tAlltar*). In the prevailing lifestyle of the prosperous West the emphasis is on food, drink, comfort; and the sparse congregations of the churches signal the recession of the idea of a future heavenly otherworld. The conflict between Crom Dubh and St Patrick is still going on.

The wonderfully impressive rite of the 'Burning of Bartle' in West Witton in Yorkshire on the Saturday night nearest 24 August keeps the Yorkshire version of Crom Dubh spectacularly alive.

A large effigy of straw and clothes, with eyes lighted by batteries, is prepared beforehand and brought to the end of the village from which the procession starts. Two men carry the huge effigy of the giant of Penhill and all is ready by 9.00 pm when people stream out from the pubs on to the street to take part in the ritual.

The men support the effigy on their shoulders as they go from one end of the village to the other and in the course of the procession there are several stops or 'stations'. These are the houses of old people and, of course the pubs, and give an opportunity to those confined indoors either through sickness, old age or just plain drunkennesss to participate in the rite, so that the giant's visit would bring them the luck of the year. At each stop a chanter sings out a formula to which the people respond.

The placenames mentioned in the ritual formula are those of the nearby area and the popular version of the story is that the Giant of Penhill was a swine-robber who was hunted down by the local population, received a particular wound at the particular area mentioned before finally meeting his end. It is possible that originally the effigy was carried to each of the places mentioned in the rite but now it is confined to the village, but still the traditional placenames are retained even though they do not correspond to the village stations. The rite takes about an hour to perform.

If we examine the ritual formulae it will be seen that they can be broken down into different parts.

Firstly, there is a statement relating to the last destiny of the Giant:

'At Penhill Crags, he tore his rags'

Then comes the invitation, in which the chanter invites the crowd to celebrate the occasion and then the crowd's response:

Chanter: 'Shout, lads, shout'.

Crowd: 'Hooray'

Chanter: 'Hip-hip'

Crowd: 'Hooray'

The procession moves on to the next stop and if there are old people in the upper storey of the house the Giant is lifted up so that they can see him. This is considered to be an important part of the proceedings.

From the pubs, bottles of beer come out for the giant-bearers and chanter, for this is a thirsty business. While the invitation and response remain the same at each station, the Statement-Formula varies:

On Penhill Crags he tore his rags.

At Hunter's Thorn he blew his horn.

At Capplebank Stee he broke his knee.

At Grisgill Beck he broke his neck.

At Vadhams End he could not fend.

At Grisgill End we made his end.

The procession of Bartle though the village, with its series of stops and ritual dialogue, finally ends when Grisgill End is reached. There, in a walled-off area by the roadside the rhyme is chanted for the last time. Bartle is laid on the ground; paraffin is poured on him; he is set on fire and he goes up on a sea of flame. The crowd cheers and dances about and the Burning of Bartle is over for another year.

What a marvellous piece of ritual this is. The ceremonial portrays the myth behind the rite quite clearly by the stops and the references to Bartle's fate at the various locations. The crowd is actively involved in the rite by accompanying the procession through the village and shouting the responses. All is spontaneous, requiring no books or leaflets, and there is a good deal of repetition – a feature common to many ancient liturgies.

Ian Taylor gives a remarkable account of his own personal reactions to the 'Burning of Bartle':

> I had been impressed by several features of the ritual: the large number of persons present (proof of the considerable extent of local and outside interest) and the seriousness of the entire event – there was very little evidence of frivolity during the hour long proceedings. The figures of Bartle and the chanter had held the almost unbroken attention of everyone from beginning to end. I felt oddly elated afterwards and my companions were similarly affected. Even in its present degenerate form a ritual of power, through the concentrated attention of its participants, had raised just a little the level of consciousness – in some of us at least … Bartle used to be pulled through the village in a cart pulled by six strong lads. The number six is a solar number – a clue to the origins of the ritual in ancient sun worship (1987, 33).

One wonders if this were originally a harvest-time sacrifice connected with the *Cailleach* or Last Sheaf to be cut down with careful and particular ceremonial.

At one time Bartle had been carried in a cart pulled by six strong boys through the village, but this custom had fallen into abeyance. As happens frequently in ancient rituals such as the *Brídeog* procession in Ireland on St Brigid's Eve (31 January) or in the case of the Mummers' Plays at the period of the Winter Solstice, the performance and organisation often belongs to a particular family native to the area for centuries or to a small group of dedicated people. This type of phenomenon is often noticed by collectors of folklore also. The local people tell the collector that, while they have no great knowledge of the subject themselves, there is a man in the area who is an expert on all things traditional. And so it proves to be. The collector meets somebody with a massive knowledge of local traditions which he is eager to impart. So that ancient lore is often transmitted, not by the many, but by the few. In the case of the Burning of Bartle, the organisation and performance of the Rite is associated with two local families – the Spence and Harker families.

As Ian Taylor observes: 'The Burning of Bartle is without doubt one of the best examples in Europe of an ancient pagan practice surviving within a vernacular tradition' (1987, 40).

The cult is very localised and the ritual associated with a local giant or divinity whose escapades are bound up with the immediate local area. The despotic and cruel characteristics of the god are highlighted along with a hint of the sacrifice of children. The element of fire is involved. The corn and milk – the Irish '*Ith agus Blicht*' – and harvest symbolism is not as well developed as in the case of Crom Dubh. However, the two gods have much in common. Greed and tyranny characterises both. They both demand exorbitant offerings involving the lives of children. They are both finally destroyed by a holy man of superior power who intervenes for the welfare of the local people. The cult is associated with a limited geographical area.

While the origins of the Burning of Bartle may lie in harvest sacrificial rituals, as in the case of Crom Dubh, a change of religion is involved in popular explanations of the event. Christianity, the new religion, takes up arms against traditional paganism – St Patrick versus Crom Cruach/Dubh; the Hermit versus the Giant of Penhill. A further complication arises, however, in the case of the Giant. Another alternative explanation of the origins of the rite surmises that it goes back to the statue of St Bartholomew in the village church of West Witton. When the Protestant Reformers arrived to wreck the church and make off with its statues and valuables, the local people had absconded with the statue of their patron St Bartholomew. Then the looters followed the trail through the places mentioned in the rite and they finally captured the statue and burned it at Grassgill End (Cooper 57 and Sullivan, 1994, 237). Here two Christian religions clash – Catholicism and Protestantism. No doubt the Protestants considered Catholicism, with its veneration of saints and sacred images, to be on a level with the cult of the Giant himself. On the face of it, there is little of the mystical in the stories of the Giant or Crom Dubh. They seem to be intimately associated with the land and its produce and with weather conditions, especially storms. Since storms which destroy the corn were a common phenomenon in Ireland towards the end of August (Lughnasa) it was advisable for the farmer to have all his corn reaped by St Bartholomew's Day (24 August). Otherwise, *Parthanán na Gaoithe* (Parthanan of the Storm) would take it all. It has to be remembered that until recent times man's control over weather conditions, blight in crops, diseases, flooding, frost and so forth, was very tenuous, and even today, despite the great scientific advances, our control over nature is far from complete. A bad harvest could decimate a community as in the case of the Famine in Ireland. In this light one can readily understand the statement of the Prose-Dinnseanchas that Crom Cróich was the god of every group that took Ireland until the coming of St Patrick. Presumably this means the Megalithic or Great-Stone Age People and the Bronze Age People, all of whom were in Ireland long before the Celts. If Crom Cróich/Cruach/Dubh is the god associated with the fertility of the land and since all people, whatever their culture, require food and drink to live, then, of course, the Prose-Dinnseanchas is quite right, thought it is uncertain if these particular names or terms were used. Presumably, the God preached by St Patrick would now look after the material needs of the people and put the bread and butter on the table as Crom Cruach had done in the past. The conversion of people to Christianity did not eliminate their need of the basic materials of life and these had to be supplied by the new God. We have a marvellous example of this situation in the Rogation Processions of the Medieval Church held on the Monday, Tuesday and Wednesday before Ascension Thursday. These often involved large numbers of priests, Religious Orders and faithful who processed through the fields singing the Litany of the Saints and imploring God to preserve their crops from disease and bless them with an abundant harvest. The custom was begun by St Mamertus of Vienne in France in the fifth century and gradually spread throughout Europe. The bishop's diocese was severely ravaged by bad weather, disease and flooding, coming at a time when the growing corn was in a particularly vulnerable condition.

The prestigious 'Litany of the Saints' sung during the procession is a superb religious composition which expresses much of the doctrine and ethos of Catholic Christianity in all its richness. While the Rogation Procession was primarily concerned with the fertility of the land, this idea was situated within the vast complex of man's relationship with God.

The great litany begins with an invocation of the Blessed Trinity – the central mystery of Christianity:

Father of heaven; have mercy on us.
God the Son, Redeemer of the world; have mercy on us.
God the Holy Spirit; have mercy on us.
Holy Trinity, One God, have mercy on us'.

From this it goes on to invoke the Blessed Virgin Mary:

'Holy Mary, pray for us'

Then the Angels are called upon: 'All you holy Angels and Archangels; pray for us.' Then the apostles, including St Bartholomew and a long list of saints. All are asked to pray for us. The saints who have passed over from the conditions of this world in which they triumphed over the evil forces separating men from God have now achieved the fullness of everlasting life with him in glory. These are the spiritual Ancestors and they have power in the Otherworld just as the Ancestors of the Megalithic People had. The statues and shrines before which people pray and light candles in Catholic churches testify to this belief. Then God is asked to deliver us from the various afflictions of life:

From your anger; O Lord deliver us.
From sudden and unprovided death; O Lord deliver us.
From lightening and tempest; O Lord deliver us.
From the scourge of earthquake; O Lord deliver us.
From plague, famine and war; O Lord deliver us.
From everlasting death; O Lord deliver us'
(Lefebvre, G., 1945, 1888ff)

In some places, as in Bodmin Riding in Cornwall, on one of the three Rogation Days, the procession went around and, as it were, redefined the boundaries of the parish, stopping at certain places or trees to hear a reading from the gospel. Before maps became popular this was a very successful way of defining the territorial limits of the parish. The practice was called 'Beating the Bounds'.

At the Bodmin Rogations, too, as in other places, an artificial Dragon was dragged along as part of the processions. It was thought that the Dragon (Satan in the Book of Revelation) was the source of evil and a causer of blight in crops. By the power of God and the prayer of the Spiritual Ancestors (the saints) the malignant interventions of the Dragon were curbed and kept under control. In some places the power of prayer in the fight against the Dragon was emphasised. On the first day of the Rogations, the Dragon preceded the Procession – showing that he was leading the group of worshippers who had grown careless in their prayers and service of God. Through this neglect, the Devil had secured the upper hand and he led them in whatever direction he wished. However, on this first day (Monday) a great deal of prayer, ritual and visitation of churches on the processional route had taken place. Accordingly, the power of God had seeped back to the people and they were gradually regaining control. On the second day (Tuesday) the Dragon had fallen back to midway in the procession. A great deal of prayer and devotion occurred again and on the third day (Wednesday) the Dragon had lost ground completely and limped along dejectedly at the end of the procession. The people were now in charge and they had defeated the wily Dragon by the use of fervent prayer. What a way to get an idea across! I suspect that this naïve, colourful, dramatic and highly visual ritual communicated the idea of the power of prayer more effectively than can ever be done by our anaemic sermons or illustrated religious instruction books. As an Antiphon in the Breviary puts it:

> *Estote fortes in bello et pugnate cum antiquo serpente, et accipietis vitam aeternam* (Be strong in battle and fight against the ancient serpent and you will receive everlasting life).

The Dragon often came to an ignominious end by burning or drowning and the place where he perished was given such names as 'Dragon Rock', 'Dragon Well', 'Dragon Pit' (Hazlitt, 1995, 62). In Co Clare, the great lake *Loch Raha* is also known as *Loch Broic Sí.*

It was here that the fearless dragon-fighter Mac Creiche finally defeated Broc Sí, after a prolonged and desperate encounter, to the relief of the local people who had suffered much from his extortions. As the monster arose from the lake, Mac Creiche threw his hat at him. The hat became huge and heavy; it descended on Broc Sí and forced him downwards into the lake from which he emerges now only on rare occasions according to local folklore (Plummer, 1925, 42-45). Mac Creiche demanded huge fees for the performance of his duties as professional dragon-fighter and one wonders if the dragon weren't more tolerable.

Considering Cromm Cróich / Crom Cruach and Crom Dubh to be essentially one and the same deity connected with weather conditions, fertility of the land and harvest, one comes across another name which clearly indicates that Crom belonged to the *Fomhóraigh* or dark gods – this is the character called Morc who is prominent in *Leabhar Gabhála Éireann*.

Morc is obviously Crom spelled backwards. It should first be explained that in ancient Ireland two types of gods were recognised – the Tuatha Dé Danann or Aos Sí and the Fomhóraigh. The Tuatha Dé Danann were the bright, generous gods like the Olympians gods of Greece (this does not mean that they were all paragons of virtue and benevolence) and the Fomhóraigh – the dark gods associated with the depths of the sea and Lochlann (Scandinavian lands) – these were the greedy oppressive gods, who, nevertheless, had a greater knowledge of the secrets of agriculture than their more civilised adversaries the Tuatha Dé Danann. Crom Dubh approximates to this oppressive group of deities and the story of Conaing's Tower, in which Morc is involved, shows signs of the same ritual layout as in the case of Maigh Sléacht.

According to the account in *Leabhar Gabhála Éireann* (Section V, *Nemed*), the inhabitants of Ireland at that time – Clann Neimhidh – were much oppressed by the Fomhóraigh Conaing and Morc who operated from their stronghold or sanctuary of Tor Conaing in the north-west of the country. Two thirds of their corn, their milk, and their progeny had to be brought to them in taxation. The men of Ireland had to convey this every Samhain night (31 October) to the

Fomhóraigh, to Magh gCetne. Finally, the people rose in rebellion and, having gathered together a large army, they attacked Tor Conaing by land and by sea. They succeeded in capturing the tower and Conaing and his family fell at their hands. But just as their victory seemed secure, Morc arrived suddenly on the scene with sixty ships. In the excitement of the ensuing battle Clann Neimhidh didn't notice the tide rising around them and in the end those not killed by the sword were drowned. Only thirty of the men of Ireland escaped and they sailed away to Greece, feeling that their case was hopeless after this terrible disaster.

The history of Clann Neimhidh continues, however, in a peculiar way. This small group of immigrants from Ireland split into two and returned to Ireland at a later stage as the Fir Bholg and the Tuatha Dé Danann. The Fir Bholg were defeated by the Tuatha Dé Danann and retired to the Aran Islands, and what are now the counties of Galway, Clare and Limerick. Meanwhile, the Tuatha Dé Danann ruled the country. But not for long. Clann Mhíle, the last Celtic invasion, arrived from Spain. They defeated the Tuatha Dé Danann at the battle of Tailtean in Co Meath, and the Tuatha Dé Danann were forced underground where they inhabit the sacred hollow hills – the Sí or Sidheáin. These are the gods of ancient Ireland and from the Sí they control the fertility of the land.

Controversy surrounds the location of Tor Inis where Tor Chonainn was situated. Some authors thought that this was Tory Island. However, Henry Morris, in a brilliant article: 'Where was Tor Inis, the Island Fortress of the Fomorians?' (JRSAI,1927, 47ff), appears to prove beyond a shadow of doubt that Tor Inis was the small island of Dernis about eight miles to the south of Bundoran. Morris describes the setting: 'The scene from this spot would suggest an epic: looking inland the solid mass of Benbulbin confronts you; behind you stretches the illimitable ocean; to the north is Mullaghmore – 'the great summit'; to the south Moneygold wooded hill and the long peninsula of Streedagh' (55). The setting corresponds to the demands of the text far more closely than that of Tory Island where there is no strand to accommodate a large army some of whom arrived by sea and others by land.

Tor Chonainn, then, was the fortress – sanctuary of Morc the

Fomhórach, the western manifestation of Crom Cruach of Maigh Sléacht of Cavan. Like Crom Cruach's sanctuary it was partially cut off from the surrounding area by water so that access to the actual sanctuary was restricted. But the *Neimheadh* or sacred site wasn't limited to the sanctuary – it extended out over the landscape to provide an area for the worshipping community in which to perform their prostrations and a place of deposition of their offerings of corn, dairy products and children. The layout is not unfamiliar – in a Catholic church the building is divided into two basic sections – the Sanctuary and the Nave. The Sanctuary is the domain of the priest and his assistants and is separated from the Nave by altar-rails and steps. The Nave is reserved for the people. This is where they congregate to participate in the liturgy by word of mouth, gesture, receiving Holy Communion and making their offerings. This is all indoors, of course, but in the Crom Cruach/ Morc system the liturgy was outdoors and involved a considerable local area. It could be called a 'Landscape Liturgy' and, indeed, the Celtic Christian rituals such as the cult of the Holy Wells and the pilgrimages to Croagh Patrick, Lough Dearg, Baile Bhóirne and so forth, which have come down to us through the centuries, are of the same nature.

In the Cavan area, then, the Crom Ritual seems to have Darraugh Rath as the sanctuary and the plain of Maigh Sléacht as the nave. Garradice Lake (Loch Ghuth Ard Theas) would constitute the watery boundary preventing free access to Crom Cruach's sanctuary.

Similarly, a watery boundary prevented free access to Tor Chonainn or the sanctuary of Morc in Sligo. But what of the other component of the sacred place – the large area where the people gathered to worship and leave their offerings of corn, milk and children? As stated in *Leabhar Gabhála Éireann*, this place was Magh Cetna/Magh gCetna and this is identified as the area lying to the east of Bundoran between the rivers Erne and Drobhais. This is still a considerable distance – about ten miles from the actual island sanctuary. This distance raises questions regarding the validity of the argument – is this too far away to be an integral part of the temple?

Leabhar Gabhála also gives the name Torinis Chétna, thereby uniting the fortress and the plain. Magh Cétna is the plain between the mountains and the sea along the coast of Sligo. According to Morris, a confusion sometimes occurs between Magh Éne / Magh nÉne, 'rich in corn', in the same area and Magh gCétna 'of the Fomorians'. It would appear then, that it was Magh nÉne which lay between the Erne and the Drobhais rivers while Magh gCétna was further south over the river Dubh. A further placename in the area was Magh nItha (Plain of Corn) and this appears to be an older name for Magh nÉne or Magh gCétna. It was here that Parthalon, who lived close to Ballyshannon, fought a great battle against the Fomhóraigh. All this leads to an area much further south past the river Dubh, to an offering site close to the island of Tor Inis which would then conform to the temple pattern of Darraugh Rath and Magh Sléacht in Cavan. By a strange coincidence a village called 'Grange' (*An Ghráinseach* – Gramary) lies very close today to Tor Inis. Though obviously of a later period, could it possibly be on the former site the Tor Inis ritual complex? Similarly the river Gráinne – also apparently related to grain – flows close to Darraugh Rath and Magh Sléacht in the Cavan complex.

As regards Tor Inis island (Dernis) itself, Morris turns to the question of Conaing's Tower situated there:

> Now for the tower. On the very highest part of the island, still called 'Cnoc a' Dúin', 'the Hill of the Dún or Fortress', there survived until about 50 years ago, the remains of a stone fort or cashel, something like Dún Aengus in Arran. It was overgrown with briars and brushwood, until it was cleared away by the uncle of the present owner; and the latter – Peter Mulligan – dug up the foundations about the year 1910, and was the first to grow a crop on the spot. The trace of the circle can still be clearly seen in the sward, which shows that it was about 33 yards in interior diameter, a dimension which I have found repeated so frequently in Irish forts that it must have some significance (54-55).

Morris gives the area of the island as 115 acres and at low tide it can be reached on foot from Streedagh on the south, by a strand three miles long, and in his time six families lived there. These, however, were fairly recent comers from the mainland which is only a short distance away.

So, in practice, we have a description of a primitive landscape sanctuary in which an unpopular but necessary harvest deity was worshipped and to whom serious offerings were made at the end of the harvest – that is at Samhain – November – the beginning of the dark half of the year among the Celts – and the time when the people were thinking of winter sowing of corn for next year's harvest. So that this was an appropriate time to approach Crom/ Morc by prayer and sacrifice. The small area between Bally-magauran and Killycluggin is particularly rich in ancients remains such as standing stones, barrows, stone circles and megalithic tombs. The spectacular dún or fort of Darraugh Rath (Derryragh) overlooking Maigh Sléacht is supposed to be the fortress of Crom Cruach while, as we have seen, he is also associated with the nearby megaliths.

So that a fortress on high ground seems to be a feature of Crom in his different manifestations whether at Maigh Sléacht, Tor Chonainn or Penhill. Perhaps significantly, Crom Cruach is known also as 'Ceann Cruaich' – 'head of the hill' and 'Pen' in Welsh is 'head' giving us Penhill – head of the hill.

So far we have discussed the possibility of a great outdoor sanctuary of the harvest god Crom in Maigh Sléacht in Cavan, in Tor Inis off the coast of Sligo and in Wensleydale in Yorkshire, and in all three areas, though widely separated from each other, much the same elements are found – a high place, a fortified, restricted area, a special space for offerings, an oppressive but necessary powerful figure who exercises control over the harvest, and while the serious sacrifices of corn, dairy produce, animal and human sacrifices are made at Samhain at the end of the harvest when produce is plentiful, is also associated with Lughnasa – at the ripening of the corn. He is associated with both the beginning and the end of the harvest. The Lughnasa festival is slightly later in Yorkshire than in Ireland, as would be expected considering how far north Yorkshire is, and there, Crom is called 'Bartle' derived from the patron of the local church St Bartholomew whose feast-day occurs on 24 August, corresponding to the beginning of harvest. We have seen that a similar tradition occurs in Ireland in the case of St Bartholomew – *Parthanán an Fhómhair*.

CHAPTER FOUR

Lough Gur: Enchanted Lake

We might well ask, then, if any other landscape sanctuary sacred to Crom occurs within the confines of the British Isles.

Lough Gur, in Co Limerick, is regarded as one of the great religious sites of ancient Ireland.

Its connection with Crom Dubh is not quite so emphatic, however, as in the case of Maigh Sléacht, as this large area with its enchanted lake, megalithic tombs, stone circles, standing stones, raths, castles and a holy well, is an awesome complex dominated by the goddess Áine whose sacred hill, Cnoc Áine, lies in the vicinity. But having asserted the sovereignty of Áine in this area, on entering the great stone circle of Grange which forms part of the complex, the first thing to strike the visitor is the huge stone jutting out above the others, and, wait for it, this stone is known as 'Rannach Chrom Dubh' (the Staff? of Crom Dubh). We will see more of this later, subsequent to a more general outline of this great archeological site near the village of Hospital – once a residence of the Knights Hospitallers (*Ospidéal Áine*), whence the name.

Here, the local people tell of the great medieval, highly Gaelicised Norman Knight, Gearóid Iarla Mac Gearailt, associated with the goddess Áine of Lough Gur and her nearby sacred hill of Cnoc Áine (Knockainey). According to the tale, which in its way breathes the mysterious, awesome spirit of the earlier days of this area, Gearóid Iarla and his wife were one night sitting in front of a blazing fire in their castle in West Limerick belonging to the powerful Fitzgerald family. He was renowned for his gift of poetry and magical ability, and to pass the time his wife asked him to show her some magical tricks. He agreed on condition that whatever happened she would on no account scream. She agreed and Gearóid Iarla turned himself into a bird which flew around the room. At this point, the cat sleeping by the fireside woke up and sprang at the bird. The woman screamed, The *geis* or magical prohibition had been broken and Gearóid Iarla could not turn himself back into a man again. He flew out the window of the castle and made for Lough Gur.

Here he met the goddess Áine. She turned him back into a man again and gathered together some Norman Knights to keep him company.

She then consigned them all to a castle underneath an island on the lake still known as Gearóid Island. There they live on in an enchanted sleep until *Lá na Cinniúna* – the day of destiny. When that day comes, at the sound of the horn, Gearóid Iarla and his Knights will arise from their enchanted sleep and set Ireland free.

This is Celtic eschatology – the dream of a small oppressed community for the return of the hero at a destined time to break their bondage.

This idea of the 'Last Days' was well known even in the early Christian church where the *Etimasia*, or painting of an empty throne waiting for the returning Christ to occupy it, dominated the ceiling of the church and, even today, at Mass, the people say: 'Christ has died, Christ has risen, Christ will come again'.

A similar tale is told of the great King Arthur. After his last battle the king died of his wounds. Four queens, dressed in black, arrive in a boat with black sails and among them is the great druidess Morgan La Fée. They carry the body of the king to the mysterious Isle of Avalon identified on a human level with Glastonbury in Somerset. Here they bury Arthur and next morning the local people are surprised at the sight of a new grave. The bishop is summoned and then Morgan La Fée arrives. She explains to the bishop that it is only the mortal remains of Arthur the King that lie in the earth, for 'his spirit', she said, 'lives on in the Isle of Avalon, and he will return again when his people have need of him'.

King Arthur's grave is pointed out in the ruins of the great Benedictine Abbey at Glastonbury with the legend of the Cross with the inscription: 'Here lies the famous Arthur, the once and future King.'

Throughout the centuries, the people of Lough Gur have heard the story of the man who entered a cave in the area. There he sees a great company of Knights asleep on the floor. A horn is hanging on the wall and out of curiosity the man takes it down and blows it. At the sound of the horn the Knights awake from their sleep and shout: 'An é an lá fós é?' (Is it the day already?). At that moment Gearóid Iarla appears and explains that it was a mistake – that the day of destiny has not yet arrived. Then the Knights lie down again and return to their enchanted sleep.

Every seven years, when the moon is full, Gearóid Iarla can be seen galloping around the lake on his white horse. The white horse has silver shoes and when the silver shoes are worn out – then will come the day of destiny and the Knights will arise from their enchanted sleep.

In discussing Gearóid Iarla Mac Gearailt and Morgan La Fée, however, the presumption is that these were basically humans who were endowed with extraordinary magical gifts which allowed them to slip in and out of the Otherworld with a facility denied to the ordinary mortal.

Áine and Crom Cruach/Dubh, however, are deities, who nevertheless, can adopt human shape and participate in human activitiess.

One of the outstanding and best-preserved sites of the Lough Gur ritual complex is the great stone circle at Grange townland, very close to the lake itself. Pottery from the Late Stone Age and Early Bronze Age (c. 2000-1500 BC) was found inside when excavated. The stones forming the circle, unlike many other circles are contiguous, that is, they are touching each other to form a boundary. Outside the circle of stones a huge embankment of earth is heaped up against the stones to support them all around so that the site looks like a rath or lios with stones on the inside of the bank. The local people actually call it 'The Lios'. One might suppose that the huge bank supporting the stones on the outside consists of clay found near at hand. However, there is no surrounding ditch and Professor Seán Ó Riordáin, who carried out the excavation of the site, makes it quite clear that the material used inside the circle to cover up the original level of the floor, and the bank it-

self, consists of gravelly clay which had to be transported across the
fields from an area closer to the lake. The bank also contained numerous small stones as if the builders were determined to construct a very solid bank all around the circle of megaliths, and, indeed, in this they succeeded admirably (cf 'Lough Gur
Excavations: The Great Stone Circle (B) in Grange Townland',
PRIA, 54 C2; 1951, 43-44,46). This is an enormous circle – the complete diameter being about 215 feet and the width of the bank is
about 30 feet (Ó Ríordáin, 1951, 42) The bank looks like a great circular grandstand from which spectators could watch the action
within the enclosure. But what was the action? If the spectators
were standing on the bank looking into the interior of the circle
what were they watching? When showing groups of tourists
around, the tourist guide must brace himself, or herself, for this
inevitable question: 'What did they do in here?' And this is a difficult question indeed.

Ó Ríordáin's attitude is not very helpful and seems to be typical of his time: 'What rites were carried on at the stone circle we
have no means of knowing and speculation is profitless' (1951, 74).

A modern tourist guide would hardly dare come out with this
curt declaration. If he did there would probably be mutterings
from the disappointed audience. He will say something to the effect that in all probability Ritual Dances were performed in the circle at certain times of the year to promote the fertility of the land.
This answer will give his audience something to think about and,
as far as it goes, it may well be part of the correct answer. But we
will see more of this later when a more detailed examination of
this marvellous site is completed.

An impressive entrance passage, allowing entry to the circle
cuts through the bank. The two entrance stones where the passage
meets the circle of stones are exceptionally large and have obviously been placed in this position to emphasise the importance of
this particular feature of the ritual complex. An impressive entrance -way is a feature of many other stone circles and this is also
a marked characteristic of some medieval churches such as
Clonfert Cathedral, Co Galway, with its elaborate doorway. In all
probability this elaboration of the entrance area is a deliberate

marker of the area of the transition between the profane and sacred worlds. It warns the worshipper, whether pagan or christian that he is now leaving the ordinary human world and entering into the world of the divine, and the world of the divine is dangerous, so he must advance cautiously and with the right dispositions. This is exemplified very simply, but very effectively, in many small country churches in Ireland at the present day. The church stands away back from the road in its own churchyard area often surrounded by elaborate wrought iron gates and railings. A path leads from the gate to a number of steps leading into a darkened porch. Here, there is a holy-water font containing blessed water for purification. He takes some of the water and makes the sign of the cross on himself with it. He splashes some of the water on the foreheads of his children and only then, after this elaborate preparation does he enter the sacred place. This arrangement is not accidental. It is a carefully planned system to enable the worshipper to part company, as it were, at least temporarily from his ordinary this-worldly preoccupations and lead him gently, step by step, into a suitable attitude for entrance into another dimension. Here, as elsewhere, a careful examination of certain observances of the Catholic and Orthodox churches will show the profound religious intuitions linking them to our most ancient forms of worship. The feeling of awe and reverence on entering a sacred sanctuary is illustrated by both the massive entrance stones to prehistoric temples and the ornate doorways of Catholic churches.

The entrance passage, at the northeast of the great stone circle at Grange, Lough Gur, begins at the edge of the bank and stone flags prevent the clay from falling down and blocking the passage. It is contemporary with the circle itself. This arrangement provides a neat pathway into the circle. Its width will allow only one person to enter at a time and we will see later that this provision may have a significance for the type of ritual performed here. The Lough Gur complex seems to differ in some rather mysterious way from that of Maigh Sléacht and it may be that a somewhat different type of religion may have prevailed here with a greater emphasis on the goddess.

The entrance path slopes upwards showing that the floor was artificially raised above the level of the surrounding fields. To the north of the entrance, but forming part of the circle, stands the massive block of stone called Rannach Chrom Dubh which links us to Crom Cruach / Dubh of Maigh Sléacht. On the other side of the circle from the entrance passage, directly opposite the entrance, the tops of two large stones come together to form a 'V' shape or notch. This formation gives the impression that it was deliberately designed to serve as a sightline for somebody looking directly through the passage-way across.

Michael Dames, in his penetrating study of the traditions of Lough Gur (1992, 77), suggests that a straight line drawn from this notch on the western side of the circle and going through the passage-way would pass over the stone platform on Gearóid Island, over 'Suíochán Áine' (the stone chair of the goddess Áine) and straight on to Cnoc Ghréine – the hill of the goddess Grian, sister of Áine, rising up behind Pallas Grean (Grian is the Gaelic for sun). This would be the point of the rising sun at Lughnasa (beginning of August) and also at Bealtaine (beginning of May). These are two major Feasts in the Insular Celtic Calendar. However, as there are so many trees and other obstructions on the way, it is difficult to be sure of this alignment but it is certainly worthy of continual study.

Similarly, by looking through the passageway across to the 'V' stones one can trace an alignment to Cnoc Fírinne near Ballingarry, Co Limerick and to the sunset at Samhain (beginning of November) and the sunset at Imbolg (Beginning of February). Samhain, Imbolg, Bealtaine and Lughnasa are the four great Insular Celtic Festivals which mark the beginning of the seasons of Winter, Spring, Summer and Autumn.

Cnoc Fírinne (Knockfeerna) is the great hill sanctuary of the god Donn – the god of fertility and death and a significant site on which Lughnasa rites were performed and to some extent continue to the present day.

It would be most intriguing, indeed, if we could be absolutely sure, without a shadow of doubt, that alignments indicated the rising or setting sun at these four dates as it would indicate that these four feasts were significant to the late Megalithic and Bronze Age peoples away earlier than the Celtic period.

Sir Berthram Windele, in his description of the Lough Gur monuments (*PRIA* 30, 1912, 286) discussed the question of alignments but was unable to give any information on the subject.

The Great Stone Circle at Lough Gur poses two of the questions which appear to be insoluble.

The first question is: 'Why did the Megalithic/Bronze Age people go to so much trouble to construct these huge monuments involving dragging large stones and clay over considerable distances with no mechanical conveniences? Why did they do it?

One might ask the same question with regard to the great medieval cathedrals of Europe such as Chartres, Rheims, Cologne, Canterbury, Ely. Why did the people of the Middle Ages undertake such enormous tasks considering that they were hardly better equipped mechanically than the earlier peoples?

The fact that we even ask this question today may be a measure of the distance we are mentally from both the Megalithic and Medieval builders.

To undertake such enormous labours, the people must have been highly motivated and the motivation must have been perfectly clear to them on a widespread and popular level.

In the case of large monuments, the work may have gone on for several generations, considering that the life-span seems to have been quite short – from about 35 to 45 years of age.

In the case of the medieval Christian cathedral and abbey builders, the motivation is clear enough. They were building this great edifice for the glory of Almighty God who would repay them for their labours by giving them an eternity of bliss in another world after death. The medieval church was strong on eschatology – the Last Things – probably because life in this world, as experienced by the ordinary person, was short and uncertain. The idea is actually well-expressed in the Third Eucharist Prayer in the modern Roman Rite of the Mass:

> Welcome into your kingdom our departed brothers and sisters, and all who have left this world in your friendship. There we hope to share in your glory when every tear will be wiped

away. On that day, we shall see you, our God, as you are. We shall become like you and praise you for ever through Christ our Lord, from whom all good things come.

This vision of an everlasting life of supreme happiness in a world beyond the grave, which is put before the Catholic faithful of today, is no different from that which inspired the medieval builders of the great cathedrals.

Even on a completely human level, one can imagine a man telling visitors with great pride that his father / grandfather / great grandfather were involved in the construction of this glorious building which reflects the glory of Almighty God to generations yet to come.

But to return to the use made of the stone circles of the late stone-age and bronze age period. Is there any clue at all to what the assembled people may have actually done at the great circle at Grange at Lough Gur? Firstly, the indications are that stone circles were only used on occasion – probably at the eight great feasts of the year. These are the Winter Solstice (21 December), the Summer Solstice (21 June), the Spring Equinox (21 March) and the Autumn Equinox (21 September) These are the 'Four Stations of the Sun'.

If we include then the more specifically insular Celtic Feasts – Samhain (1 November), Imbolg (1 February), Bealtaine (1 May) and Lughnasa (1 August), we have the eight major occasions on which a ritual may have taken place at Grange Stone Circle. It may not even be as often as that and the paucity of use is indicated by the fact that according to archeologists the finds of crockery, brooches, and everyday utensils of domestic life are notoriously meagre at stone circles, indicating that they were not in daily use.

One of the most enthralling things so often remarked by anthropologists and students of comparative religion is the extraordinary similarities in ritual customs and beliefs which occur among widely separated peoples.

One school of thought attributes this phenomenon to the similar reaction of different peoples to the same or similar basic conditions which can occur in a pre-scientific community.

Another school of thought favours a more diffusionist theory, arguing that there was once a common centre from which peoples and ideas and rituals emanated to different areas of the world and were, in the process of time, gradually modified to suit local conditions.

Perhaps it was a mixture of the two approaches and, indeed, the ancients may have been greater travellers than we give them credit for and spread their own usages far and wide.

At any rate, in this largely unsolved question, the fact remains that there appears to be a remarkable unity among mankind in its early stages with regard to religious customs. The incredibly widespread use of Megaliths among peoples who have no known connection with each other, is an example of this phenomenon.

So, taking this phenomenon into account, and eager to give some kind of reasonable answer to the question 'What did the prehistoric people do here at Grange Stone Circle?', let us take a giant step in the footsteps of a Catholic Missionary Priest of the African Missionary Society, to the Yoruba Tribe of Nigeria.

In his book *Yoruba Religious Carving – Pagan and Christian Sculpture in Nigeria and Dahomey* (Chapman, London, 1967), the author Father Kevin Carroll, gives an illuminating description of a Pagan Feast near the village of Egosi.

When the heavy rains set in and the yam roots are ripening in the ground, the date of the masked dances is announced by the master of the Feast, the 'Aworo'.

There is a long period of preparation for the Feast and the people are very conscious of its approach and use it as a time indicator – twenty days to the Feast, fifteen days and so on, until the vigil when they greet each other: 'We salute you for the Feast.' The Christians follow the same procedure.

Preparations are going on by way of procuring extra food for the occasion, washing and repainting the masks to be worn by the dancers and making preparatory sacrifices to propitiate the spirits.

From the hills and forests comes the sound of the slit drums made from trees with a full length slit and the interior gouged out.

Father Carroll describes his experience of the rite:

Suddenly we came out from the narrow path, dark under the trees, into the open light of the clearing where the masks would appear, and we saw the fruit tree which gives its name to the feast – Udi osan (at the foot of the osan tree). The arena was a slightly tilted saucer in a saddle of the hills, partly encircled by a bank overhung with trees which was used as a stand by the people. Inside the bowl there were several smooth swellings of rock which the people also used as stands. The grass of the glade was green at first but by nightfall it had been churned into mud. A channel had been cut into the bank at one side and it led to the 'sacristy' where the mask carriers assembled and dressed out of sight of the people. Here sacrifices were made and blood poured on the faces of the masks (p 64).

In this detailed account, there is no mention of megaliths and we are not speaking of a megalithic culture, but on the other hand, the arena, with its saucer-like shape, and bank on which the spectators stood, bears a remarkable resemblance to the stone circle at Lough Gur.

Another striking feature of this outdoor sanctuary is the channel cut into the bank leading outside the arena to a kind of sacristy or dressing-room in which the actors put on their masks out of sight of the people. It was here also that the preliminary sacrifices (probably of hens) were made to secure the good will of the spirits.

This layout bears a remarkable resemblance to the banked circle at Grange with its carefully arranged narrow passage leading in and out of the circle. Perhaps this narrow passage was the path to the dressing-room where the actors vested and put on their masks.

Father Carroll goes on to describe the scene witnessed by himself and his companions. They noticed that there was a kind of 'royal box' reserved for the Aworo and the older men who accompanied him, somewhat isolated from the jostling crowd.

The priestesses, messengers of the spirits, gathered under the sacred osan tree and some moved around crumbling cakes as peace-offerings to the spirits. These women moved with reverence and knelt to greet the Aworo.

Meanwhile, groups of 'soldiers' dressed in the dark clothes of hunters marched to and fro across the arena throwing spears into the air and catching them as they fell and uttering discordant cries.

Two companies of brightly-dressed girls performed a woven dance between rocks and trees, sometimes moving with a rhythmic walk, swinging their hands together, at times holding hands in groups of four.

Meanwhile, the people, participants rather than spectators, were filling up all the available space on the banks and rocks and an air of expectancy was building up as they looked towards the entrance passageway into the circle from the dressing room.

It was from here that the masked figures, each representing a god would emerge, one by one, into the arena to parade and dance while the people shouted their acclamations.

The dressing-up and purification of the huge masks by preliminary sacrifice was conducted out of sight of the people and the build-up of atmosphere was like that experienced in a theatre moments before the curtain rises.

To continue the account of the scene in Father Carroll's own words:

'Is it coming? Have they finished the sacrifice?' they asked each other.

Suddenly the girls moved towards the entrance to the sacristy and we knew a mask (masked figure) was about to come out as they chanted:

'Uyi, Uyi, se e r'uyi o, uyi nla, uyi o'
'Glory, glory, do you see the great glory'

Then the mask came out, a dog-eared 'Elefon' mask, the head glistening with the scarlet of fresh-clotted blood; it came out slowly and then ran suddenly like a bull in a Spanish arena and everyone cleared before its rush until it was arrested and controlled by the young men in charge of it. Then the people took up the refrain for this mask, 'Oja Iesi', princess of Ieshi. The fierce mask was surmounted by the gentle figures of a woman and child coloured with red and yellow ochres, black and white. As they sang, the people swayed in time with the rhythm, shoulder to shoulder in their close packed ranks. Money and children are the first and chief requests of the Yoruba people and they called on the spirit of the mask for

these things:
'Princess of Ieshi,
O re, o ye, ora o.
I like money, I like children.
Give me a fine child,
Princess of Ieshi,
Ora – o –'

The rhythm of the song was controlled by the drums; not the 'dundun' or 'gangan' talking-drums of the northern influenced Yoruba, but the heavy barrel drums of the old areas' (Carroll, 1967, 67).

The next masked figure was waiting impatiently to make its entrance, as the deities paraded, one after another, like models on the catwalk.

Princess Ieshi, however, hugged the limelight, as it were, and was in no hurry to leave. When she finally left, the next mask entered the arena with a more gliding, menacing, stride than its predecessor. Each mask has its own typical behaviour.

Presumably this is to portray the different character of each divinity.

A succession of masked figures followed in rotation, the body being covered with palm fronds except for the legs and arms.

This yellow-green cloak make a stark contrast to the daub of scarlet blood on the mask.

As each mask retired, the girls followed it with a long drawn cry of praise:
'U – u – u – u – yi –.'

As dusk descended on the ritual scene, there was a break in which all waited expectantly for the final entrance – that of the great mask 'Oluwa'. Father Carroll describes the event:

The great mask 'Oluwa' was about to appear but it kept us waiting to allow tension to build up. Then it came out suddenly, moving quickly around the arena, a horizontal , spiral-horned mask, eight feet long, painted with ochres and black and white. Oluwa is 'the feared, the terror of the district, the killer of the beautiful', and the people broke into the menacing chant:

> 'It is fear that comes,
> With a viper for his robe;
> It is fear that comes,
> With a python for his scarf;
> It is fear that comes'

Suddenly the long mask broke away from the arena, running away with its followers down the path which leads to the hilltop of Utala, two miles away. In front ran a man striking a gong to clear stragglers from the path. Oluwa will be kept in the cave at Utala's top, covered with slabs of stone until it is needed again. When the sound of the gong died away down the hillside the crowd broke up and we made our way home as the darkness settled around us (1967, 67-69).

The masked feasts are dying, due no doubt to the onward march of westernisation. Father Croll, who has contributed such a vivid description of the rites, has made some use of masks, together with the rich poetry and beautiful religious music which accompanies them, in the development of Christian drama.

This approach, of course, has a long and venerable tradition in the Catholic Church. It does, however, involve inherent difficulties in preserving the cultural past in the light of a radically changed philosophical environment.

We might describe this Yoruba ritual as a parade of the gods in which the divinities, one by one, manifested themselves to their people and received their homage.

It was a liturgy of dance, of displays of emotion, of intense excitement, and states of ecstatic trance are hinted at in the feature of the assistants restraining the dancing god. This ecstasy may have also extended to those of the congregation who joined in the dance as happened elsewhere.

The large crowd, gathered together in a sacred place, with a common objective – to make contact with superworldly forces of fertility and well-being – could be temporarily transferred by the mesmeric rhythm of the dance into a state of trance – a brief experience of eternity in the company of the spirits. The Mysteries of Dionysus of Greece, with their enormous following and tradition of dance, may have antecedents going back to prehistoric ages.

While the Yoruba rite of Nigeria as described, is modern and does not involve megaliths, the architectural layout of the site at Lough Gur bears a remarkable resemblance to what has been described in the Yoruba area.

At least, it gives some idea of what might have taken place in the Grange Stone Circle.

At a certain time of the year, and the Summer Solstice (c. 21 June) is the date most in evidence, crowds of dancers representing outlying communities and villages who were warned of the approach of the Feast well in advance, could have been summoned by drummers and horn-blowers on the surrounding hills and their route directed by beacon-fires. Large amounts of food for the feast would have been collected beforehand. Those people who had the intellectual and organisational ability to design and build the massive sacred sanctuary certainly had the ability to organise what took place within it. It may have involved the sacrifice of animals.

From the studies made of peoples who have maintained archaic lifestyles into modern times, it is clear, above all, that the dance played an enormous role in their lives. While the Christian priest said 'Let us pray', his prehistoric counterpart said 'Let us dance'. We will see later, when discussing the case of the megalithic culture of Malekula in the New Hebrides, how vital the dance was in the life of the community and its power of binding together in a cohesive body the various groups separated by mountain, hill and lake. The proliferation of sacred sites of various kinds around the Maigh Sléacht, Ballymagauran area of Cavan, for instance, may indicate a large number of small communities separated from each other by hills, bogs and lakes. This type of terrain which made travel difficult would naturally result in a multiplication of localised shrines, with a more centralised sanctuary for very solemn occasions in which a pilgrimage was involved. And this is indeed what is suggested by the Co Cavan landscape.

One of the characteristics of the Lough Gur landscape, also, is the number of hills dotted around the lake: Knockfennell, Knockadoon, Knockroe, Grange Hill, Knockderc, Knockbolg,

Barnaschagh Hill and others. These could have been used as sites of beacon fires to direct pilgrims to the great sanctuary of Lough Gur.

We have seen already that the Summer Solstice seems to have had a special importance in this area and was associated with the goddess Áine at her sanctuary at Cnoc Áine near the modern village of Hospital (*Ospidéal Áine*) just a few miles from Lough Gur. Here, people carried lighted torches – 'Cliars' – of hay around her sacred hill and afterwards threw them into fields and orchards. Legend tells us that on this holy night Áine with her *Bantracht*, or company of female Tuatha Dé Danann, could be seen on the hill when she appeared, took off her ring, and invited people to look through it.

While the bonfire was a vital part of the Summer Solstice celebration, and still remains so in the few places where it is still observed, it may have served as a beacon also on other occasions to direct pilgrims to the ritual site, while accepting that at the Summer Solstice the primary purpose of the bonfire, lighted sometimes near a dolmen, seems to have been to encourage the sun to keep on shining vigorously to ripen the corn even though it had reached its highest point in the heavens and now its power was declining. Following the principle: 'As above, so below' the worshippers were saying: 'As our fire blazes on earth, so may you blaze in the sky to ripen our corn.' The 'rat, tat, tat' of drumming imitated the patter of rain on the hard parched land, and the ancient belief appears to have been that such ritual imitation had a causative effect – that it actually caused rain to fall. Vigorous ritual dancing and rhythmic stamping of the ground may have been seen as an incitement to the earth to increase fertility and production. In this connection, could we perhaps formulate the principle: 'Simulation equals stimulation.'

To us today, brought up as we are on logical and scientific modes of thought, this type of thinking is decidedly curious. But supposing a different philosophy prevailed in which the Universe was a unity and each part was connected with every other part, and in which each part affected every other part, one can see that highly concentrated ritual, which imitated certain phenomena, might actually produce the effect it imitated.

Now, to take an example of ritual from parts of Europe where the heat at the Summer Solstice is causing the ground to harden up to an extent that cultivation is impossible and farmers are worried about the possibility of ploughing as the time for Winter sowing of grain approaches.

This intense and malevolent heat in the period immediately after the Summer Solstice (21 June) was something of a puzzle to people, as the sun was actually rising further south each day and losing its power, so that the days were getting shorter. People naturally expected that the weather would grow colder. It was not known then that the earth acted as a kind of battery or storage container for the sun's heat and was now giving it back with a vengeance.

In these intensely hot areas, then, the purpose of the rite was the opposite of what it was in a cold area such as Ireland. It was to reduce the heat of the sun, to calm down its torrid fervour, so that the rain could soften the soil and let the farmers go ahead with their cultivation.

So, the ritual took a different form. A great wooden wheel was stuffed with straw and combustible material and taken up to the top of a steep hill overlooking a lake or river and then set on fire and sent rolling down the hill until it plunged into the lake below where its fire was extinguished. What a wonderfully explicit way of expressing what the people of those hot areas wished would happen to the sun.

An elaborate form of this midsummer rite prevailed at Lower Konz, a village overlooking the great Moselle river, centre of the Moselle wine industry in Germany. Frazer gives an elaborate account of the rite which involved many details found also in other places:

> A quantity of straw was collected on the top of the steep Stromberg Hill. Every inhabitant, or at least every householder, had to contribute his share of straw to the pile. At nightfall the whole male population, men and boys, mustered on the top of the hill; the women and girls were not allowed to join them, but had to take up their position at a certain spring half-way

down the slope. On the summit stood a huge wheel completely encased in some of the straw which had been jointly contributed by the villagers; the rest of the straw was made into torches. From each side of the wheel the axle-tree projected about three feet, thus furnishing handles to the lads who were to guide it in its descent. The mayor of the neighbouring town of Sierck, who always received a basket of cherries for his services, gave the signal; a lighted torch was applied to the wheel, and as it burst into flame, two young fellows, strong-limbed and swift of foot, seized the handles and began running with it down the slope. A great shout went up. Every man and boy waved a blazing torch in the air, and took care to keep it alight so long as the wheel was trundling down the hill. The great object of the young men who guided the wheel was to plunge it blazing into the water of the Moselle; ... As it rolled past the women and girls at the spring, they raised cries of joy which were answered by the men on the top of the mountain; and the shouts were echoed by the inhabitants of neighbouring villages who watched the spectacle from their hills on the opposite bank of the Moselle (Frazer, 1923, 623).

CHAPTER FIVE

Midsummer Fires on St John's Eve

In this marvellous description of the Midsummer Bonfire on St John's Eve in the Moselle area, Frazer shows that much the same pattern prevailed right across Europe from Ireland to Russia. It was a great communal, popular, celebration and dancing, shouting, circumambulation of the fire, jumping over the flames, putting small stones in the fire, the use of special herbs such as vervain, mugworth and larkspur were known in many places. Spring wells were also a feature of the celebration so that, not only fire, but the element of water was involved. In Ireland special torches made of bunches of straw or oil-soaked rags or sods of turf steeped in oil or grease and borne aloft on poles or pitchforks were lighted from the bonfire and carried around through the fields so that the sacred fire would endow them with fertility and protection from disease. The old saying was: *Tine chnámh agus sop Sheáin ar gach ardán* – a bonfire and John's torch on every high place (Danaher, 1972, 145-146).

The St John's Eve fire festival resembled very closely the Bealtaine Fires of May Eve in their attention in some places to the protection from disease of cows and livestock. Sometimes the bonfire was divided into two so that cattle could pass between the two fires – *Idir dhá thine Bhealtaine* – as at May Eve, or it could be arranged that the cows were put into a field over which the smoke from the bonfire spread. A variety of different ways could be found in which people, fields, houses and livestock could be brought into contact with the sacred Midsummer Fires to ensure their prosperity during the coming year. This was also a great occasion of pilgrimage to Holy Wells dedicated to St John the Baptist, but undoubtedly of pre-Christian origin, as also of Fairs and Markets which drew large numbers of people from surrounding areas to one central venue. In short, the Summer

Solstice, marked by a decisive solar phenomenon – the turning back of the sun from its northern progress – became also here on earth a vital ritual and social occasion with major cosmic overtones with the uniting of the above with the below. Nor did the church miss this really spectacular event. Both in the Catholic and Eastern Rite churches the Feast of St John the Baptist (24 June) – coinciding with the Summer Solstice – is one of the great feasts of the Liturgical Year. The birth of Our Lord was fixed at the Winter Solstice (25 December) – the shortest day of the year but from then onwards the days are growing longer with increasing light. And Christ said: 'I am the Light of the World; anyone who follows me will not be walking in the dark; he will have the light of life' (John 8:12).

So, it was fully appropriate that the Birth of Christ should take place at the turning point of darkness to increasing light.

On the other hand, we know from the scriptures that St John the Baptist was six months older that Our Lord. So, his Feast was appropriately fixed on 24 June – the Summer Solstice – the longest day of the year. However, at this point, the sun turns and begins to rise a little further to the south each morning. In other words, the sun is losing its power – it is decreasing. An this natural phenomenon corresponds to St John's description of himself in contrast to Christ: 'He must grow greater, I must grow smaller' (John 3:30).

Despite the Catholic Church's many protests about the addiction of the faithful to pre-Christian practices, the Blessing of St John's Fire sneaked its way into the official book for the administration of sacraments and sacramentals, the *Rituale Romanum* and was approved for the Diocese of Tarbes: *Benedictio Rogi quae fit a Clero extra Ecclesiam in Vigilia S. Joannis Baptistae* (The Blessing of the bonfire which is performed by the priest outside the church on the Vigil of the Feast of St John the Baptist). The text of the blessing shows how the church veered the thought away from the fertility of the land and directed it rather to eternal light and life in the world to come:

Domine Deus, Pater omnipotens, lumen indeficiens, qui es conditor omnium luminum; novum hunc ignem sanctifica, + , et praesta; ut ad te, qui es lumen indeficiens, puris mentibus post hujus caliginem pervenire valeamus. Per Christum Dominum nostrum (Lord God, almighty Father, undying light, you are the creator of all lights; sanctify this fire, and grant, that we may be able to reach you – the undying light – after the darkness of this world. Through Christ, Our Lord.)

This wonderful, classical-style prayer unites ideas of the sun, of God the creator of all light, of God himself as the undying or never-decreasing light, of purity of mind and of the final end of man in union with God himself, and contrasts all this with the darkness which we experience here on earth.

Now, it is interesting to compare this official ecclesiastical prayer with a folk-blessing in use by *Giolla na Tine* (Attendant of the Fire) – the Master of Ceremonies at the St John's Eve Ritual in rural Ireland:

> *(Lasaim an tine seo) in onóir do Dhia agus do Naomh Eoin, agus chun toraidh agus chun tairbhe ar ár gcur agus ar ár saothar, in ainm an Athar agus an Mhic agus an Spioraid Naoimh, Amen* (Danaher, 1972, 139). (I light this fire) in honour of God and of St John, and for results and for help for our sowing and our labour, in the name of the Father, and of the Son and of the Holy Spirt. Amen.

This prayer, said at nightfall by a lay-person to accompany the lighting of the fire, is perfectly Christian, but unlike the ecclesiastical composition of the clergy is more directly concerned with the fruitfulness of the earth – that the labour involved in sowing the corn and other crops would result in a fruitful harvest.

The Feast of St John at Midsummer when celebrated fully was a highly developed rite. The great folklorist, Kevin Danaher (Caoimhín Ó Danachair) gathers together the disparate elements of the rite from various parts of the country and in this way shows the important place which this feast held among the people until fairly recent times in his major work, *The Year in Ireland* (Cork 1972).

In Athea, in Co Limerick, the bonfire was lighted near the Holy Well and the graveyard bringing together the elemental ideas of fire, water and the ancestors.

Kevin Danaher mentions a large variety of different practices from a number of areas throughout the country.

Sometimes the Bonfire was kindled in proximity to a Cromleac and one wonders if this suggests a connection between the Midsummer Rites and the pre-Celtic Megalithic People.

Children took burning branches from the fire and threw them as high as they could into the air while others threw lighting branches into the fields and orchards. Fire is the great source of purification and here we have an example of the purification of the air and earth from disease and contamination by the application of the sacred fire to these elements at the turning point of the year. The system is continued in the ritual of the Catholic Church in both the Latin and Eastern Rites when during the celebration of the Eucharist the priest incenses the altar all around with burning incense to purify the sacred area from all demonic influences. The famous Irish artist, Jack Yeats, has a painting of the children of Belmullet throwing lighting branches high in the air at Belmullet at Midsummer Eve in a display of primitive fireworks.

Kevin Danaher describes just how spectacular the celebration of the rite could be:

Special torches made of bushes, of bunches of bogdeal slips, of tightly bound bundles of reeds, or of bunches of stray or oil-soaked rags or sods of turf dipped in oil or grease and borne aloft on poles or pitchforks were lit at the fire and carried around and through the fields and gardens. Often each member of the household had such a torch, and they formed a little procession in making the circuit. The torches were variously called 'Sop Seáin', 'cliars', 'wisps' and other local names. Sir Henry Piers saw them in Westmeath in 1682:

'On the eves of St John Baptist (23 June) and St Peter (28 June), they always have in every town a bonfire, late in the evenings, and carry about bundles of reeds fast tied and fired; these being dry will last long, and flame better than a torch, and be a pleasing divertive prospect to the distant beholder; a stranger would go near to imagine the whole country was on fire.'

Amhlaoibh Ó Súilleabháin remarked on them in Callan in 1831: *Teine cnámh agus sop Seaghain ar gach ardán* – a bonfire and a John's wisp on every height' (1972, 145-146).

Noxious weeds and medicinal herbs were also associated with St John's Feast. A bundle of weeds, of the type considered to be inimical to crops, was thrown into the fire. This is also the custom in Cornwall where a great revival of the Midsummer Bonfires has taken place providing a remarkable spectacle both for locals and tourists.

With regard to medicinal herbs, St John's Worth (*Luibh Eoin Baiste*/Hypericum), the beautiful yellow shrub in flower at that season was prized highly. 'Both the flowers and leaves are used for a tea to help liver complaints' (Twitchell, 1971, 119).

The herbs could be gathered between 23 June and 4 July. This latter day was the Old St John's Day as the calendar had lost contact with the sun to the extent of 11 days and had to be corrected.

Danaher cites an eighteenth-century medical work to help a child who gets fits or spasms while asleep:

> An lus mór 's an fothrom a bhaint idir dhá fhéil St Seáin agus á mbruith ar uisge trí teorann, á gcur suas a mbuidéal agus a gcumhdach go mbiaidh ócáid agat leo ....(foxglove and figworth to be gathered between the two feasts of St John, boiled in the water of three boundaries, bottled and kept until required) (1972, 148).

Where three boundaries met, or where three streams met, was a sacred place and water taken from there had curative qualities. Here we have an example of the combination of a sacred time, (the Summer Solstice) and a sacred space (three streams/boundaries) as the setting for a medical preparation. Here the religious context is very clear. The cure of the sick child is not in the natural ingredients of the herbs alone but in the mysterious intervention of the Otherworld. The mystique of the three streams is also well known in Gaelic Scotland.

In the treatment of the 'Evil Eye', in the case of a female sufferer, a man went to a place where three streams met. Putting his right knee on the side of the stream, he put three quantities of water into a wooden bucket in the name of the Trinity.

The 'Sacred Silence' associated with archaic rites was observed – the celebrant spoke to nobody on his way to the *neimheadh* or sanctuary, be it the enclosure of three boundaries / streams or a stream over which the living and the dead passed embracing the idea of the *táirseach* or threshold between the two worlds.

The man on his arrival at the house where the patient was, placed a wife's gold ring in the bucket, a piece of silver and copper and gave some of the water to the patient to drink. Some of the water was also sprinkled on her while the remainder was poured over a rock. This formula is only efficacious when passed from male to female and female to male. Unlike the principle of an exclusively male priesthood in the Catholic and Orthodox churches, the rule here is different and follows the natural mutuality of the sexes (Carmichael, 1972, 42). This obviously archaic rite, or variations of it, was much used in parts of Gaelic Scotland as a treatment for the Evil Eye (*Súil Bhálair*) – a much-feared disease throughout Europe in times past, as evidenced by the painting of an eye on boats in Italy. It was believed that some people had the 'Evil Eye' and by staring at some other person, or at a cow or other animal, could seriously damage their health.

In the herbal cure quoted earlier, two important herbs are included – Foxglove – *An Lus Mór*, also called by the significant name of *Méirín Púca* – the Púca's thimble – the Púca being the supernatural horse who gallops around the roads at Samhain and can only be got rid of by leaving a basin of whiskey for him to drink outside the door. At any rate, this is the beautiful colourful herb (*digitalis*) used in the treatment of heart disease and is usually very poisonous.

The other herb to be prepared for medical purposes such as the treatment of bruises, etc. is Figwort (*Scrophularia nodosa*) *Fothrum*. Now, this name may be significant, as *Fothrum/Fothram* means 'Noise', a great clamour, etc, and in Scotland, it was known, not only as 'farum / forum' = *Fothram* but also as 'torranan' or 'Lus an Torranain' – the herb of the 'Thunderer', in other words, this is the herb of the great noisy one, the Thunderer. This may well be the well-known Celtic Thunder god of Gaul – Taranis – and in the intense heat of the Summer Solstice period when thunder storms occur – what better time could there be to prepare the herb which shares his name?

When these varied strands of tradition are combined, we see that the Summer Solstice/St John's Day was an immensely important festival and calendrical marker with its counterpart the Winter Solstice/Christmas at the opposite end of the year.

The celebration of these Feasts today in a more robust style than is usual should help to restore a lost consciousness of our links with the natural world of which we are part.

A peculiar tradition links the Hymn of Vespers with musical notation. The Hymn is to be sung during Vespers, the Evening Prayer of the Church, or while standing around the bonfire. It was composed in the eighth century by Paul the Deacon, a Benedictine of Monte Cassino. Certain syllables of the first verse – Ut, Re, Mi, Fa, Sol, La – stand for our modern Doh, Re, Mi, Fa, Soh, La:

> Ut queant laxis resonare fibris,
> Mira gestorum famuli tuorum,
> Solve polluti labii reatum.
> Sancte Joannes.
> (That thy servants may be able to sing thy deeds of wonder with pleasant voices, remove, O holy John, the guilt of our sin-polluted lips)

The idea is based on the fact that Zachary, John's father, lost his voice on account of his disbelief in the angel's message to him (Luke 1:19) and that it was restored to him at the naming of John –'his tongue was loosed' – *laxis fibris* (Luke 1:64). For this reason, singers prayed to St John as their Patron asking him to improve their voices (Britt, 1922, 256-257).

Another part of this remarkable eighth-century hymn by Paul the Deacon is sung at the Office of Lauds – the Morning Prayer of the Church – in Benedictine Monasteries on the Feast of St John (24 June) and this particular portion contains a verse which appears very clearly to give St John the character of a great and powerful Otherworld figure, who, although now inhabiting a different region or state (heaven) is now more capable of producing results here on earth than he actually was while he was here among us in this world. He is more powerful dead than alive.

This remarkable and exciting idea connects the Christian St John the Baptist with the ancient Ancestors who, as we have seen, were described so fluently by the renowned Egyptologist Rundle Clarke as 'the custodians of the source of life, the forces of vigour, sustenance and growth. Hence they were not only departed souls but still active, the keepers of life and fortune. Whatever happened, whether good or evil, ultimately derived from them' (1959, 119-120).

The Ancestors may be presumed to be deified mortals – not all mortals but only those of a superior type such as the founders of a community, for instance, a little group of people of outstanding vision and ability who moved into an uninhabited area and with immense labour and industry cut down the trees, levelled the ground and made the site suitable for agriculture to sustain a settled community which with increasing numbers evolved into a tribe. These outstanding individuals could indeed be recognised as fathers of their people and when they died were given huge megalithic tombs which became shrines to which the people would come to pray. For the local people would understand that their great Ancestors, after their heroic earthly life was over, moved on to another dimension where they had immense power – greater than they ever had on earth – and they could use this power to assist the tribe they had left behind in matters of fertility, health, good hunting, peaceful relations with other tribes and so forth – in other words all the normal things required to make life on earth sustainable, and in this the wants and needs of archaic man were probably much the same as our own – food, shelter, security, peaceful living of family life. Early man, sitting in front of his fire, after a good supper, with his wife and children and neighbours around him listening to a *seanchaí* (storyteller) telling far-fetched stories may be little different from his modern counterpart sitting in front of his fire, after a good supper, with his wife and children around him watching a far-fetched soap-opera on television.

But, it does appear that, for megalithic man and for much later peoples, the cult of the Ancestors continued to be of vital importance and the great megalithic monument of temple was the place where the Ancestors could be contacted. It does appear that only outstanding personalities became Ancestors and this may explain the small numbers of the dead found in megalithic tombs. Perhaps the practice of the Catholic Church gives a clue to a pre-historic system.

Many Catholics would not consider themselves, nor would anybody else consider them to be particularly devout; neverthe-less, when they die they hope to scrape a pass admitting them to heaven – the Lord is merciful – in much the same way as an un-enthusiastic University student hopes to scrape a pass in the ex-aminations. But, in the Catholic Church, to become a canonised saint is a different matter and the candidate is required to have practised heroic virtue. Once officially declared a saint by the pro-cess of canonisation, then the faithful are encouraged to pray to him / her for their various needs, for the saint has now the power to help them. The system bears a remarkable resemblance to what we know of the ancient cult of the Ancestors.

Now, to return to the particular case of John the Baptist and the hymn for Lauds on his feastday. The relevant verse is as follows:

Nunc potens nostri meritis opimis,
Pectoris duros lapides revelle (repelle),
Asperum planans iter, et reflexos
Dirige calles (Britt, 1922, 260).
(Now that you are made powerful by your rich merits, pluck out / drive away the stony hardness of our hearts, level the rough paths and make the crooked roads straight.)

This verse obviously reflects the account of John's in Luke 3:3-5. He tried to change people's attitude, to soften their hearts of stone, to level out the rough straying character of their dispositions, and to prepare them for the coming of Christ among them. He had a large following and was very successful. Nevertheless, in the words *Nunc potens* (Now you are powerful) it seems to be implied that it is now, when he is dead, that he is really powerful and man-ages to get things done in a way in which he couldn't when he was alive.

A further example of this type of thinking was demonstrated a few years ago when the relics of St Thérèse of Lisieux (The Little

Flower) were carried around to various churches for veneration by the faithful.

Now, during her lifetime, St Thérèse lived as an unknown person in an obscure convent in France. Who, except for a small local group, ever heard of her when alive? But when she had died and became canonised her cult spread through Western Catholicism to make her one of the most invoked and renowned of saints. It is now that she is really powerful for she has passed over to the Otherworld and her influence comes back to assist those who still in this world require help and call upon her. Surely, this cult of the saints is the great and precious inheritance of the Catholic and Eastern Rite churches which links them to the religious thought of untold ages of the past. And how moving it is to go into a church of the Byzantine or Coptic Rite and see the priest going around with his censer throwing up clouds of aromatic incense at the Ikons of the saints, welcoming these great ancestral figures to the celebration of the liturgy along with the High Priest Christ himself and the congregation of the faithful lighting candles before them. Here the heavenly Otherworld breaks into the human world to transform it and transfigure it into the divine pattern.

When one considers the bare churches of the West from which in many cases statues and pictures have been eliminated, and sees at the same time the gradually diminishing congregations and the absence of young people, churchmen must certainly ask themselves if some serious mistakes haven't been made in the reform of the liturgy after Vatican II.

In the great seventeenth-century poem 'Tuireamh na hÉireann' a long and impressive list of the Irish saints is given – local saints, the guardians of their people:

> Colum mac Criomhthainn is Colum mac Féilim,
> Ailbhe Imlig is Diaglán Déise,
> Ciarán Chluana is Ciarán Cléire,
> 's an té do bheannaigh in-Árainn Éanda,
> Eimhín, Áine, is Fiacha Sléibhte,
> Sionán Innse Catha na péiste (O Rahilly, ed, 1977, 80)

The tradition is continued at the 'Rounds' at the Holy Wells on

the saint's feastday. The importance of local saints becomes particularly clear in areas such as Baile Bhóirne in the West Cork
Gaeltacht where the great Gobnat whose elevated shrine on the hillside overlooks the inhabited area below, still, like a tutelary goddess
of old, protects the people of Baile Bhóirne and Cúil Aodha, as she
saved them long ago from the advancing plague at Goirtín na Plá
and from the villainy of the horse-thief An Gadaí Dubh.

In the post Vatican II years, the church, no doubt, had excellent
reasons for focusing attention to the place of Christ in the work of
our redemption as the supreme Mediator between God and men.
But in the process of emphasing one particular doctrinal aspect
another may become obscured. It is very difficult to maintain a
balance and in this instance the cult of the saints may, in some
places, have suffered a decline with statues thrown out, pictures
taken down to provide bare walls and create a cold rational
atmosphere. But somehow the reforms, undertaken with the best
of intentions, haven't always worked, and in throwing out the
saints have we also thrown out the sinners?

At any rate, these thoughts have arisen from consideration of
the feast of the Birth of St John the Baptist at the Summer Solstice.
With the feast of the Birth of Christ, six months later, at the Winter
Solstice, and the Conception of John at the Autumn Equinox and
the Conception of Christ at the Spring Equinox, the two principal
figures of the New Testament are brought into vital association
with the astronomical year, for these are the pivotal points in the
journey of the sun throughout the year and the marking points for
our calendars. So, these feasts direct our attention not only to the
earth in which the historical events took place – to the spacial dimension – but to the sky – the temporal dimension. It is an awesome
vista – a crossing of the boundaries between sky and land.

A very elaborate celebration of the feast of St John known as
'The Pardon of Fire' was a feature of Plougaznou in Brittany. A
huge stack of combustible material stood near the church, and
with much ringing of bells and firing of muskets, representative
groups from the surrounding parishes, carrying their distinctive
banners, gathered together as darkness was falling. The great
banner of St John from the home church came out to greet the visi-

tors and the banners, carried by strong men in native dress, bowed in courteous greeting to St John and to each other. Hymns were sung, drums beaten, and greetings exchanged among the large gathering. As a climax to the rite, a fuse was lighted. This – the 'dragon of fire' – travelled, spluttering and hissing, up to the top of the church and then down again traversing what was known as the 'way of the dragon'.

The congregation watched with baited breath as the fiery dragon hissed his way along the ground again and at last disappeared into the centre of the piled-up mass of fuel.

Then, there was a mighty flash of fire, as with a boom, the whole thing burst into flames. The congregation roared 'An Tan', 'An Tan' (The Fire, The Fire) and old men fired their ancient guns into the air to add to the commotion.

In this outdoor celebration of the Feast of St John at Plougaznou, we can pick out some elements characteristic of archaic ritual performances.

Firstly, there is the sacred place, the *neimheadh* or sanctuary in which the pilgrims have assembled year after year for generations.

And then there is the sacred time, the Summer Solstice, when the sun turns and retraces its steps. For ancient peoples who followed the course of the sun closely, this must have been an awesome event.

The rite took place at sunset, the transition period between day and night when the boundaries between different dimensions of reality grow thin.

The large banners brought by the surrounding parishes represent the saints to whom these areas were dedicated. These are the local Spiritual Ancestors and at the turning of the sun they gather together to greet each other and honour their great leader St John. It is another form of saluting the Ancestors from that of the Byzantine and Coptic Rites where the priest incenses the Ikons and the people light candles before them.

Even in the austere Roman Rite of Mass in its Tridentine form the welcoming of the Spiritual Ancestors was not omitted. The celebrant kissed the altar-stone containing relics and said:

> We beseech you, O Lord, by the merits of your saints whose relics are here, and of all the saints, that you may forgive all my sins.

By way of modifying the Roman Rite of Mass in accordance with African culture, an invocation of the saints was introduced into the Zaire Rite to accommodate the African attitude to the Ancestors.

The priest invites the faithful to unite themselves to the entire communion of saints. He says:

> Brothers and Sisters, we who are living on earth are not the only followers of Christ; many have already left this world and are now with God. But together with them, we make up one great family. Let us join ourselves to them, and especially to the saints, so that this sacrifice may gather us all together into one body.

All stand, and the celebrant makes the following prayers:

> C. Holy Mary, be with us; you who are the Mother of God, be with us. Here is our prayer; be with us, and be with all who celebrate Mass at this time.
> People: Be with us, be with us all.
> C. Saint N (the patron saint or saints), be with us; you who are the patron of our parish, be with us. Here is our prayer …
> People: Be with us, be with us all.
> C. Holy people of heaven, be with us, you who see God, be with us; here is our prayer …
> People: Be with us, be with us all.
> C. And you, our ancestors, be with us, you who have served God with a good conscience, be with us. Here is our prayer …
> People: Be with us, be with us all.
> (Thurian, M., and Wainwright, G., 1983, 205)

In a remarkable commentary on the Zaire Rite of Mass developed as a result of Vatican II, Edouard Flory Kabongo comments on the African mentality which the rite endeavours to express:

La personne humaine est posée en rapport au cosmos, au monde des esprits et de génies. L'homme est a la fois du monde des Vivants et des Morts; il est esprits, animaaux, vegetaux, terre ... il est l'univers en miniature ... c'est a dire dans sa double dimension cosmique et anthropologique. Dans la première, l'homme vit en communaute avec la creation tandi que dans la seconde, l'homme vit en communauté avec l'humanité. Ces relations avec le cosmos et avec l'humanité ne sont seulament de communauté, mais aussi de communion ...

Tout dans le monde africaine est intimement lié. Le monde est d'un seul tenant. Tout ce qui existe y est étroitement et nécessairement lié et coordonné. Le monde est comme une immense toile d'araignée don't on ne peut toucher un fil sans la faire vibrer tout entière. L'homme n'est pas seulement une partie de monde, mais le resumé du monde. Il ya entre l'homme et le monde une dialectique , un influx vital. La destinée de la personne humaine exprime la destinée du cosmos. Assurer la victoire de la vie dans l'homme c'est assurer la meme victoire dans l'univers.

('Rite Zairois et dynamique d'une eglise locale ou particulière en Afrique subsaharienne', *Questions Liturgique*, 87; 2006, 287-288)

(The human person is placed in relationship to the cosmos, to the world of spirits and gods. Man at the same time belongs to the world of the Living and the Dead; he is spirits, animals, plants, earth. He is the universe in miniature, that is to say in his double dimension of the cosmic and anthropological. As regards the first, man lives in community with creation while, as regards the second, man lives in community with humanity. These relations with the cosmos and with humanity are not just a matter of community but of communion.

In the African world all things are joined intimately. The world is of one tenant only. All that exists there is tightly and of necessity bound together and coordinated. The world is like some immense spider's web in which one cannot touch one thread without making the whole web vibrate. Man is not only a part of the world, but the resume of the world ... Between man and the world there is a dialectic, a vital influx. The destiny of the human person expresses the destiny of the cosmos.

To assure the victory of life in the man is to assure the same victory in the universe)

These profound philosophical ideas are further developed by
the author's treatment of the concept of what constitutes man. In
Western thought ,in general, it is the individual mind that makes
the man – *Cogito, ergo sum* (I think, therefore I am). In African
thought, however, a man becomes a man through relationship
with other men – *Cognati sumus, ergo sum* (We are related, therefore I am). By being a member of a family, a clan, a tribe, a person
achieves manhood.

A curious incident, reminiscent of this philosophy of relationship, occurs in a late Irish romantic story which still contains some
archaic features. In *Toraíocht Dhiarmada agus Ghráinne* the great
hero Diarmaid Ó Duibhne is persuaded, against his better judgement, to elope with the princess Gráinne who is betrothed to his
military leader Fionn Mac Cumhaill. At last he has sex with her
and the text makes the comment: 'Is ansin do rinne Diarmaid
déadholais Ó Duibhne bean de Ghráinne, iníon rí Éireann, ar
dtús' (Ní Shé, 1971, 32). (It was then that Diarmaid Ó Duibhne of
the white teeth first made a woman of Gráinne, the daughter of
the king of Ireland). The inference seems to be that previous to this
sexual relationship, she was not fully a woman. It was only as a
result of a relationship that she achieved full status as a woman.

The African text is obviously less specific. It is concerned with
a totality of relationships – parentage, tribal, relationships with
the living and the dead, with animals, with vegetation and with
the Ancestors, which might include the notion of God as the primordial ancestor. It might be remarked that the Irish god, Donn, (in
Caesar's terms *Dis Pater*) was regarded as the great father / ancestor god of the Irish from whom they descended and to whom they
would return after their death to his otherworld home, *Tech
nDoinn*, Bull Rock, off the coast of Kerry.

In the African anthropological system, then, vertically, the
person is related to God and the Ancestors.

Horizontally he is related to family, clan, tribe, so that he is, as
it were, the hub of a whole system of relationships like spokes
emerging from the hub of a wheel.

Have we here, in an African context, the Primordial Tradition, the ancient philosophical system common to archaic societies, over space and time, in which essentially, all was one?

Before leaving the Feast of St John and the Summer Solstice, perhaps a further look should be taken of the rite of the Fire-Wheel rolled down a hill to fall into lake below. As we have seen, one interpretation of this Summer Solstice rite was to see it as ritual in imitation of the sun descending in the sky, rising a little further south each morning with a corresponding shortening of the day – a gradual loss of power. In very hot areas this was to be welcomed and the ritual simulation would act as a form of stimulation to strengthen the process. The dreaded *Dies Caniculares* or 'Dog Days' occurred around this time, c. 14 July to 5 September, which with their torrid heat made life practically impossible for dogs and men.

But, the ritual may have another meaning. A key to its meaning may be suggested by the mixing of fire and water.

Ancient creation myths speak of the sun shining on the primeval flood and, from the interaction of fire and water, giving birth to the world hill from which created things emerge. In other words, could we have here an ancient creation rite taking place at one of the most significant points of the year, the Summer Solstice?

Up to now, my argument has been that the rite, whether in its bonfire or fire-wheel form, was to control the sun – to make the sun shine brighter in cold countries like Ireland to ripen the corn at Lughnasa (c. August) and in hot countries to cool its ardour and let the ground soften for the Autumn cultivation and sowing of corn.

A symbol, unlike a sign, is open to many different interpretations, and in the mixing of fire and water in the rite of the Summer Solstice, it is possible that there is a distant echo of an ancient creation story in which the sun god shines on the waters of chaos and from this commixture of fire and water the world mountain arises and from the world mountain vegetation springs to be followed gradually by animals, birds, humans and the rest of creation as we know it today.

In common experience, it is seen that heavy rain followed by intense heat from a blazing sun will soon cause luxurious vegetation to spring up from the land.

The idea is deeply embedded in the marvellously numinous ritual of the Blessing of the Baptismal Font containing the water for baptisms at the Easter Vigil (Holy Saturday Night) in the Roman Liturgy (Tridentine Rite).

The prayer of blessing speaks of the joy of the church at the number of baptisms taking place on this holy night all over the world, and these newly-baptised are the reborn ones who have been born into a new type of existence from the baptismal font – the womb of Mother Church. The highly sexualised vocabulary of the Latin original makes it clear that baptism is a birth into a new form of life with God, in the same way that in ordinary human birth the baby passes from the enclosed life of the womb to the greater world outside. In other words, from the church's point of view, an unbaptised person is living in a very enclosed world having as its boundaries the dimensions of this present limited exist-ence and which will come to an end for him at physical death. But the baptised person is transferred into the extended world of God which knows no boundaries. He has passed over to a different type of existence as the baby passes from the womb to the outside world. In the Catholic Church today, for the most part, the bapt-ism of a child is of course a very refined, genteel affair in which the baby is beautifully clothed and three small drops of water are poured over his head while admiring relatives look on. The bless-ing of the Baptism Font, however, is very different in tone and speaks of the archaic, the primitive, the numinous, an initiation rite which transfers a man to a different dimension of reality.

At the centre of the ritual is the dipping of the lighted Paschal Candle into the water of the font as the fire-wheel of the Summer Solstice plunges into a river or lake.

The argument is that from this mingling of the two elements of fire and water new life will arise – a new creation. The Summer Solstice then, if the argument is valid, would be a renewal of cre-ation – a re-contacting of the primeval act of creation so that the world today would be renewed and re-invigorated by its contact with the primeval event. The creation-event is seen as a birth rite in which the earth mother is fecundated by the sun god and from this union the world is born.

The elaborate blessing of the font containing the water for baptisms in the *Missale Romanum* (1570) on Holy Saturday operates along these lines:

The priest prays: 'May he (the Holy Spirit), by a secret admixture of his divine power make this water fruitful for the regeneration of men, to the end, that a heavenly offspring, conceived in sanctification, may emerge from the immaculate womb of the divine font, reborn new creatures.'

(Qui hanc aquam regenerandis hominibus praeparatum, arcana sui numinis admixtione foecundet; ut sanctificatione concepta, ab immaculato divini fontis utero, in novam renata creaturam, progenies caelestis emergat.)

There is an obvious reference here to the Conception of Christ and the angel Gabriel's announcement to Mary: 'The Holy Spirit will come upon you and the power of the Most High will cover you with its shadow. And so the child will be holy and will be called Son of God' (Luke 1:35). A new creation is about to take place.

The Latin original contains a surprising number of words of sexual connotation: *regenerandis, foecundet, concepta, utero, renata, progenies emergat.*

After many references to water and its separation from land, in other words the Creation scene, the highly ritualised section occurs:

'Here the priest dips the Paschal candle in the water, and resuming the tone of the Preface says: 'May the power of the Holy Spirit descend into all the water of this font.'

He then withdraws the Candle from the water, sinks it in to a greater depth, and repeats on a higher tone: 'May the power of the Holy Spirit descend into all the water of this font.'

Withdrawing the candle from the water again, for the third time he dips it in to the bottom of the font singing on a higher tone: 'May the power of the Holy Spirit descend into all the water of this font.'

Then, the priest breathes three times on the water in the form (shape) of the Greek letter *psi* singing:

'And make the whole substance of this water fruitful for re-
birth.' *(Hic Sacerdos paululum demittit Cereum in aquam: et re-
sumens tonum Praefationis, dicit:*

   'Descendat in hanc plenitudinem fontis, virtus Spiritus Sancti.'

   *Deinde extractum Cereum de aqua, iterum profundius mergit,
aliqunto altius repetens: "Descendat in hanc ..." Postea Cereum
rursus de aqua extractum, tertio immergens usque ad fundum, al-
tiori adhuc voce repetit: "Descendat ...", ut supra. Et deinde sufflans
ter in aquam, secundum hanc figuram "psi", prosequitur:*

   *'Totamque hujus aquae substantiam, regenerandi foecundet ef-
fectu').* (*Missale Romanum* (1570), *Sabbato Sancto*.)

In this magnificent example of archaic ritual drama the power
of the Holy Spirit symbolised by the fiery candle is united with the
water to produce a fruitful matrix from which a new creation (the
baptised) will rise up as the Primordial Hill emerged from the
waters of chaos under the action of the sun.

The letter *psi* probably stands for the word 'psyche' – 'soul',
shaped somewhat like a cross. The celebrant breathes three times
on the water in this form and this recalls the Holy Spirit hovering
over the water in the Creation story in the Book of Genesis. As the
text of the Blessing says: 'At the very dawn of creation, your Spirit
breathed on the waters'.

It seems a pity that this striking, numinous piece of ritual is
drastically reduced in the new reformed *Missale Romanum* of
1970.

Perhaps this archaic usage did not coincide with the sensit-
ivities of the late twentieth-century reformers with a leaning towards rationalisation and streamlining. Reformers, no doubt, are
men of their own period of history and find it difficult to adjust
completely to the mind-set of another age.

CHAPTER SIX

The Mystery of Fire and Water

We might wonder if there is the debris of an ancient mid-eastern creation myth hidden away in the story of the first invasion of Ireland by the Egyptian woman Ceasair as recorded in *Leabhar Gabhála Éireann* (Book of Invasions).

According to the story, the Egyptian woman Ceasair arrived in Ireland to escape the biblical flood. The argument was that there would be no flood in Ireland; the flood was a punishment for sin and there was no sin in Ireland, therefore there would be no flood.

The reason why there was no sin in Ireland was not that the Irish were better than everybody else but that the island was un-inhabited at this time – there was nobody there to commit sin.

At any rate, Ceasair arrived from Egypt with fifty women and three men, Fionntan, Ladhra and Bith.

On arrival, the women summoned a meeting to decide how the three men were to be divided among the fifty women. This Assembly must have been the archetype for our modern *Dáil Éireann*.

The first session decided that the fifty women be shared among the three men so that each got seventeen. However, Ladhra soon died – from 'an excess of women'. The women summoned a second session of the Dáil and it was decided that the two remaining men get twenty-five women each.

Again, the solution was short-lived. Bith died from the same complaint as Ladhra and to avoid the inevitable, Fionntán adopted the old formula *Is fearr rith mhaith ná droch-sheasamh* - a good run is better than a bad stand – so he ran away and hid in a cave at Tul Tuinne above Loch Dearg. Ceasair died of a broken heart.

Fionntan, however, escaped, as the waters never reached him at Tul Tuinde (Tulach Toinne – the hill of the wave). He underwent many transformations, becoming an eagle, a wild boar, a deer, in turn and finally a salmon. During all these transformations he retained his human mind and memory and stored up his experiences in these various mutations. At last, as a salmon, Fionntan was caught by a queen's fisherman. She ate the salmon and found herself pregnant. She had a child and, of course, this was Fionntan re-incarnated. From his birth he remembered all his past-lives' experiences and was able to pass on to the Christian scribes the stories of the various groups who invaded Ireland – the Partholonians, Clann Neimidh, Fir Bholg, the Tuatha Dé Danann, Clann Mhíle. So, it is through Fionntan and St Finnian and his scribes that we know the ancient history of Ireland (Macalister, 1939, Part 11, 177ff).

Possibly, Fintan/Fionntan may signify 'white fire' – the sun, while Ladhra the mariner may be a symbol of the primordial sea and 'Bith' the earth/world. So that through the action of the sun shining on the sea of chaos, 'Bith' the world arises and creation begins.

Macalister comments: 'There is no room for doubt that the Ceasair legend is a tattered fragment of a Flood myth, such as is told almost universally throughout the world. The story usually follows a uniform course: Deity determines to destroy mankind, but instructs a favoured mortal to make a ship for his own salvation; the flood comes and departs, and the ship grounds on a hill; by certain devices, which differ with different stories, the world is re-peopled' (1939, 11, 172).

In the Irish version, Ceasair is Noah's grand-daughter, but being a wild girl, her grandfather will not allow her into the ark, so the druids of Egypt advise her to build her own boat and sail for Ireland to escape the flood. The area around Loch Dearg on the Shannon, with the Arra Mountains in the background, seems to be the Irish scenario for the legend.

The Noah's Ark story was popular among tellers of pious tales, and even to this day Allied Irish Banks display Noah's Ark as their logo. The meaning isn't particularly subtle: 'Just as Noah, his family and friends were safe and sound in the ark despite the surrounding chaos, in the same way your money will be safe and sound with AIB.'

The Liturgy of the Easter Vigil in the Latin Rite is particularly insistant on the creation. The First Reading from the Book of Genesis (Chap 1) opens with the dramatic words:

> In the beginning God created the heavens and the earth. Now the earth was a formless void, there was darkness over the deep, and God's spirit hovered over the water. God said, 'Let there be light, and there was light.'

The story goes on, then, to describe in more detail the work of God over six days in providing the structure of the Universe.

This creation narrative provides the background for the Blessing of the Baptismal Font as we have seen above; it is the myth behind the rite.

The newly baptised is a new creation. He emerges from the waters of the font as a new creature of God as the world-mountain (Bith) emerged into the light from the primeval waters of chaos.

Unfortunately, today, because of attenuated ritual forms, infant rather than adult baptism, lack of instruction and other reasons, few Catholics appreciate the magnificence of the vision presented at the Easter Vigil.

The seasonal ritual re-enactment of the creation, both for Pagans and Christians, brought them back to the matrix of power to bring renewal and fresh vigour to their world.

The idea is captured in the Blessing of the Water on the Feast of the Epiphany (6 January – Winter Solstice according to some computations) in the Byzantine Rite:

> By your divine will you brought forth all things out of nothingness into being; by your might you control all creation; by your providence you govern the universe, you, who from the four elements, established the whole world, and with four seasons set up the cycle of the year (Raya, 1958, 302).

By seasonal mimetic ritual, then, the ancients entered into the primeval event of creation and so made contact with the matrix. This recharging of the world-battery from the primary source at sacred seasons of the year renewed the earth and all within it. No wonder, then, that ancient people spent so much time and energy in performing ritual dances. It was the way of making sure that the world would endure, and continue on a healthy, fertile course.

In the newly revised ritual of the Blessing of the Water for the Epiphany (6 January) in the Maronite Rite of the Catholic Church, the priest takes three lumps of burning charcoal and plunges them, one after the other, into a large vessel of water, saying:

May this water be purified in the name of the Father;
May it be sanctified in the name of the Son;
May it be blessed in the name of the Holy Spirit'.

Then the priest sprinkles the faithful with the water to bring protection, peace and blessing on them and on their homes (*Qurbono: The Book of Offering. The Service of the Holy Mysteries according to the Antiochene Syriac Maronite Church, Season of Epiphany*, Brooklyn, New York, 1993; 18-19).

Both in the Catholic/Eastern Orthodox and the residue of prehistoric rites that remain to us, the mysterious ritual mingling of fire and water points to an archaic vision of creation and the desire of the ancients to immerse themselves in this primordial event – this return to the womb of the world symbolised by the female form of some of the megalithic monuments – to be renewed, reborn.

Even in Brú na Bóinne (Newgrange), so much is uncertain. What of the great stone basins found inside? What did they contain? Was it the ashes of the dead, or was it water upon which the shaft of sunlight would fall at the Winter Solstice to represent the creation event on a minor scale, possibly another version of the equally uncertain phenomenon of the debris of a mid-Eastern creation myth at Lough Dearg (*Loch Deirgdheirc*) on the Shannon involving the sun shining – represented by Fionntan, the white fire, on the lake, and the Arra Mountain – representing Bith, the world; while Ladhra represented the waters of chaos from which the world mountain emerged through the fertilising action of the sun.

The number of questions surrounding the ancient peoples of Ireland and the archaic monuments scattered around the country is truly amazing but definitive answers are few. Down through the generations they have preserved their mystery and it is by gathering a clue here and a clue there and putting them all together that we arrive at some kind of conclusion though it may not be the right one. And then there is the large number of local variations in a general theme to be considered.

We consider, for instance, the tremendous number of Holy Wells throughout the country – there may be more than 2000 – some of which are still visited by pilgrims on the 'Pattern Day'. They perform the ancient ritual in the traditional manner with slight variations for the particular place.

(a) If possible, the pilgrim approaches the Holy Well from the North, the area of darkness.

(b) The pilgrim kneels before the well and recites the opening prayer mentioning the name of the saint to whom the well is dedicated:

(c) *Go mbeannaí Dia dhuit, a Bhríghid (Ghobnait/Phádraig) Naofa; Go mbeannaí Muire dhuit, is beannaím féin duit. Is chugatsa a thánag ag gearáin mór phéine, is ag iarraidh cabhrach ar son Mhic De ort.*

(May God salute you, O Blessed Brighid; may Mary salute you and I salute you myself. It is to you I have come complaining of my affliction, and requesting help from you for the sake of the Son of God.)

The pilgrim, then prepares to 'make the Rounds', that is to perform the *Cor Deiseal* or right-handed (sunwise) walk around the well, the required number of times. In Munster it will often be the sacred number 3 or a multiple of 3 – 9 (3x3).

To count the number of rounds, which is difficult if the number is large, such as 9, the pilgrim may use one of two methods. He / she, marks a standing stone near the well with the sign of the cross after each round is completed or, instead of this, he / she may pick up 9 small stones (pebbles) and drop one after each round. When the pilgrim's hand is empty, then he has completed the ritual number of rounds.

The pilgrim must always keep the well at his right-hand while walking around it. The pilgrims walk in single file and in most places they say certain prayers such as the 'Our Father', 'Hail Mary' and 'Glory be'.

When the rounds are completed, the pilgrim makes an offering. This is something small which the pilgrim will have with him.

There is usually a ledge or little stone aperture beside the well where these offerings are laid – things such as Rosary beads, biros, combs, holy pictures, safety pins and such-like. Pins feature also in the Brídeog Procession of St Brigid's feast. When the Mummers entered a house, and performed a little dance to introduce the new season of Spring at the Feast of Imbolc (1 February) the people of the house sometimes stuck some pins on the Brídeog or doll carried in the procession. Some Holy Wells were called 'Pin Wells' as in the case of Wooler in Northumberland. 'Lovers would go to the Pin Well at midnight and throw a bent pin into the water, wishing for a speedy marriage or some other lover-like wish. Also there was a May Day procession to the well, when those present would also drop a bent pin into the water and make a wish' (Bord, J. and C., 1985, 170). The bending of the pin meant that it was taken out of profane use to be dedicated to the goddess from whose womb in the depths of the earth the life-giving water sprang. In folkloric tradition the loosening of all pins and ties was associated with childbirth.

Then the pilgrim drank the water three times from the mug beside the well.

The pilgrim may then hang a piece of cloth which has been in contact with his body on the *Bile* or sacred tree nearby. In this way he transfers any ailment he may have to the tree. In addition, while the pilgrim has to go away, the piece of cloth hanging on the *Bile* continues his prayer in his absence as the candle lighted by a devout woman in church continues her prayer when she has gone home.

A Holy Well is easily recognised by the pieces of cloth left beside it by pilgrims, and some Holy Wells are known as 'Rag Wells'.

Finally, the pilgrim may take a bottle of water home with him for those unable to travel.

At many pilgrimage sites, such as that of Naomh Gobnat at Baile Bhóirne, the rite is quite complex as several other features such as the grave of the saint, a *Gallán* or standing stone, a stone oratory, etc, are involved.

Perhaps the most prominent feature of the Holy Well Rite is

the *Cor Deiseal* or sunwise circumambulation around the Holy Well and grave of the saint.

This is a well-known ritual action of the Celts. The Greek writer Athenaeus (c. 200 BC) said of the Celts: 'and they do reverence to the gods, turning towards the right' (*kai tous theous proskunousin, epi ta dexia strephomenoi*) (Tierney, 1960, 247, 225).

What is meant is the Celtic custom of circumambulation or walking around a person or statue of a god or some sacred thing such as a well, a standing stone, a sacred hill, a fire, a house, a farm, etc, to honour it. The idea occurs in the eighth century text *Lúireach Phádraig* (St Patrick's Breastplate) where the person wants to protect himself '*fri himchellacht nidlachtae*' (Stokes, W., and Strachan, J., 1903, 357) – 'against the circumambulations of idolatry', in other words walking around the statue of a god. This is the way of honouring the sacred object and it must be performed *deiseal* – in other words, the performer keeps the sacred object at his right-hand side as he goes around – makes the rounds. In this way he follows the course of the sun and puts himself into harmony with the movement of the cosmos. This *Cor Deiseal* or sunwise / clockwise ritual turn is well known to the Celts of Scotland and to the Hindus of India. It is a moving experience to see pilgrims today going around a Holy Well, *deiseal*, and recall that a writer had described this in Greek over two thousand years ago.

In their book on Lough Derg, (Dublin 1988) Deirdre Purcell and Liam Blake show some fine pictures of barefooted pilgrims moving in single file around the penitential stone 'Beds', keeping them at their right-hand side.

An American pilgrim commented: 'In Lough Derg, the church is reaching backwards to an ancient tradition, opening up the past with rites which have not changed for 1500 years ... I think the Celt had a faith which was very natural, based on nature, close to the streams and rivers of the earth. So for them to do penance, it would have to be physical and close to nature too' (p 77).

We may notice that while Lough Derg and Croagh Patrick are renowned for their penitential character, practices such as walking barefoot on rough ground and through streams feature also in the rites performed at other sacred sites. This recalls the worship

of Crom Cruach/Dubh of Maigh Sléacht in a pre-Christian context. Hard physical penance was a feature of both religions.

The connection between the Holy Wells and the ritual Celtic
Calendar is particularly apparent in the case of the Barony of
Duhallow (*Dúiche Ealla*) in north-west Co Cork, where a ritual calendar appears of be laid out on the local landscape. Here, we have
the extraordinary phenomenon of a sacred sanctuary of the Triple
Goddess, now Christianised, and covering a large, more or less,
square area of about six square miles north of the road between
Banteer and Rathmore. The area is hemmed in on the west and
south sides by the River Blackwater and on the east side by the
Dalua. High ground around Taur and Maoileann on the north
provide a natural enclosure for the *neimheadh* or sanctuary, as a
high wall may enclose the more conventional type of church or
temple. But, here, there is no building but rather four Stations,
three of which have Holy Wells as markers and these are at three
corners of the square. The fourth corner is marked by the village of
Kishkeam. This is the corrupted form of the original Irish *Coiscéim
na Caillí* – a very significant name indeed for it means 'the footstep
of the Hag' – the Hag being the goddess of the land in her winter
aspect at the decay of vegetation during the winter months beginning at Samhain (1 November).

The Christian story behind this remarkable site is that three
nuns or religious women settled in this area and from them the
pilgrimages that are a feature of the place are derived. Their
names are St Lasair (Feast 6 February); St Iníon Bhaoi (Feast 6
May) and St Laitiaran (Feast 25 July). There is a tradition that at
some point the three sisters went underground and I take it that
this refers to Samhain and Winter where vegetation disappears
under the earth. The other dates are obviously the old Insular
Celtic Feasts of Imbolc (1 February); Bealtaine (1 May); Lughnasa
(1 August). This leaves us with the four points of the Landscape
Sanctuary to which the dates correspond:

PLACE	GODDESS ASPECT	SAINTS	DATE
Coiscéim na Caillí	Cailleach	Saints go underground	Samhain
Cill Lasrach	Brídeog	Lasair	Imbolc
Drom Tairbh	Bábóg	Iníon Bhaoi	Bealtaine
Cuilinn	Tailte	Laitiaran	Lughnasa

In his great poem *An tan bhí Éire saor gan spleáchas*, Dónal Ó Conchúir (Ó Cadhla, 1984, 9-12) describes the three sisters as coming *Ó Shasana anoir* – from England from the east, and settling down in Dúiche Ealla in the three named places a few miles from each other. An angel came and constructed paths for them for easier communication. In the poem, and indeed even today in the numbers who come to Cuilinn Uí Chaoimh for the pilgrimage, it is Laitiaran who receives the most notice, possibly because of the well-known fire episode – which is attributed to St Brigid also:

> Laitiaran a thagadh gach maidin go ceárta
> Bhí suite i ngaireacht dá teach mar ráitear
> Is síol na tine gan spás ina gúna
> Is ní dhóití filleadh dhe, miota ná blúire.
> (Laitiaran used to come every morning to a forge which is said to be situated near her house. She carried the blazing embers of the fire on her dress and not a single thread of it was burned.)

The purpose of the practice was to kindle her own domestic fire from the forge where the blacksmith would have a fire lighting day and night. The miracle of the non-burning of her dress was a testimony to her great holiness.

Then, one day, the inevitable occurred: The blacksmith remarked on her beautiful legs. Laitiaraan looked down on them with great pride and immediately, because of this sin of pride, the fire burned her dress.

She proceeded to curse the blacksmith and because of this curse the blacksmith's trade never again flourished in Cuilinn Uí Chaoimh.

At any rate, the local pilgrimage is held on 25 July or the Sunday nearest to it – the old Festival of Lughnasa – to celebrate the ripening of the corn.

The Holy Well at Cullen is in a graveyard near an old church ruin. An ancient whitethorn tree, to receive the pieces of cloth, stands beside it and there is a large heart-shaped stone in the graveyard called *Cloichín na Cúirtéise* – the courtesy stone – to which the pilgrims bow when making the rounds. Here, as at other Holy Wells, a woman stood by the well, handed the mug full of water to the pilgrim and if necessary explained to strangers to the place how the rite was to be performed. One wonders if this were a last remnant of *Bandia an Tobair* – the goddess of the well, returning from the Otherworld to her people on this sacred occasion. Here is a combination of the sacred time, the sacred place, the burial site of the ancestors, the elemental rock, the life-giving liquid emerging from the womb of the Earth Mother, the archaic ritual, the goddess herself being celebrated in her Corn Spirit aspect.

According to the tradition, Laitiaran was the youngest of the three sisters. The name is difficult. Some surmise that it has something to do with iron (*iarann*) and that this would explain her connection with the forge. Strangely, in the curse attributed to St Laitiaran by Dónal Ó Conchúir, she uses the word *milliarainn* – meaning 'destroyer of iron' – perhaps an echo of her own name in the opposite sense. Like other ancient Irish saints, her curses possess great dramatic force:

A Thaidhg mhilliarainn mo chiach mo chráiteacht
Mar tharla riamh fá iadh do cheartan
Mar dhearcas lem ré thú, a sméirle chiardhubh,
Mar chloiseas do chlaonphus bréagach briathrach.
(O Tadhg, you iron-destroyer; my torment, my misfortune that I ever came inside the door of your forge; that I ever laid eyes on you, you beetle-black villain; that I ever heard your lying, voluble, crooked-mouthed speech.)

The poem continues in this vein and if St Laitiaran could pray as intensely as she could curse, she deserves all the devotion that the people of Duhallow shower upon her.

Lasair is directly connected with fire as the name means 'flame'. As the name of the third saint 'Iníon Bhaoi' was sometimes written 'Iníon Bhuí' (as by Dónal Ó Conchúir) it was thought that her name meant 'the yellow daughter'. However, it is most likely that Iníon Bhaoi means the daughter of Baoi – a proper noun. In Co Clare there is the well-known ruined church – Killinaboy – with its Síle-na-Gig, remains of a Round Tower and a Tau-shaped Cross associated with Iníon Bhaoi. For some time Iníon (Inghean) Bhaoi was a common name for women in Co Clare.

Then, there is the great goddess of the Beare Peninsula, Co Kerry, whom the church tried somewhat unsuccessfully to convert to the life of a nun.

In her great poem *Aithbe damsa bés mora*, the Cailleach describes herself: 'Is mé Caillech Berri , Buí' – 'I am Buí, the Old Woman of Beare'.

Now, in this area of what we have called the 'Ritual Landscape' the word *Baoi/Buí* occurs in several places – *Iomaire Baoi* (the ridge/furrow of Baoi), *Gort a' Tuí Baoi* (the field of the straw of Baoi), *Bóthar Baoi/Buthaire Baoi* (the road/bonfire of Baoi). Then at *Drom Tairbh* (the mountain ridge of the bull) at Bealtaine, the pilgrims gather at the Holy Well to celebrate *Iníon Bhaoi* (daughter of Baoi)

If, then, the daughter of Baoi is celebrated at Bealtaine (beginning of May) and the goddess has a life-cycle of one year – then we must look for her mother six months earlier, and sure enough, there is the *Cailleach (Béarra Buí)* at *Coiscéim na Caillí* representing Samhain and the death of vegetation in Winter. So that mother and daughter stand at opposite corners of the square and *Bóthar Buí* joins them. The mother becomes the daughter, and the daughter becomes the mother in perpetual alternation in the annual cycle, as in the Solar Calendar, the young god Aonghus Óg – the young son/sun – becomes the old son/sun at the Summer Solstice, and at the Winter Solstice the old son/sun, An Daghdha, becomes the young son/sun Aonghus Óg. And so it will go on for ever and ever. In the Solar Calendar it is Father and Son who are involved and the 'Turn' takes place at the Winter and Summer Solstices, while in this Celtic Calendar of Dúiche Ealla it is Mother and Daughter who are involved, as in the case of Demeter and Persephone in the Elusinian Mysteries of Greece, and the 'Turn' occurs at Samhain and Bealtaine.

As has been said, there is a tradition in the area that the three saints went underground at some part of the year. This is undoubtedly Samhain when vegetation disappears. The argument is that in this area of Dúiche Ealla there was a great outdoor sanctuary of the goddess of fertility with, fundamentally, four stations representing the four seasons, and the four aspects of the goddess in her annual cycle of life. The people went on pilgrimage to these Four Stations, in turn, at the appropriate time, to celebrate the annual life-cycle of the goddess and thus become one with her. In the ancient way of thinking, the goddess must have stood for the ordered succession of the seasons with the agricultural prosperity which this ensured. Was some mystical union with the goddess achieved by this procession liturgy which made the people themselves an embodiment of this annual cycle of nature?

In Winter, beginning with Samhain, when gaunt leafless trees predominate and the earth is bare and barren, the goddess in her 'Hag', *Cailleach*, form presides and this is linked to Kishkeam (Coiscéim na Caillí). The pilgrimage to Kishkeam at Samhain celebrated her death, for she was the personification of the seasons. Yet, this funeral pilgrimage was penetrated by hope, for, glancing to the east, the people knew that in three months' time, at Imbolg, they would be going to Cill Lasrach to celebrate her rebirth with the coming of Spring.

Significantly, a little to the south of Coiscéim na Caillí, there is a hill called *Cnoc an Bhuthairín* – the hill of the little bonfire. One wonders if this were the hill on which the Samhain Bonfire was lighted, which would also serve as a beacon fire to direct the pilgrims.

Next on the calendar is the Celtic Feast of Imbolc, *Lá 'le Bríde*, 1 February, the beginning of Spring and the start of the farmer's year. All of nature shows signs of reawakening after its winter sleep. The buds begin to appear on the trees, the grass begins to turn green, the days grow noticeably longer with increasing light, everything speaks of renewal and new life, it is the season of rebirth. The goddess returns to life. She is the personification of Springtime, the child, the 'Brídeog'. In some places today, and formerly in many more, a straw doll called the 'Brídeog' was carried from house to house to symbolise the goddess or the saint going around to give her people new hope for peace and prosperity for the coming year. At Imbolc, while the growth of vegetation, of lambs and calves is still weak, the goddess is in her 'Brídeog' or baby form.

Three months pass by, and in those three months the goddess, along with nature, grows and develops. The Celtic feast of Bealtaine arrives at the beginning of May when all nature is in bloom. Corn crops are well advanced though subject to blight and various diseases caused, in medieval thought, by the poisonous breath of dragons. To combat this, the church organised the colourful and dramatic Rogation Processions in which crowds of people led by a bishop or priest processed out into the fields sprinkling the corn with holy water and singing the Litany of the Saints on the Monday, Tuesday and Wednesday before the Feast of the Ascension of Our Lord into Heaven. This noisy and popular dragon-fighting operation brought the Christian Faith into vital contact with the ordinary cares and pre-occupations of the population.

Processions with 'King and Queen of the May', dancing around the Maypole, collecting the dew from the grass were all features of the celebration of Bealtaine. From this latter custom we have the rhyme:

The fair maid, who,
On the First of May,
Goes to the fields
At break of day;
And washes in dew
From the hawthorn tree
Will ever after,
Handsome be',

And, we still have the Rann of Bealtaine:

Babóg na Bealtaine, Maighdean and tSamhraidh,
Thugamar féin and Samhradh linn;
Samhradh buí faoi luí na gréine
Thugamar féin an Samhradh linn

(Young woman of May, virgin of summer; we brought the
summer with us. Yellow summer under the rays of the sun; we
brought the summer with us)

In his marvellous book, *The Avebury Cycle*, (London 1977, 154 ff),
Michael Dames stresses the importance of the May Wedding between god and goddess at Bealtaine, which would result in the
birth of a child – the corn, wheat, oats, barley – at Lughnasa, the
next feast at the beginning of August when the harvest would be
ripening. This, of course, was an element that would not be
stressed in the transition to church observance. Nevertheless,
hints of the Bealtaine Wedding may be discerned in the songs
Thugamar féin an Samhradh linn (Ó Baoill, 1986, 95) and in *Cuach mo
Londubh Buí* (Ó Baoill, 1975, 42)

Dames comments: 'The flowery image of the communal May
wedding set within the great ditch and bank (of Avebury,
Wiltshire) once hung about the Neolitic Obelisk.'

Indeed, there is good reason to believe that all Neolithic
henges were designed for the May wedding. Of the Stanton Drew
henge (Somerset), Stukeley wrote:

> This noble monument is vulgarly called the Weddings; and
> they say 'tis a company that assisted at a nuptial solemnity
> thus petrified (turned to stone). Other Circles are said to be the
> Company dancing, and a separate parcel of stones standing a
> little from the rest are call'd the fiddlers, or the band of musick.

He went on: 'I have observed that the appelation of Weddings,
Brides and the like, is not peculiar to this place, but applied to many
others of these Celtic monuments about the land' (1977, 154).

The pilgrimage to the Holy Well of Iníon Bhaoi takes place
every year at Bealtaine with considerable numbers taking part.
While the pilgrimage at Imbolc to St Lasair's Well takes place no
longer, it may not be entirely obsolete. The well had been covered
over but has been restored, and a native of the area told me that
when he passed it recently he noticed pieces of cloth hanging from
the *Bile* or sacred tree beside it. This means that St Lasair's Well is
still being visited. But often it happens that ancient traditions are
preserved only by the few.

The next Station is that of Lughnasa at the Holy Well of St Laitiaran at Cullen –Cuilinn Uí Chaoimh –called after the Clan of Ó Caoimh (O'Keefe), the traditional lords of this area. This seems to have been always the largest of the pilgrimages and remains so today, though it has lost something of its former profusion of music, dance and games.

This Lughnasa Pilgrimage in honour of St Laitiaran at Cuilinn Ui Chaoimh celebrates the First Fruits of the Harvest. At this time, part of the corn is ripe and the god/goddess/saint is asked to ripen the remaining part and so provide an abundant harvest. This links the sanctuary of Dúiche Ealla with the other great Lughnasa pilgrimages of Croagh Patrick, Loch Dearg, Mt Brandon, Liscannor Well, Cnoc Fírinne and others, as well as the world-famous Puck Fair.

At Imbolc, the corn has been sown and has sprouted.At Bealtaine it has grown to strength. At Lughnasa it has ripened to a rich yellow, and harvesting is the next operation.

At Samhain, it is gathered into the barns, it is threshed and some of the grain is kept for next year's sowing, some for animals, some of the barley for making whiskey and most for milling for flour. Perhaps, Samhain was never a great pilgrimage occasion to Coiscéim na Caillí, being superceded by the ordinary Rites of Samhain with its ritual extinction of domestic fires to be relighted from the great Samhain bonfire, (Compare with the quenching and re-lighting of candles at the Easter Vigil) its practice of divination, its Mummers or *Geamairí* going from house to house collecting money or goods from generous householders. On this night of Samhain, the barriers between this world and the world of the Celtic gods and goddessess, the Tuatha Dé Danann or *Aos Sí,* broke down and they could enter our world and we could be abducted into theirs. It is likely that those masked figures with turnip-lanterns who go from house to house represent the Tuatha Dé Danann coming to collect their taxes for having given an abundant harvest. If they are well-treated they will give another abundant harvest next year, for in Irish tradition the *Aos Sí* retreated underground into the sacred hollow hills (*Sí*) and from there they control the fertility of the land.

And what a marvellous scenario this is – the life-cycle of the corn, linked to the life-cycle of the goddess and celebrated in pilgrimages to sacred places according to the cycle of the seasons.

From Coiscéim na Caillí, at Samhain, the people glance eastwards in the direction of Cill Lasair, and they know that in three month's time they will be back there to celebrate the return of the goddess in the new and budding vegetation. And so, the seasons and the aspects of the goddess will succeed each other through everlasting ages – the Myth of the Eternal Return.

Another tradition of the area holds that the three sisters had a brother called St John of Mushera – a height in the nearby Boggerah Mountains – and his feastday is that of St John the Baptist, 24 June, the Summer Solstice. Here the male element is introduced from outside and two versions of the calendar are blended – the three sisters having the Insular Calendar and St John having the Solar or Solstice/Equinox calendar. In her internationally renowned book, *The Festival of Lughnasa*, (Dublin 1982) Máire Mac Néill remarks:

> How it happened that a namesake with the same feastday was assigned by popular belief to a height on the Muskerry hills and to fraternity with a trio of Duhallow saints presiding over quarterly feasts of the old Gaelic year is one of the many beckoning and elusive problems of our folklore research. It strongly suggests a calendar myth as background. It is perhaps worth bearing in mind that a neighbour height to Mushera has the significant and now familiar name of Seefin (271). Seefin occurs as a placename in many elevated places from which there is a great view. The original is *Suidhe/Suí Finn* –the chair / seat of the great hero Fionn Mac Cumhail.

Without going outside this small district of Dúiche Ealla, one can, by performing the four pilgrimages at the apriorist times, put oneself into harmony and empathy with the life of nature as personified in the life-cycle of the goddess. At a period of history in which we face an acute ecological crisis, it is a first step to recovering a lost link to the earth and the mysterious, life-giving cycle of the seasons.

This ritual calendar which expresses the different aspects of the life-cycle of the goddess of fertility can be seen within a much wider context.

A considerable amount of research has been done on the religion of the Megalithic peoples of Europe and it has emerged that the worship of the Great Goddess, the *Magna Mater* the *Mór-Ríoghan*, the *Tellus Mater* was of great importance to them, and the stylised form of a woman's body may be seen in some of the monuments such as the court-tomb at Shanballyedmond, near Rearcross, Co Tipperary. This argues to the existence of a largely female religion that was concerned with the growth of crops, the increase of stock – cows, sheep, goats, the general fertility of the land, the birth of children – the general preservation and continuation of the race.

And, as it is the female who gives birth, it was only natural that the divinity should be thought of as female, and that the principle of reproduction and growth should be conceived of as a feminine principle embodied in the idea of the Great Goddess, the mother of all manifestations of life, in plant, animal, and human forms. The prehistoric mentality is described by Marija Gimbutas:

> Most Old European sacred images symbolise the ever changing nature of life on earth: the constant and rhythmic interplay between creation and destruction, birth and death. For example, the moon's three phases – new, waxing and old – are repeated in Trinities of deities: maiden, nymph and crone; Life-giving, death-giving and transformational deities; rising, dying and self-renewing deities. Similarly, life-giving deities are also death wielders. Male vegetation spirits also express life's transitional nature; they are born, come to maturity, and die, as do plants (2).

> The images of Old Europe are those of the earth's vitality and richness. The transformative processes of nature are symbolically manifested in sprouting seeds, eggs, caterpillars and butterflies, and in such 'life columns' (symbols of rising and spontaneous life) as trees, springs, and serpents, which seem to emerge from the earth's womb. Sacred images represent both the miracle of birth – human, animal and plant – and the awe

and mystery surrounding the cyclic destruction and regeneration of life' (idem 506-507)

Having lived their lives in empathy with the cycle of the goddess, the curled up bodies in the foetal position in the tombs may indicate a desire to return to the womb of the Mother to be reborn.

The Gallo-Romans sometimes depicted the triple goddess on a plaque showing the three ladies with enormous hairdos seated and having on their laps baskets of bread and fruit. A folklore account of the Spring activity of the goddesses which gives the impression that they held meetings among themselves to decide how the early growth of vegetation should be advanced comes from Gaelic-speaking Cúil Aodha, not far distant from Díiche Ealla:

> Deireadh na seandaoine go mbíodh nithe ag cuimhneamh ar bheith ag fás Lá 'le Bríde, go mbíodh cailleach a' cur aníos agus beirt cailleach ag a gcur síos, agus nuair a thagadh Lá 'le Pádraig bhíodh beirt chailleach ag cur aníos. Ach nuair a thagadh an chéad lá d'Abrán bhíodh an triúr cailleach d' aonbhuíon chun bheith ag cur neithe aníos.
>
> Deir na feirmeoirithe gur mithid cuimhneamh ar obair an earraigh nuair a thagann Lá 'le Bríde agus 'sé ceol na n-éun a chuireann so i n-iúl dóibh' (*IFC* 900; 89-90)

(The old people used to say that things would be thinking of growing on St Brigid's Day; that one Veiled-One would be pushing the vegetation upwards (above the ground) while two Veiled–Ones would be keeping it down.

Then, when St Patrick's Day arrived, two Veiled-Ones would be pushing it upwards. But when the first of April came, the three Veiled-Ones would join forces to push the vegetation upwards. The farmers say that it is time to think of the Spring work when St Brigid's Day arrives and it is the music of the birds that reminds them of this.)

The four Celtic feasts were also connected to the economic life of this area of Dúiche by the fact that four Annual Fairs, held in Dromagh, were assigned to them in a slightly modified form:

1. 20 February – Imbolc; 2. 20 May – Bealtaine;
3. 20 July – Lughnasa; 4. 20 November – Samhain.
(*Seanchas Duthalla*, 1991, 48)

Michael Dames, again in his enormously enlightening work, *The Avebury Cycle*, quotes the English eleventh-century scribe, Byrhtferth of Ramsey, comparing the four points of the farming year, or seasons, to the human life-cycle: 'Spring and boyhood correspond; early manhood and summer are alike; autumn and manhood are allied; winter and old age are periods of decay' (1977, 16).

In performing the ritual of the four pilgrimages to the sacred sites at the appropriate dates, the pilgrims are inserting themselves into the divine pattern, as Christians who follow the life of Christ in the performance of the rituals of the Liturgical Year are inserting themselves into the divine pattern of the life of Christ. Obviously, the picture is clearer in the case of the goddess as her yearly life-cycle corresponds exactly to the four seasons of the natural year.

The process of operations of the agricultural year and the fate of the corn personified as John Barleycorn is wonderfully set out in the traditional English folksong which may also contain an echo of the Purusa Creation Myth:

There was three men came out of the west,
Their fortunes for to try,
And these three men made a solemn vow,
John Barleycorn should die.
They ploughed, they sowed, they harrowed him in,
Throwed clods upon his head,
And these three men made a solemn vow,
John Barleycorn was dead.

Then they let him lie for a very long time
Till the rain from heaven did fall,
Then little Sir John sprung up his head
And soon amazed them all.

> They let him stand till midsummer,
> Till he looked both pale and wan,
> And little Sir John he growed a long beard
> And so became a man.
>
> They wasted oer a scorching flame
> The marrow of his bones,
> But a miller used him worst of all,
> For he crushed him tween two stones.
> (Kennedy, P., *Folksongs of Britain and Ireland*, London 1975; 609, 627-628)

Here, the ploughing, harrowing, sowing, burial of the corn is described, the death of the seed in the ground, the rain which brings John Barleycorn back to life above ground to the amazement of the farmers as this great mystery of death to life has amazed all peoples since time began. Then, the corn develops and ripens to be harvested and used for different purposes – the grain itself for re-sowing and for horses, for bread and for the making of beer. Here we see echoes of the great Purusa myth: Purusa, cruelly dismembered, not destroyed but transmuted, changed into a multitude of forms as the Indonesian goddess, Hainuwele, was dismembered and the different parts of her body buried in the earth where they grew and mutated into different food-plants for the benefit of mankind.

On Plough Monday (6 January) the people of Haxey in Lincolnshire celebrate John Barleycorn in raucous song as they drink the ale into which he has been mutated. He lifts the spirits of all, even of the widow 'though the tear were in her eye'. He subdues the drinkers by making them drunk and shows, that after all his tribulations, he is still 'the stronger man' (Dames, 1977, 16-17).

A curious piece of folklore surrounds the Dúiche Ealla sanctuary and may possibly be connected with the local placenames. As we have seen, 'Cnoc an Bhuthairín' and 'Buthaire Baoi' suggest ritual bonfires, while 'Iomaire Baoi' and 'Gort an Tuí Baoi' suggest a tillage plot and a corn field, and with the repetition of 'Baoi' might suggest a farm attached to an established temple or *neimheadh* of 'Baoi.'

Now, the Holy Well and pilgrimage site of St Iníon Bhaoi is at Drom Tairbh – the ridge/hill of the Bull. Legend has it that each year, probably at Bealtaine, a bull-calf was sacrificed in honour of the goddess. The calf entered the Otherworld, the world of the Ancestors where the power of fructification lay and so contributed to the fertility of the land of Dúiche Ealla, as in the story of King Conaire Mór in *Togail Bruidne Dá Derga*, the 'Tarbhhfheis' took place. This was a rite of divination – to give the electors of a new king an idea of who would be a suitable candidate for the kingship of Tara. A bull was sacrificed and a seer who was strictly bound to truth ate the flesh of the sacrificed bull, fell into a heavy sleep and, in a vision, saw the figure of the one who should be king. He then proceeded to describe him to the officials. The sacrificed bull had entered into the *Alltar* – the Otherworld of the gods where knowledge was available among the Ancestors, and then, by communion with the bull, knowledge of the future king was passed on to the seer, and by the seer to the electors.

In the case of Dúiche Ealla, no doubt, it was the fertility of the land that was involved.

A common surname in the area is Ó Laoghaire. The name can be broken down to 'Laogh' (calf) and 'Aire' (attendant/minister/carer) – the 'Calf-Carer – and the tradition says that there was a branch of the family known as 'Ó Laoghaire Baoi'. It seems then, that there was a branch of the family who inherited the position of Carer of the Bull-Calf of Baoi each year until the appropriate time came for sacrifice.

Ó Laoghaire Baoi would then have a very important part to play in the cult of the three sisters in Dúiche Ealla.

As well as Dúiche Ealla, there is another case in which Three Holy Sisters are venerated. This is at 'Tobar na mBan-Naomh' at Teelin in Co Donegal. The Turas is made on Bonfire Night, 23 June, the Feast of St John the Baptist, the Summer Solstice.

The three are known locally as Ciall, Tuigse agus Náire – Sense, Understanding and Modesty. If the weather is fine, devout pilgrims remain at the well until dawn. In this case, unlike Dúiche Ealla, there is only one well, so that the calendrical character of the site is not so obviously marked out. Nevertheless, it is highly significant that the Turas takes place at the Summer Solstice when the sun is at the highest point of his annual journey and from this on is gradually going into decline. The Station on Bonfire Night suggests that it was originally a pagan sanctuary, christianised by early missionaries.

CHAPTER SEVEN

The Tradition of the Three Sisters

Fishermen when sailing out from Teelin Bay, lower their sails by way of salute on passing Tobar na mBan-Naomh, take off their caps and ask for help and protection from the Holy Women.

Enrí Ó Muirgheasa, in his authoritative article 'The Holy Wells of Donegal' (*Béaloideas*, 1936, 143-162) informs us that there is another well near Tobar na mBan-Naomh and that an alternative tradition said that it was to this well that the fishermen saluted. This latter well was called Tobar na gCórach – interpreted as 'Well of the Fair Winds'. 'When Teelin boats were storm-stayed at Sligo, Ballina, or Belmullet, if this Tobar na gCórach were cleaned out it would bring favourable winds, but there was a danger that a member of the family that cleaned the well would die' (149).

In all of this matter of Holy Wells it may be asked why they were so important to people in the past and why so many of them have remained, in a somewhat Christianised form, so popular among people today.

In such a wet country as Ireland, one would hardly expect such devotion to water. But different factors have to be considered. If the Holy Wells go back untold ages into the Megalithic period when, as is so often pointed out, the climate was much warmer and drier than it is today, then it may be that the presence of a well was of vital importance to the local population. This is not a wholly satisfactory explanation, however, for a Holy Well is not generally used for domestic purposes; an ordinary well, not considered holy, is the type of well in use for domestic purposes. Apparently, it is tradition, and the practice of ritual, which point out that this particular well is a 'Holy Well' while another well only a short distance away is an ordinary domestic well. Many stories assert that the water from a 'Holy Well' will not boil, or that evil will follow from lack of respect for it. This idea goes back a long time. The Rennes Dinnseanchas tells the story of Bóinn – the River Boyne:

> Boand, wife of Nechtan son of Labraid, went to the secret well which was in the green of Sid Nechtain. Whoever went to it would not come from it without his two eyes bursting, unless it were Nechtan himself and his three cupbearers, whose names were Flesc and Lámh and Luam.
>
> Once upon a time Boand went through pride to test the well's power, and declared that it had no secret force which could shatter her form, and thrice she walked withershins round the well. Whereupon three waves from the well break over her and deprive her of a thigh and one of her hands and one of her eyes. Then she, fleeing her shame, turns seaward, with the water behind her, as far as Boyne-mouth, (where she was drowned). Now she was the mother of Oengus son of the Dagda (*Rev. Celt.* 15 (1894), 315-316).

Here, out of contempt, Boand performs the *Cor Tuathal* or left-handed (withershins) turn around the well instead of the *Cor Deiseal* or right-handed (clockwise) turn which follows the course of the sun. The *Cor Tuathal* is the unlucky, cursing turn and the well punishes Bóinn for her disrespect. Significantly, she is left with one eye, one hand and one leg. The Fomhóraigh or Dark Gods, the enemies of the Tuatha Dé Danann, are often depicted as having only one eye, one hand and one leg. The Boyne rises at Sí Neachtain, a sacred hill in the Barony of Carbury, Co Kildare.

This may be the same well as the Well of Segais, source of the Boyne. Around it grew nine hazel trees. The hazel nuts fell into the well and were eaten by the salmon. This conveyed wisdom to the salmon and to those who ate the salmon the wisdom was transferred to them as in the case of Fionn Mac Cumhail.

In this case, the *tobar diamhair* or mysterious well was '*i n-urlaind in Sidhe Nechtain*' – in the lawn or forecourt of the Sí. Here there is a very close connection between the Holy Well and the Sí or sacred hollow hill of the Tuatha Dé Danann / Aos Sí. One wonders if this were a common feature – the close siting of the well and the Sí and perhaps the exclusive use of the Holy Well by the Aos Sí under normal circumstances, only to be used by the humans on those sacred occasions when the barriers between the two worlds are removed such as at Samhain, Bealtaine, Summer Solstice, etc.

when the Tuatha Dé Danann and humans co-mingle. One thinks immediately of the great Sí of Áine at Lough Gur in Co Limerick with its St Patrick's Well as part of the complex, or indeed St Gobnat's Well at Baile Bhóirne in Co Cork, where the great St Gobnat is venerated as the protector of her people to a degree of which any tutelary goddess might well be proud.

Logan mentions a tradition of three nuns in the Ardagh, Co Longford area also:

> I have heard a legend about three nuns, accompanied by a big spotted cow, 'like an Ayrshire,' who were going from St Brigid's Well at Ardagh, Co Longford, towards Slieve Golry (1980, 42).

Here, it will be noticed that the reference is to St Brigid and that according to the *Sanas Chormaic* there were three Brigids – daughters of An Daghdha, king of the Tuatha Dé Danann. They were 'Bé leighis', 'Bé éigse' and 'Bé ghaibhneachta' – Lady of Medicine, Lady of Poetry and Lady of Metalwork' (Stokes, 1862, 8). Here they appear again accompanied by a big spotted cow – symbol of the fertility of the land. This cow, 'like an Ayrshire' is probably a folk version of the *Glas Gaibhleann* – the magic cow, white with red ears, which often accompanies St Brigid and other notable personalities. She gives enormous quantities of milk to her followers but departs on being insulted. The goddess, as patron of the arts, is linked to the *Aos Dána*, the druids, filí, bards – the learned class of Celtic society, while her association with cows links her to the Bó–Airí, the farmers and food producers.

Another significant point in this account is the connection between St Brigid's Well in Ardagh and Slieve Golry, and the fact that the three women were going from the well to the mountain. St Brigid's Well is located at the north-eastern foot of the hill.

Slieve Golry – *Sliabh gCalraighe* – from the ancient tribe of the Calraighe – is only 650 feet high but commands a spectacular view of the surrounding countryside and was one of the best-known sites for the celebration of the Festival of Lughnasa on the first Sunday of August known as 'Bilberry Sunday'. Large groups of people climbed the hill to pick *Fraochán*, bilberries / whortleberries, the wild fruits of the beginning of the harvest season. Dancing, flirting and general amusement on the hill made it a memorable occasion for all. The mountain was supposed to be the hunting ground of a giant.

The name of the giant was King Midas of the Mountain and he is said to have cellars and corridors all leading to a castle in the interior of the mountain. There is a tradition of a tunnel leading from the top of the mountain to these internal buildings and children attending the Festival of Lughnasa were warned to stay with the others in case the giant pulled them down into the interior. Máire Mac Néill remarks on similar beliefs that were to be found in other sites such as Ard Éireann, Caher Roe's Den, Knockfeerina, Slieve Bloom, Keeper Hill and Dún Briste (1982, 238).

Apart from the Lughnasa celebrations, however, Sliabh gCalraighe is identified with Sí Bhrí Léith, the home of Midhir, one of the best known of the gods of the Tuatha Dé Danann. It is sometimes surmised that he is a Celticised form of the Iranian god Mitra whose cult was strong among the soldiers of the Roman Empire and travelled with them to such an extent that it was a serious rival of Christianity. However that may be, Midhir Bhrí Léith, Eochaidh Aireamh and Aonghus Óg of Brú na Bóinne along with the goddess Étaín are central figures in perhaps one of the most haunting and mysterious romances in the whole of ancient literature – *Tochmarc Étaíne* (*Eriu* 12, 1938, 137-196).

This long, complicated and intensely moving love story in three parts leads into the magical tragedy, *Togail Bruidne Dá Derga* – The Destruction of Da Derga Hostel – in what might be called 'The Étaín Cycle'.

Perhaps the procession of the three sisters from St Brigid's Well near Ardagh, to Sliabh gCalraighe, as recorded in the folklore account, is an echo of the Dúiche Ealla tradition of the three sisters going underground for part of the year. This would certainly be at Samhain when vegetation has descended into the barren earth. Perhaps the three sisters at Ardagh, likewise at Samhain, vacated the upper world and using the tunnel, descended to meet Midhir in his castle in the hidden depths of the Sí of Brí Léith. In a similar way, in Greek mythology, Persephone descended into the

Underworld to Pluto during the barren months of the year, to return again at the appropriate season to restore the fertility of the land.

The tradition of internal tunnels, corridors and a castle in which the Tuatha Dé Danann / Aos Sí live and carry on their ordinary social life, mentioned in the case of the Sí of Brí Léith, occurs also in relation to other sacred hollow hills notably that of the god Donn Fírinne at his Sí at Cnoc Fírinne (Knockfierna) near Ballingarry, Co Limerick. This area remained Gaelic-speaking for longer than many other areas and retained a rich corpus of folklore relating to the god Donn associated with death, weather conditions and the fertility of the land. The various traditions of the area were gathered together by Dr Kate Muller-Lisowski in her remarkable monograph: 'Contributions to a Study of Irish Folklore; Traditions about Donn', (*Béaloideas* 18, Uimhir 1-11, Meitheamh-Nodlaig 1948, 142-199).

Donn Fírinne (Donn of Truth) – he is popularly known as Donn of Truth as, by means of cloud formations over the hill, he warns the local people of impending bad weather, and he never leads them astray. Like the god Donn mentioned in *Leabhar Gabhála Éireann* whose Sí is at Tech nDoinn – a rock (An Tarbh) on the south coast of Kerry and who said: 'To me, to my house you shall all come after your death', the Donn of Cnoc Fírinne is also associated with life after death. 'One of the folklore collectors writes: 'The day before old C… died, just after the priest had a last interview with him, and as he looked through the low open window on Knockfierna, he told me that he would be up there soon, on the whaleback "Black Hill", east of the cone where Donn was supposed to marshal his men.'

Mr Liam Danaher, our informant, adds the comment: 'I was struck by the strong hold this stark paganism still held over minds which after fifty generations of Christian baptism still clung to older beliefs' (*Béaloideas* 18, 143).

Donn is known by several names: Donn na Duimhche (Donn of the Sandhills), Co Clare; Donn na Binne (Donn of the hilltop), Co Fermanagh; Donn Chnuic na nOs (Down of the fawns), Co Cork, etc.

They may be all local manifestations of Donn, the Irish god of the dead, perhaps corresponding to Caesar's 'Dispater': *'Galli se omnes ab Dite patre prognatus praedicant idque ab drudibus proditum dicunt.'* (The Galls all assert their descent from *Dis pater* and say that is the druidic belief) (Tierney, 1960, 244, 273).

Many people in the Ballingarry district believed that there were underground tunnels from Cnoc Fírinne to the mouth of the Shannon, to Tory Hill and other places. This resembles the situation at Sí Bhrí Léith. But perhaps the most extraordinary story of Cnoc Fírinne is that recorded by David Fitzgerald in 1885 concerning, as it were, the interior life of the sacred hill.

According to the account, a new farmer and his wife settled down near the Sí of Cnoc Fírinne and were very careful to divert the dirty water from the farm so that it flowed away from the Sí. The former owner of the farm had been very careless in this matter. This change did not go unnoticed by Donn. He invited the farmer to his castle (which of course had not been visible before) and showed him around. He took him to a room in which were a large number of boys studying 'the mysteries of the creation since the stars began to shine'.

Donn asked the farmer if he recognised any of the students. The farmer replied that he recognised his brother who had died nine years previously. Donn gave him the boy to take away with him.

Then, Donn's wife took him to a hall in which a large number of girls were studying 'the virtues and weaknesses of women since Adam and Eve'. Among them he recognised his sister who had died twelve years earlier. Donn's wife gave her back to him and when they emerged from the Sí they both recognised their brother. The castle vanished and the farm became prosperous. (*Béaloideas* 18, 163-164)

This was Donn in a mood of benevolence. He was, however, often ill-tempered and violent. An old woman, believing she heard the voice of Donn roaring in the storm, shrieked: 'Dia idir sinn agus an t-olc, tá sé ag lasadh le feirg' (May God be between us and harm, he is on fire with fury.)

The local people, in a general way, were afraid of him and he had powers of retaliation. Gifts were made to Donn at Bealtaine and Samhain, so that while the people paid their respects they kept at a safe distance from him. In this and in may other respects the situation resembles the cult of Crom Cruach and some scholars wonder if Donn and Crom are not variations of the one divinity.

Another Lughnasa tradition associated with Donn Fírinne is his organisation of a ritual hurling match each Autumn. This was a contest between his own Aos Sí at Cnoc Fírinne near Ballingarry, and the Tuatha Dé Danann of Áine Cliach of Lough Gur and Cnoc Áine near Hospital (*Ospidéal Áine*) in East Limerick. Unlike modern hurling, this was 'cross-country' hurling. The ball was thrown in half way between the two mystical sites and each team battled over fields, bogs, rivers and streams, trying to get the ball back to their own Sí. If Áine's team got the ball back to Cnoc Áine, then the potato crop would be excellent in East Limerick that year but would languish in West Limerick in Donn's area, and vice versa (MacNéill, 1982, 591-592). Here we have a very interesting phenomenon of a supernatural hurling match played by supernatural hurlers, among whom a small number of outstanding human hurlers might be included, battling, not for medals and a silver cup, but for the fertility of the land in the local area under the patronage of the local god or goddess.

To return then to the question of the Three Saints in Munster.

An alternative tradition in the south-west Cork-Kerry area gives a different three saints and assigns them to the same feasts though at different locations. These are:

St Gobnat, at Baile Bhóirne, at Imbolc (11 Feb);

St Crobh Dearg, at Cathair Chrobh Dearg (The City Well), at Bealtaine.

St Laitiaran, at Cullen (Cuilinn Uí Chaoimh) at Lughnasa.

While this formulation does not follow the neat four-square path of the Dúiche Ealla arrangement it still maintains the three major feasts and was probably convenient for many pilgrims as regards the distance they were required to travel.

There is the well-known and highly popular pilgrimage to St. Gobnat's Shrine (*Relig Ghobnatan*) at Baile Bhóirne at Imbolc. Here it is 11 February which is really 1 February – the calendar having been corrected, as it had lost alignment with the sun by 11 days.

Workers in Britain rioted in the streets shouting 'Give us back our 11 days' – as they had lost 11 days' pay.

Crov Dearg (*Crobh Dearg*), however, is something of a puzzle. According to the traditions, she is the sister of St Laitiaran and St Gobnat (MacNéill, 1982, 579). But the name is peculiar – 'Red Claw' and some writers have suggested some connection with the Celtic goddesses of war, Macha, Badhbh and MórRíon who fly shrieking over warriors in battle. It is difficult to reconcile this with the peaceful saints of Dúiche Ealla. Nevertheless, there is an account of St Brigid, in the form of the Badhbh (scald-crow) inciting the soldiers in the ancient story 'Cath Almaine'. This is obviously a throw-back to Brigid the goddess.

The Holy Well (the City Well) associated with St Crobh Dearg is attached to the great stone fort Cathair Chrobh Dearg situated on the northern slopes of *Dhá Chíoch Dhanann* – the Paps. It would appear that lines of even length drawn from the Paps would meet at the Cathair to form the triangle mentioned earlier in association with Kildare and other sacred sites. The dating of this construction, like many others of its kind, such as Staigue Fort, is uncertain. Diarmuid Moynihan, who did a local study of the area of Sliabh Luachra, seems to suggest that this was an ancient ritual site connected especially with the Festival of Bealtaine (1 May) and the formerly very large and popular Christian pilgrimage to the Cathair and Holy Well at Bealtaine is a Christianisation of the pre-Christian ritual (2003, 31) According to Cormac Mac Cuileannáin, the great intellectual and king-bishop of Cashel in the tenth century, the people drove their cattle between two fires at Bealtaine to keep them healthy and free from disease for the coming year.

Similarly, at Cathair Chrobh Dearg people brought their cattle from long distances and got them to drink the water from the Holy Well. The pilgrimage still continues but with severely reduced numbers. But it does seem that here we have a genuine survival of an extremely ancient ritual.

Again it is suggested that as well as being a ritual site and remaining one, it also became a residence of the Kings of Ciarraí Luachra. Moynihan sees local placenames such as *Ath an Rí* and *Cosán an Rí* (Ford of the King/Path of the King) as significant. But what of the odd name? Could it possibly have any connection with Cathal Crobh Dearg Ó Conchúir, King of Connaught, who founded Ballintubber Abbey, Co Mayo, in 1216? This is the great abbey which managed to survive attacks and persecution throughout the centuries and has been restored as a centre of pilgrimage. It is sited on the pilgrim path to Croagh Patrick, *Tóchar Phádraig*.

Again, it is claimed, like many other sites, that Cathair Chrobh Dearg was the Teamhair Luachra or Luachar Dedadh mentioned so frequently in ancient literature, but this is uncertain. There is no denying, however, that this was, and to some extent remains, a highly important ritual site involving a saint/goddess who is one of a trio of saints/goddesses on the central feast of Bealtaine, the beginning of the bright half of the year, with the performance of a rite at a Holy Well at which cows and cattle are involved as mentioned in *Sanas Chormaic* over a thousand years ago. Patrick Logan (1980, 129-130) quotes O'Donovan's account of Cathair Chrobh Dearg:

> In the townland of Gortnagowan in the East division of this Parish (Kilcummin parish, Co Kerry), there is a caher or circular stone fort called Caher Crobhderg, ie the fort of the Redhanded. In the west side of it is a holy well at which stations are performed by the peasantry on May Eve: who also drove their cattle into the fort and made them drink of the water of the holy well which is believed to have the virtue to preserve them from all contagious distempers during the ensuing year.

Logan (1980, 130), quotes Wilde with regard to the May Day practice of drawing a little blood from cattle at Rathcroghan, Co Roscommon, the royal seat of the Kings of Connaught:

> When I was a boy I used to visit on a May morning the great Rath at Crohan, near the rampart of which the cave's mouth (Hellmouth door of Ireland) is situated and when all the great Connaught oxen of the extensive plains around were driven in to be bled, the peasantry gathered in with pots.

Taking a little blood from animals and from people (notice the

red and white pole outside a barber's shop) was standard treatment but what makes this account unique is that it was part of a
Bealtaine ritual at Cruachan beside *Uaimh na gCat* (Cave of the
Cats) or *Uaimh Chruachán*, the entrance to the dangerous
Otherworld which features so largely in the mysterious ancient
story *Eachtra Neara* (*Rev. Celt.* X , 215ff) In the darkness of the night
of Samhain when demons are abroad, Neara, the hero of the story,
binds up a hanged man and carries him around on his back seeking water as he was very thirsty when he was hanged, or so the
dead man tells him, for the hanged man is neither dead nor alive –
this is the 'betwixt and between' period of Samhain when it is neither summer nor winter, neither day nor night. This is *Oíche na
hAimiléise*, the night of chaos when the barriers between the *Alltar*
and the *Ceantar* have collapsed and the inhabitants of the two regions coalesce. Eventually, the human Neara finds his way into
the Sí of Cruachan and is well treated by the Tuatha Dé Danann
and is given a beautiful *Bean Sí* for his wife. While Neara fared
rather well, Uaimh Chruachan was a dangerous place from which
supernatural birds, cats and pigs emerged, all of whom were up to
no good.

Speaking of the great Connaught cemeteries, Professor
Michael Herity mentions a curious phenomenon which , perhaps,
may be a feature of other sacred sites:

> Like the cemetery at Rath Cruachan, Carnfree is surrounded
> by a great empty zone in which no later monuments were
> built: this excludes the ringforts, mundane habitations of the
> first 1000 years after Christ, which were kept at least 400 to 500
> metres away from the sacred central area on top of the ridge …
> This empty area between is thus a zone of avoidance delimit-
> ing a sacred region around the cemetery and inauguration
> place (*Rathcroghan and Carnfree*, Baile Átha Cliath, 1988, 26).

Since there are numerous earthen enclosures in this area of
Rath Cruachan, the one mentioned by Wilde into which the cows
were driven for blood letting at Bealtaine must have been quite a
large one with a level interior and one gap – a ringfort or Lios.
While it is not mentioned, one wonders if the traditional rite of

Bealtaine – the passing of the cows between two fires, *idir dhá Thine Bhealtaine* – was not practised at the same time. This could be done, as it was in some farms, by lighting a fire at each side of the gap in the earthen ring on the outside, so that as each cow emerged from the interior of the rath she passed automatically between the two fires of Bealtaine and was thus fortified against the diseases of the coming year.

In all of this we can see a pattern emerging from the two ritual sites, Cathair Chrobh Dearg in Co Kerry and Rath Cruachan in Co Roscommon.

At both sites, the ritual takes place at Bealtaine and is closely connected to the health of cattle.

In the case of Rath Cruachan, the cattle are bled, while in Cathair Chrobh Dearg they are sprinkled with water from the Holy Well just beside the Cathair. Again, it is unknown if the passing between the two fires took place. Cathair Chrobh Derg seems to be much more Christianised; it was and is a place of pilgrimage and St Crobh Dearg is one of the trio of local Saints – Gobnat, Crobh Dearg and Laitiaran.

In comparing this arrangement to that of Dúiche Ealla, the system is as follows:

Gobnat replaces Lasair-Imbolc at Baile Bhóirne.

Crobh Dearg replaces Inion Bhaoi-Bealtaine at Cathair Chrobh Dearg.

Laitiaran remains unchanged – Lughnasa at Cuilinn Uí Chaoimh.

Here, as the rite of passing between two fires has been mentioned as a traditional and widespread feature of the Feast of Bealtaine, we might wonder if any remnant of it remains, apart from those who deliberately practice it to continue the custom of their ancestors.

Strangely, I believe that it may be found in an adapted form, in a place where one would least expect it – among the rituals of the Catholic Church.

The 'Blessing of the Throat' on the Feast of St Blaise, on the third of February, is a well-known and popular practice in the Catholic Church of the Roman Rite. Following the *Rituale*

Romanum, the priest, wearing alb and stole, says a prayer of bless-ing over two candles and sprinkles them with holy water. The blessing prayer recalls that as a reward for the great sufferings which this bishop and martyr endured, among other privileges, God gave him the power to cure diseases of the throat for those who practise the rite with faith.

A legend asserts that St.Blaise cured a boy who had swallowed a fish-bone and was choking.

After the blessing and sprinkling, what happens next is de-scribed in the rubric of the *Rituale Romanum* of the year 1895 and 1915:

> *Deinde sacerdos terminata Missa, deposita casula, et manipulo, ac-census duobus cereis, ac in modum crucis aptatis, apponens illos sub mento gutturi cujusvis benedicendorum, ipsis ante Altare genu-flectentibus, dicat:*
>
> *'Per intercessionem sancti Blasii, Episcopi et Martyris, liberet te Deus a malo gutturis, et a quolibet alio malo. In nomine Patris, + et Filii, et Spiritus Sancti. Amen'*
>
> (Then, the priest, the Mass being ended, and his chasuble and maniple being laid aside, and two candles having been lighted and fastened together in the form of a cross, placing them under the chin of the throat of each one of those to be blessed, while they kneel before the altar, he says:
>
> 'Through the intercession of St Blaise, Bishop and Martyr, may God set you free from disease of the throat, and from every other evil. In the name of the Father, and of the Son, and of the Holy Spirit. Amen.')

Now, when we come to the *Collectio Rituum* for all the dioceses of Ireland published in 1960 (Dublini, MCMLX, 256) there is one sig-nificant difference – the word *accensis* (lighted) is omitted and fol-lowing this, in the practice we follow today, the candles are in-deed fastened together by a ribbon to form a cross, and placed on the throat, but the candles are not lighted, whereas in the *Rituale Romanum* of as late as 1915 they were lighted. When one thinks about it, it use of unlighted candles seems rather odd.

I remember asking a priest who had worked in Belgium about

this. He told me that there it was taken for granted that the Blessing of the Throat was given with lighted candles as the former *Rituale Romanum* had stipulated. What was the purpose of this change in the *Rituale Romanum* and the consequent diminution of the force of this Rite? Presumably it was thought that there was the practical danger of setting fire to people's hair. When I mentioned this to my friend he assured me there was no danger. He said that in Belgium they used very long slim candles and the flame was away above the person's head.

Now, when we examine this curious Rite more closely and its popularity among the faithful, we are immediately reminded of passing between the two fires of Bealtaine as a well known popular practice.

Cormac's Glossary explains the usage in this way: '*bil-tine*, i.e. a goodly fire, i.e. two fires which Druids used to make with great incantations, and they used to bring the cattle to those fire (as a preservative) against the diseases of each year' (Stokes, 1862, xxxv). Fire is the great purificator and at the end of a long dark and wet winter people felt the need to cast off the colds and chills and enter into to the cheerful period of summer renewed. The purpose of dividing the fire into two was purely practical. While humans circumambulate the fire *deiseal* (keeping the fire at their right hand as they move around; following the course of the sun) cows can not be persuaded to do this, or to jump over the fire and absorb its purifying heat and smoke. They can, however, be driven between two fires and many farmers just lighted a little fire at each side of the gate and drove their cows through into the next field. Children, no doubt, also carried their pet dogs or cats in the same way between the two fires. Sir William Wilde describes the practice among the humans:

> If a man was about to perform a long journey, he leaped backwards and forwards three times through the fire, to give him success in his undertaking. If about to wed he did it to purify himself for the marriage state. If going to undertake some hazardous enterprise, he passed through the fire to render himself invulnerable. As the fire sank low, the girls trip across it to procure good husbands; women great with child might be

seen stepping through it to ensure a happy delivery, and children were also carried across the smouldering ashes, as of old among the Canaanites (1853, 49).

The fire-ritual was considered to be widely-embracing in its effects as is evident from Sir William's commentary. It is evident also that Sir William had watched very carefully the rite being performed and had consulted the local people about its meaning. It gave protection in travel, in hazardous enterprises, good luck to young women on the look out for husbands and safety in childbirth.

Similarly, the Blessing of St Blaise is far wider than just protection from diseases of the throat – it says: '*et a quolibet alio malo*' (from every other evil).

The lucid and engrossing research on the goddess done by Professor Pamela Berger (*The Goddess Obscured*, London 1988) shows the popularity of this Armenian saint particularly in Belgium, France and Germany where he seems to take over the care of fertility of land and women traditionally associated with the goddess; and as a male saint more easily accepted by a male orientated church than a woman. His name in French 'Blaise' resembles 'Ble', 'wheat,' and women, on his feastday 3 February, the beginning of the agricultural year and Feast of Imbolc/Brigid among the Irish, brought a bucket of wheat to the priest to be blessed, giving half of it to the priest and mixing the blessed wheat with the seed to be sown in the field at Spring sowing. Young women watched his statue carefully in the church and if the saint seemed to wink at them it meant that they would soon be married. Elaborate processions of carts depicting the various operations of the farmer's year took place around the countryside. In some of these areas where the pageantry of St Blaise lasted on until interrupted by the First World War, the fertility role of the great goddess continued in a thinly obscured way in the form of devotion to a male saint. This presented no great difficulty for the official church, and anyway St Blaise, being a great and powerful saint in his own right, could no doubt influence God in matters of fertility and general health and prosperity. Here, as in the case of St Brigid, the exact demarcation between saint and goddess is often obscure and a cause of some misgivings to theologians. The ordinary people, however, are less exercised by these considerations and when life prospers are well content with their lot irrespective of its source. Traditionally, they rarely bother to distinguish if it is the local saint or the local goddess is responsible for their good luck.

If we compare then, the Rite of the Blessing of the Throat on the Feast of St.Blaise, 3 February, in the Catholic Church and the Bealtaine Blessing among the Celts of Ireland, it is clear that there are certain similarities and dissimilarities.

Firstly: the church rite is indoors while the Bealtaine rite is outdoors in accordance with Celtic custom as seen in pilgrimages to Holy Wells, and sacred places, Bonfire Night (23 June), etc.

Secondly: both rites are on the sacred Celtic day of Imbolc (1/3/February) but the fire element is transferred from Bealtaine (1 May) to Imbolc.

Thirdly: two candles in the church take the place of the two fires of Bealaine, two fires being impractical in the church building.

Fourthly: the purpose is basically the same – protection from disease during the coming year with particular emphasis on throat diseases in the case of St Blaise, but as we have seen, in the European context, the general fertility of land and women was stressed as among the Celts.

Fifthly: the Blessing of the Candles for the Church Rite, *Benedictio Candelarum in Festo S. Blasii Episcopi et Matyris (Rituale Romanum)* mentions the touching of the throat and the candle (lighted). This would correspond to the contact of the person with the smoke and heat of the fires and the torches lighted from the fires and thrown into the fields in the Celtic system.

It does seem that the Blessing of the Throat in the Catholic Church on the Feast of St Blaise is an adaptation by the church of the Celtic Rite of *Dhá Thine Bhealtaine* though it is unknown precisely how this could have come about.

In practice, it may be suggested that two large candlesticks with long fat lighted candles be used and set down on the floor of the church so that each one receiving the Blessing could walk between them while the priest in alb and stole, standing nearby, recited the formula of blessing with the sign of the Cross as each one passed through.

The prayer-formula in the *Rituale Romanum* 'for deliverance from diseases of the throat and every other evil' reflects, no doubt the 'great incantations' (*cotinchetlaib moraib*) of the druids mentioned by the King-Bishop Cormac Mac Cuileannáin.

The great collector of folklore in Scotland Alexander Carmichael, the author of the masterpiece *Carmina Gadelica*, remarks on the life and mentality of the people of the Highlands, out of his vast experience of their ways:

> Perhaps no people had a fuller ritual of song and story, of secular rite and religious ceremony, than the Highlanders. Mirth and music, song and dance, tale and poem, pervaded their lives, as electricity pervades the air. Religion, pagan or Christian, or both combined, permeated everything – blending and shading into one another like the iridescent colours of the rainbow. The people were sympathetic and synthetic, unable to see and careless to know where the secular began and the religious ended – an admirable union of elements in life for those who have lived it so truly and intensely as the Celtic races everywhere have done, and none more truly or more intensely than the ill-understood and so-called illiterate Highlanders of Scotland (1972, Vol 1, xxxii –xxxiii).

The Feast of St Blaise is celebrated with great ceremony and rejoicing in the city of Dubrovnik on the Croatian coast every year on 3 February. He is the Patron of the city and is said to have warned the Officials well in advance that the Venetians were preparing to attack them. His canopied relics are carried through streets swarming with people and a great assembly of priests and bishops (Travirka, A., *Dubrovnik*, Forum 1998)

CHAPTER EIGHT

The Age of the Megaliths

We have seen something of the rituals and religious ideas of the Celtic people of Ireland in the previous pages and something of the way in which the new religion of Christianity gradually blended with the old in some respects and in particular in the case of calendar customs. The three saints of Dúiche Ealla, immersed in the traditional insular Celtic Calendar of Samhain, Imbolc, Bealtaine and Lughnasa, is a good example of this process.

We began with the story of Crom Cruaich, then there followed an account of the ancient Celtic gods and goddesses, their sanctuaries, their relations with the people and the land, and the gradual extension of Christianity while the old religion was not entirely abandoned; indeed, an adaption and re-ordering of certain rituals took place in order to accommodate the new religion. This is fairly familiar territory as so many vestiges of it remain to the present day and the study of local customs and folklore can bring further enlightenment. This area of our past is not so far away.

However, there is another part of Ireland's ancient story yet to be revealed and this is so far away from us that it is veiled in obscurity. This is the age of the megaliths and many people will be aware of this prehistoric period from the fame attached to Brú na Bóinne and the bend of the Boyne. It is here at Newgrange that the rising sun at the Winter Solstice, the shortest day of the year, sends a ray of light through the long passage of the mound into its inner chamber. This awesome event is recorded by Professor O'Kelly, excavator of Newgrange, at the Winter Solstice Sunrise of 21 December 1969:

> At exactly 9.45 am (BST) the top edge of the ball of the sun appeared above the local horizon and at 9.58 am the first pencil of direct sunlight shone through the roof-box and right along the passage to reach across the tomb chamber floor as far as the

front edge of the basin stone in the end-chamber. As the thin line of light widened to a 17cm band and swung across the chamber floor, the tomb was dramatically illuminated and various details of the side- and end-chambers as well as the corbelled roof could be clearly seen in the light reflected from the floor. At 10.04 am the 17cm band of light began to narrow again and at exactly 10.15 am the direct beam was cut off from the tomb. For 17 minutes, therefore, at sunrise on the shortest day of the year, direct sunlight can enter Newgrange, not through the doorway, but through the specially-contrived narrow slit which lies under the roof-box at the outer end of the passage roof. Further observation has shown that direct sunlight penetrates to the chamber for about a week before and a week after the solstice but not as fully as on the few days centring on the 21st.' (O'Kelly, C., *Concise Guide to Newgrange*, Cork 1991, 24)

In the great megalithic cemetery of Loughcrew (*Sliabh na Caillí*) – the mountain of the hag – which may have been the original Tailteann, the Equinoxes of Spring (23 March) and Autumn (22 September) when day and night are of equal length, are marked dramatically by a ray of the rising sun lighting up the enigmatic engravings on the back stone of Carn T. Magnificent pictures of this event are given by Martin Brennan in his outstanding work, *The Stones of Time* (Vermont 1994), 90-101.

The beam from the rising sun at the Equinoxes travels through the passageway and focuses on the back stone (Stone 14) to light up the profusion of images carved on it.

The most prominent are what Brennan calls the 'circular radial sun sign' of which there are four. Each one consists of a central dot surrounded by a ring (circle), and around the circle a number of what looks like leaves branch out like the leaves of a flower or plant. All this is enclosed by a large ring. Apart from the surrounding ring, they look like flowers with extended foliage. One 'flower' has 9 'petals', another has 8; another 6 and another 8; another has four but has no surrounding ring. Could these be simply the 'flowers of Spring' on which the beam of light is directed like a spotlight on the ballerina? On the other hand, the same phenomenon occurs at the Autumn Equinox when vegetation is on the wane. Perhaps it indicated the beginning and end of the half-year period of the growth of plant life.

This, however is not the interpretation generally accepted, if indeed, there is any certain interpretation of these mysterious symbols. Nevertheless, it would seem natural that the engraving spotlighted by the carefully contrived ray of sunshine on a significant calendrical date would be of special importance.

These two examples of orientation and megalithic art occurring together at megaliths are chosen as an introduction to the pre-Celtic period.

These two areas, Brú na Bóinne and Loughcrew with their large cemeteries and solar alignments are among the best-known of all megalithic sites in Ireland and Newgrange and Knowth on the bend of the Boyne attract huge numbers of visitors every year.

This massive megalithic site known as Brú na Bóinne (the mansion of the Boyne river) is a high ridge situated at a bend of the Boyne river in Co Meath, about 8 km inland from Drogheda.

On the hilly ridge sloping down gently to the Boyne – the sacred river *Bó Fhinn* (the white cow, symbol of fertility), three enormous cairns or mounds are situated on a more or less West-East direction, each about a mile distant from each other. Around these are other smaller mounds often called 'satellite tombs'.

Firstly, beginning at the western end of the ridge there is Knowth (*Cnogba*) with its satellites, then, not exactly in a straight line but to the south is Newgrange and at the Eastern end in Dowth (*Dubhadh*) which is not yet excavated.

The complete complex is known as Brú na Bóinne and is well known in ancient Irish Literature and associated with Celtic gods such as An Daghdha, Aonghus Óg, Manannán Mac Lir, Midhir and the goddesses Bóinn, Eithne, Éadaoin and Curcóg.

While archeologists know that Newgrange, for instance, is a structure built by the megalithic people c. 3300 BC, nevertheless it is peopled by deities of the Celts who, it is believed, drifted into Ireland about 500 BC – about three thousand years later. So, it does seem that the Celts took over the sacred places of the megalithic peoples. In Ireland and in England one is reminded of the Protestants taking over medieval Catholic Cathedrals and using them as their own. This historical event sometimes leaves vestiges of the former religion intact in its architecture and art, thus giving valuable clues to the nature of the original form of belief. Holy water fonts, statues or paintings of the Blessed Virgin Mary, remains of the twelves crosses on the walls signifying a consecrated church are all reminders of the building's Catholic past disapproved of by the Reformers but still managing to survive.

The reason for mentioning this is to point out that the replacement of one religion or set of beliefs by another is a common phenomenon and is seldom complete. Vestiges of the earlier religious system may still remain in archeological remains, in folklore, in placenames, in seasonal rituals and in general folk-memory for untold ages. By piecing all these elements together, we are, perhaps, on the way to some understanding of the life and mindset of the ancient people who constructed the mighty monuments of Brú na Bóinne. As an example of this we have already noted the local farmers' knowledge of the entrance of the beam of sunlight into Newgrange at a special time of the year.

In view of the outstanding importance of the monuments in this area, and to accord it international recognition, the United Nations Educational, Scientific and Cultural Organisation (UNESCO) has designated Brú na Bóinne a World Heritage Site.

Newgrange, which is best known on account of the striking phenomenon of the entrance of a beam of sunlight through the long stone passage into the central chamber at the Winter Solstice (21 December), is a Passage Tomb. Huge standing stones form a covered passage by which you can walk into a stone chamber at the end. To the right and left and at the end are smaller chambers so that the whole has a cruciform look. The apartment to the right is larger than that of the left and this curious phenomenon is noted also in other passage tombs though the reason for this is unknown. The central chamber has a corbelled roof. The whole unit is covered with a massive cairn or mound of stone and clay estimated to weigh about 200,000 tons. This gives some idea of the enormity of the task undertaken by the megalithic builders of over 5,000 years ago. A ring of huge boulders encircle the mound and were used as kerbstones to prevent the clay of the mound from slipping down to the ground. The huge standing stones for passage, roof and kerb may have been found fairly close at hand but the white quartz and granite used for the front or southern portion of the mound came from a great distance in those days – the white quartz from the Wicklow Mountains and the granite from the Mountains of Mourne.

When the sun shines on the southern façade it seems to blaze and can be seen from afar. For this reason it was known as *Teach Bán Aonghusa* – the white house of Aonghus – Aonghus, son of An Daghdha, being the Celtic god of Brú na Bóinne.

The transportation of stone and earth to the site by manpower and perhaps oxen must have been a formidable undertaking. We can see *what* the megalithic people did, but it is a lot more difficult to say *why* they did it.

The time and labour involved in the construction of the tomb implies a large population group, a well-organised disciplined body with specialised groups to undertake different aspects of the work. Moreover, it suggests a community of wealth in which people could be spared from the ordinary demands of farming at least at certain times of the year. No doubt, the fertility of the land in the area, the 'Golden Vale' of Co Meath, which could support large herds of cows, sheep, pigs and goats, relieved people from the subsistence farming of poorer areas. At any rate, the monuments of the Boyne Valley are more elaborate in ornamentation, larger and more spectacular than many of those in other regions of the country. Perhaps, the nearest we can get to an idea of their construction is the building of the great cathedrals of medieval Europe. A powerful motivation must have inspired the builders in both cases.

Monuments such as Newgrange and Knowth are generally called 'Passage Tombs' as they contain relics of the dead. However, this term may be too exclusive, suggesting that the sole purpose of the monument was a kind of graveyard. Perhaps future research may show that it served other purposes also. While a dead bishop may be interred under the floor of his cathedral, the cathedral serves the faithful in many other ways – the celebration of the liturgy of the Mass, baptisms, confirmations, funerals, marriages. In Newgrange, the connection with the dead is clear. In each of the recesses of the central chamber there is a stone basin which held the remains of the dead – exactly how many is unknown due to disturbance. Excavation revealed the remains of at least five people, mostly cremated, along with grave-goods of chalk and bone. A common feature of these monuments is that they contain so few burials/cremations. The Passage Tomb cannot be compared to a modern cemetery on the edge of a town and destined to be the last resting-place of all the citizens. It does seem that the megalithic tomb was for an elite of some kind. We might well ask what happened to the population at large. Perhaps they were cremated and the ashes sprinkled around, leaving no trace or, as is more likely, the ashes of ordinary people was spread around the megalithic tombs so that in death they would be in close proximity to their ancestors in the tomb, as Christians liked to be buried near the tomb of some great saint.

The three recesses of the chamber at Newgrange have a stone basin each while the right-hand recess has two, one inside the other very large one. It is thought that these held the remains of the dead and the associated offerings. However, another view suspects that these basins held water which reflected the sunbeam on to the walls of the chamber at the Winter Solstice.

Martin Brennan (1994, 82-85) points out that at Dowth the setting sun shines dramatically into the western passage to illuminate the chamber at the Winter Solstice. This means that great significance was given to the Winter Solstice (21 December) considering that both the rising and setting of the sun are marked on that day. If, for instance, a cloud obscures the rising sun in the morning and prevents the light from entering Newgrange, there is a chance that the skies may be clear in the evening to allow a beam from the setting sun to enter Dowth about a mile away.

The Spring and Autumn Equinoxes (21 March and 22 September), periods of equal day and equal night are marked at Knowth.

Strangely, the Summer Solstice (21 June), is less in evidence even though this is marked by bonfires at Oíche Fhéile Eoin, 23 June, in many parts of the country down to the present day. This is an important day in the Christian Calendar as it is the Feast of St John the Baptist and the longest day of the year.

Newgrange is obviously a very specialised monument on account of its precise orientation towards the rising sun at the Winter Solstice and the extraordinary phenomenon of the sunbeam making its way down the interior passageway to illuminate the central chamber. The knowledge, sensitivity to symbolism, astronomical and engineering skills displayed at such a remote age is quite staggering.

Such precision is not always present in the case of megalithic monuments and often a general orientation is all that is required.

A parallel may be drawn between the megalithic tradition and the tradition of the Catholic and Eastern Rite church in the orientation of a church. The general rule, unfortunately not always adhered to, is that a church should face the east. This means that the main door of the church is at the western end and the people face the east for worship. The altar is at the eastern end of the church. The present fashion in the Catholic Church of the priest *versus populum* or facing the people across the altar, and so facing the west, is not a situation beloved by many liturgists who see it as a deviation from the age-old tradition of priest and people all facing in the same direction towards the east, the place of the rising sun, of new life, the symbol of the resurrection of Christ from the dead and entrance into a glorious Otherworld. In other words, the priest and his congregation form a united body on a pilgrim path to the mysterious Beyond to enter into union with the glorified Christ and the angels and saints – the Ancestral Spirits.

This tradition is not the same as the Jewish custom of turning towards Jerusalem or the Moslem tradition of turning towards Mecca, for it is noticeable that priests of Eastern Rite living to the east of Jerusalem still face the east – the rising sun – for the performance of the liturgy.

The orientation, while always towards the east, often takes into consideration the feastday of the saint to whom the church is dedicated. For instance, if the church is dedicated to St John the Baptist, then it may be orientated towards the rising sun at the Summer Solstice – the feastday of St John.

It would be an interesting exercise to examine to what extent ancient Irish churches conform to this pattern: it would involve finding out the name of the saint to whom the church is dedicated, the date of his feastday, determining the time of the rising of the sun on that day; looking through the east window from the back of the building to see if the sun shines through it to illuminate the church at the appropriate moment.

In his outstanding work, *Temples of Stone* (Cork 2007), Carleton Jones gives an Orientation Diagram of the Court Cairns/Tombs in Co Mayo. The vast majority are directed towards the east but not rigidly so. Many are orientated north or south of east, very much as in the case of churches or Christian burials which conform to the same type of orientation. The Irish phrase *Cosa an mhairbh soir* (the feet of the dead person to the east) illustrates the way the coffin is carried and subsequently buried so that at the end of the world when Christ returns in glory from the east the dead will rise up and be facing him to welcome him as he arrives.

The orientation of the Court Tombs is judged from the interior of the tomb looking through the court or open semi-circular space in front of the tomb proper and which probably formed the area for the performance of the funeral rites. The Court Tomb looks very distinct, as from the eastern end of the long gallery in which the dead were contained standing stones stood out at each side to form a semi-circle. The whole monument has the appearance of a cow's head and horns. As the cow in prehistoric times was the great symbol of fertility and well-being from whom the Boyne river seems to be named – *Bó Fhinn*, the white cow – and the great river of the sky the Milky Way – *Bealach na Bó Finne* (the path of the white cow) – perhaps it is not unduly imaginative to see the outline of the cow in this type of monument.

The Court Tomb is very common in the northern part of the country and is very rare in the south where it is found notably at Shanballyedmond at Rear Cross, Co Tipperary.

Having seen the strong tendency towards an eastwards orientation in the case of the Court Tombs it comes as a surprise that a different orientation occurs in the case of another type of tomb – the Wedge Tomb.

In the legend of the much later Cormac Mac Airt, King of Tara, the question of orientation arises. Cormac, who has become a Christian before the time of St Patrick, instructs his people to bury him at Ros na Rí rather than at Brú na Bóinne with his royal ancestors and that in death he should face the east, the place of the rising sun, in the Christian manner. However, according to the legend, his servants ignored his wishes and carried his body to the Boyne intending to take it over the river to bury it at Brú na Bóinne along with the former kings of Tara. Ros na Rí (Hill of the Kings) is the area south of the Boyne and more or less directly across the river from Brú na Bóinne. According to Geraldine Stout, author of the authoritative book, *Newgrange and the Bend of the Boyne* (Cork 2002, 70), the kings of Tara had their residence at *Cleiteach* on the site of what is now Rosnaree House almost directly south, across the river, from *Sí Chnogba* (Knowth). There was an ancient ford here near the modern Breo House.

According to the story, as the servants attempted to carry the coffin across the ford, the river swelled up and carried it off to lay it gently at Ros na Rí and there it was buried in accordance with Cormac's wishes, as Sir Samuel Ferguson put it:

'But bury me at Ros na Rí and face me to the rising sun.'

However, if one thinks of former kings of Tara being interred in the chamber at Newgrange, would they not be looking out through the passage facing the rising sun in the east at the Winter Solstice along with the group of visitors who now gain admission to the tomb for this extraordinary occasion? As a Christian, one would think that Cormac had little to complain about, considering that within Newgrange he would be looking out to the rising sun in the east on the time of Christ's birth. One wonders if there are churches in Ireland orientated towards the rising sun on the 21/25 December – the Winter Solstice – so that the congregation in the nave of the church could see the sun rising through the east window as the priest begins the Mass of Dawn with its superb Entrance Antiphon and Collect:

A light will shine on us this day, the Lord is born for us; he shall be called Wonderful God, Prince of Peace, Father of the world to come; and his kingship will never end.

Almighty God and Father of light, a child is born to us and a son is given to us. Your eternal Word leaped down from heaven in the silent watches of the night, and now your church is filled with wonder at the nearness of her God. Open our hearts to receive his life and increase our vision with the rising of dawn, that our lives may be filled with his glory and his peace, who lives and reigns for ever and ever. (*Roman Missal*, Dublin 1974, 40).

Newgrange, with its marked orientation towards the rising sun at the Winter Solstice, appears to be rather unique and specialised in the way of sky and earth relations, for in the case of many megalithic monuments the orientation does not seem to mark some significant solar event such as the equinoxes and the solstices nor the Celtic feasts of Samhain, Imbolc, Bealtaine and Lughnasa which occur between them. The tomb may be orientated towards a distant hill or mountain and it is significant that a part of Sliabh Eibhlinne (mountain of the goddess Eibhle) is called *Máthair-Shliabh* – Mother Mountain – and small tombs may have their passages in the direction of the large central one.

On account of the astronomical sophistication of Newgrange and the worldwide interest it has aroused, the hundreds of other smaller sites may be thought of as of lesser value, but perhaps the megalithic monuments of Brú na Bóinne and Loughcrew with their spectacular orientations and megalithic art may stand apart from the rest of the country as forming some specialised centre for ritual, pilgrimage and research on a parallel with a great medieval monastery as a centre for liturgy, pilgrimage, study and artistic pursuits.

Tim Wallace-Murphy (London 2005, 9-10) attempts to trace the line of thought from the archaic figures of the goddess, such as that of Laussel in the Dordogne not far from the cave-paintings of Lascaux through the famous paintings down to the later megalithic period. He suggests that the massively extensive megalithic site of Avebury and Silbury Hill in southern Britain may be 'A massively landscaped hymn of praise to the fertility of "Mother Earth".' What a marvellous description this is – a poem of praise of the Earth-Mother, not in words but in superb magnificent landscape architecture.

A recognition and celebration of the goddess of the earth as the 'Great Mother' – the origin, source and sustainer of life in all its forms – must surely stand as a key notion in ancient thought to be expressed in various ways in statuary, architecture, painting and ritual.

In this era in Ireland, in the transition from a hunter-gatherer society to the megalithic period, the domestication of cattle and growing of cereals developed and a more sedentary type of existence began. This involved a move towards the enclosure of fields, the idea of private property and a certain control of nature not present in the past regime of a hunter-gatherer society where people were dependent to a much larger degree on untamed nature. From hunting wild animals and the use of roots and herbs for food to a settled lifestyle in which food could be stored for the rainy day must have been a mighty step with enormous social consequences. Nevertheless, some see it as a traumatic break with nature – the beginning of the trend towards alienation from the earth which is reaching crisis point in our own day. What is rarely mentioned, and what must have been a major improvement in the progress of human development, is the introduction of clothing as we know it today. In a relatively cold climate such as Ireland people could hardly have gone around completely naked and must have used animal skins for clothing. One had, as it were, to wait until a large animal presented itself for killing before getting a new suit, and the animal may have been in no hurry.

All of this changed with the introduction of large flocks of sheep and the realisation that their wool could be used for clothing. In later Irish tradition the phrase *Cosc ar Chasaibh* is often found in association with the feastdays of certain saints such as Brigid and Gobnat of Baile Bhoirne. This 'prohibition of turning' has proved to be something of a puzzle. What it means in practice is that no work involving the turning of wheels was allowed on the saint's feast. Spinning seems to be the archetype for this – the saint or goddess who preceded her being considered to be a culture heroine who first introduced spinning to the human race and so improved their lot immensely. It was considered only right and proper, then, to refrain from spinning on the goddess's own day as a mark of honour and respect. So, the *Cosc ar Chasaibh* custom may have its roots in a very archaic period, in the megalithic age itself.

In the hunter-gatherer period, men and women must have felt themselves to be close relatives of the animals, who like themselves were forced by their own natures to kill smaller animals and eat vegetation to keep themselves alive. One is reminded of the many animal-headed gods of Egypt. The numbers of people in this pre-megalithic age in Ireland must have been very small and being semi-nomadic left no great visible remains or, as it were, put down no permanent roots but followed the herds and foraged in the areas providing an abundance of herbs for eating and medicine. Intense cohesion within the group, teamwork and detailed organisation, was necessary for successful hunting upon which life depended. When a hunter died it is thought that he was not given burial as we understand it, but rather left on the ground to be devoured by wild beasts and carrion birds and this may be the origin of the later megalithic custom of leaving the bodies of the dead exposed on a platform for the carrion birds such as the Celtic *Badhbh* to denude to the skeleton in the process called 'Excarnation'. Then the bones could be cremated and the ashes placed in the tomb. In this, the megalithic people may be returning to the practice of an earlier age, following the well-known phenomenon of a later race still attached to the old ways of their predecessors.

It can be noted also, that a profound religious intuition may be involved in this archaic practice of excarnation.

The primitive hunter depended largely on the wild animals and birds that he killed for his sustenance, and the art of hunting, according to later cultures, laid down very precise rules, such as killing only the weakest animals, killing only what was immediately necessary for food, and so forth. A quasi-understanding existed between the hunters and the animal herds.

One may see then, the exposure of the hunter's corpse to be devoured by the wild beasts and birds as a kind of return gift to them. Throughout his lifetime the animals, through the gift of their bodies, have supplied him with food. And now, his death and his exposure is his return gift to them – a recognition of what they have contributed to his welfare.

This idea too, may lie behind the archaic custom of 'Hunting the Wren' still observed in Ireland. As described by Sir James Frazer in *The Golden Bough* (London 1923, 536-538), the ritual was particularly elaborate in the great medieval city of Carcassone (France) and extended over a long period. In its simpler and better-known form, 'Hunting the Wren' takes place in many parts of Ireland, being particularly popular in An Daingean, Co Kerry, where it involves musicians, disguise and processions through the town. Sadly, however, the wren, which should form the centre of the proceedings, is now missing and this changes its whole nature making it merely a popular pageant rather than a serious rite carrying a serious message to mankind.

This was not always the case. In *The Year in Ireland*, Kevin Danaher quotes a January 1894 note in *The Graphic* entitled 'With the Wren Boys in Dingle': 'The Wren Boys, having killed a wren tie it to a holly bush on a pole. Two of them decorate their heads and shoulders with straw and wear masks with single eyeholes. These also carry large bladders tied to sticks with which to clear the way. Two others, also masked, dress in petticoats and are supposed to represent dancers; six more carry flags, while one plays a fife and another a drum' (Mac Donagh, *Green and Gold: The Wrenboys of Dingle*, Brandon 1983, 49-50).

Hunting the Wren occurs as a celebration of the Winter Solstice (21 December), the day on which the sunbeam enters Newgrange. In practice it takes place on St Stephen's Day (26 December) which is also a big occasion for the fox hunters on horseback. One wonders if there is any connection.

Essentially, the rite consists of killing a wren – a tiny bird who resides in hedges and cannot fly very well but who is very prolific and who lives in a house-like nest. Then the dead wren is tied by the leg to a holly bush and carried around from house to house by masked figures. Musicians generally play a major part and the group stop outside each house they visit and recite the ritual formula:

The wran, the wran, (wren) the king of all birds,

On St Stephen's Day he was caught in the furze;
Although he is little his family is great.
I pray you, dear lady, give us a trate (treat).
Up with the kettle and down with the pan,
Give us some money to bury the wran.

The housewife then makes her contribution and the wrenboys/girls move off to the next house.

In Wales, the dead wren was carried in a specially constructed little wooden house adorned with ribbons and the bearers pretended they were carrying a heavy coffin. In the Isle of Man, at the end of the day, the wren was buried in the local graveyard.

The money collected from the various houses in the locality was later spent on a party or 'Wren-Ball', on a parallel with the 'Biddy-Ball' of the *Brídeog*.

Speaking as an observer at the Dingle Wren celebration, the author, Steve MacDonogh, describes the experience: 'The Wren is drama which has not only dispensed with the proscenium arch, it has dispensed with the theatre. Indeed, it is a kind of drama which predates either structure. And in terms of the much discussed relationship between audience and players, it is an event in which there is no such distinction. A drama of participation, then, and an experience of belonging to a people and a place' (1983, 87). He describes the extraordinary scenes taking place in Dingle when the Wren Boys arrive on the streets: 'At the corner the shape of the hobby horse emerged, a white form suspended in the air where it turned, its dark carrier at first merging with the darkness ... Then the banner, held aloft, spanned the street as it negotiated the corner, borne by stocking-masked figures. And now the followers on the pavements, costumed, masked figures, some linking arms, others cavorting and dancing, some weaving drunkenly with heads down, others jaunty, arms waving. The sound built, swirling around the tangle of buildings at the corner as the band entered the street. The silent stage of minutes earlier had become a sea swarming with bizarre images, the air thick with cacophony. Light and life had entered – raw and crude, energetic and raucous; a celebration, a festival, a shared drama. Details of the experience might be forgotten, the experience would not' (1983, 82-83).

While, with the absence of the funeral parade of the wren from house to house with its ritual significance, may be lost in Dingle, the extraordinarily primitive and archaic character of a singularly ancient rite lives on and the participants are seized by the influx of raucous life-force. Why did I introduce this extraordinary local phenomenon of the wren in a discussion of the 'hunter-gatherer' and megalithic periods in Ireland? Because it may well be that in the rite of 'Hunting the Wren' we may have a precious relic of an incredibly ancient ritual which enshrines and illustrates the religious thought-processes of pre-historic people in Ireland.

The rite can be divided into two parts – the hunting and killing of the wren which takes place beforehand, and secondly, the funeral procession of the wren with its various stops or 'Stations' at private houses to collect contributions of money or drink.

Mr and Mrs Hall, visiting Cork about 1840, described it thus: For some weeks preceding Christmas, crowds of village boys may be seen peering into the hedges, in search of the 'tiny wren'; and when one is discovered the whole assemble and give eager chase to, until they have slain , the little bird. In the hunt, the utmost excitement prevails; shouting, screeching and rushing; all sorts of missiles are flung at the puny mark' (Danaher, 1972, 243).

Some versions of the 'Rann' or poem recited outside each house visited contain the words:

'We hunted him up and we hunted him down.'

A priest, commenting on the practice in his parish recently, remarked to me:

'These big fellows should be ashamed of themselves going out and killing a tiny wren.'

However, this difficulty had been anticipated in certain areas: 'In some cases the wren-boys carry round little toy-birds on a decorated bier, and they themselves have ribbons and coloured pieces of cloth pinned to their clothes' (Danaher, 1972, 246).

The wren-boys were not always welcome in the growing re-

spectability of nineteenth century towns. Amhlaoibh Ó Súilleabháin of Callan, Co Kilkenny, remarked in 1828:

> '*Grathain an bhaile ag imeacht ó dhoras go doras, le dreoilín i gcrann*
> *cuilinn, ag iarraidh airgid chun bheith ar meisce um dheireadh lae. Is*
> *olc an nós a thabhairt dóibh í'* (De Bhaldraithe, 1976, 52).
>
> (The rabble of the town going around from house to house,
> with a wren in a holly bush looking for money so that they can
> be drunk at the end of the day. It is a bad custom to give it
> (money) to them.)

What is the meaning of this singular rite which even in a de-
based form still has the ability to reach some hidden depths of the
human psyche?

A major examination of the rite has been made by Sylvie
Muller and her findings condensed in her long article 'The Irish
Wren Tales and Ritual: To Pay or Not to Pay the Debt of Nature' in
Béaloideas 64-65 (1996-1997), 131-169.

While Irish, Manx and Welsh have *Dreoilín, Drean* and *Dryw*
which may be connected to *Draoi* (druid), other European languages associate the wren with kingship: French *roitelet*, Italian *re-
golo*, Greek *basileus*. Then there is the well-known legend explaining this association.

According to the legend, the birds decided that they wanted a
king to rule over them – a 'King of All Birds'. The bird who could
fly highest would be chosen. A contest was arranged. The little
wren knew that he had no chance whatsoever. When nobody was
looking, the tiny wren jumped up on the back of the powerful
eagle. All the birds took off and the mighty eagle soared up above
all the others. When he had reached his zenith, the wren took off
from the eagle's back as from a launching pad and was seen to
soar above all. From this, the wren was declared to be 'King of All
Birds'.

This brings us back to the idea of the ritual killing of the Divine
King when he showed signs of aging or infirmity or at the end of a
set number of years on the throne, as discussed at length by Sir
James Frazer in *The Golden Bough*. Sir James gives numerous examples of the custom, especially from Africa, and examines the

rationale behind the usage. Fundamentally the theory was that the fertility of the land, the peace and prosperity of the kingdom depended on the health, ability and effectiveness of the god-king. If the king grew old, sickly or had a some physical defect, this reduced the fertility of the land and rendered his reign ineffective. Moreover, his spirit would be affected by the weakness of his body and when passing on his spirit to his successor at his death, his successor would receive a weakened, attenuated spirit leaving him ill-prepared for his royal duties. Even in the much later Irish tradition the king was required to be *gan mháchaill* – without a physical blemish – and according to the legend, even the great king of Tara Cormac Mac Airt, whom we mentioned in relation to his burial at Ros na Rí near Newgrange, had to resign from the kingship after losing an eye. Similarly in the case of Nuadha, king of the Tuatha Dé Danann, after he had lost an arm in battle. The physician Miach provided him with an artificial arm and he is still known as *Nuadha Lámh Airgid* – Nuadha of the Silver Arm.

Frazer makes a comparison between the regicide system and the legend of the priest-king of Nemi from which comes the title of his great work *The Golden Bough*. The sacred tree at the lake of Nemi in Italy, the sanctuary of the goddess Diana, was guarded by a runaway murderer who had made his way to Nemi, killed the reigning king-priest-guardian, cut a branch of the tree – or the mistletoe on it – and took up his position as the new guardian – the *Rex Nemorensis* – king of the grove. He then began his anxious vigil until a younger and stronger runaway criminal arrived and killed him.

Speaking of the Samorin (king) on the Malabar coast of India, Frazer remarks: 'It was an ancient custom for the Samorin to reign but twelve years, and no longer. If he died before his term was expired, it saved him a troublesome ceremony of cutting his own throat, on a public scaffold erected for that purpose' (1923, 275).

Perhaps the best-known example of regicide is the case of William II, (William Rufus), king of England who was the third son of William the Conqueror. He was killed on 2 August, a significant date, referred to in the records as 'the morrow of Lammas' (Lughnasa), the great Celtic Feast at the beginning of the harvest

called after the god Lugh Lámh Fhada, and falling half-way between the Summer Solstice (21 June) and the Autumn Equinox (22
September).

The story was that Rufus, a very effective and popular king,
belonged to the 'Old Religion'. His period of office had ended,
and according to the story, an 'accident' was arranged. The king
and his loyal courtiers went off to the New Forest, Hampshire, for
a deer hunt. But during the hunt the king stepped 'accidently' in
front of an arrow meant for a deer and so ended his life and his
reign as 'Divine King'. William Rufus' body was taken to
Winchester by way of Otterbourne, where today, King's Lane and
King's Mead record the event (Bord, 1982, 159-163).

To return then to the question of the *Dreoilín* or Hunting the
Wren as it is known in Ireland at the present day. Is there some
connection with the custom of regicide in which the king is put to
death when the period of his reign is over?

There are some obvious connections. A king is involved in
both cases – a real human king and the wren - the King of All Birds.
Moreover, the rite is performed on a sacred day of the ancient calendar – the Winter Solstice. As in the case of William Rufus a hunt
is involved. Could it be that the wren who is killed in the hunt
stands for the king who is killed in the forest to make way for his
successor, the new King?

Frazer describes the very elaborate form the rite took in
Carcassone in southern France in the early nineteenth century. On
the first Sunday of December young people went to the hedges to
hunt the wren and whoever killed the wren was declared King.
They returned to the town in procession led by the King who carried the dead wren hanging from a pole. On the evening of the last
day of the year, the Wren Boys marched through the town to the
sound of the fife and drum and the light of torches, the King carrying the dead wren on a pole. An interesting ritual then took place
as they stopped at each house. One of the Wren Boys wrote on the
door with chalk *Vive le roi* (Long live the King) and the date of the
year about to begin. The usage is strangely reminiscent of that at
the beginning of the Easter Vigil in the Roman Rite where the
priest, using a sharp knife, traces the letters Alpha and Omega

and the date of the current year on the wax of the large Paschal Candle, saying: 'Christ yesterday and today; the beginning and the end; Alpha and Omega (the first and last letters of the Greek alphabet); all time belongs to him, and all the ages; to him be glory and power, through every age and for ever. Amen.'

Then the priest inserts five grains of incense in the candle, saying: 'By his holy and glorious wounds may Christ our Lord guard us and keep us. Amen.'

Then the Paschal Candle is lit from the new fire as the priest says: 'May the light of Christ, rising in glory, dispel the darkness of our hearts and minds' (*The Sunday Missal*, Collins Publishers, London 1975, 209).

The faithful then light their candles from the Paschal Candle and the light and life of the Risen Christ communicates itself to them.

What a fabulous piece of dramatic art this is, outside the door of the church with the faithful gathered around in the darkness of the night and the new fire of Easter, symbol of renewed life, blazing in the background. This is theatre at its most basic, using only the most elementary props of fire, water, darkness and light.

The open-air setting, at midnight, when it is neither day nor night, situates the rite in a threshold position between two worlds and its primitive character conveys something of the mysterious process in which the life of God is communicated to the human race through the death and resurrection of Christ, the God-Man.

Similarly, in the rite of Hunting the Wren, something of the spirit of the dead king would go out to enrich the people who contributed to the expenses of the funeral on the ritual path to the graveyard, or whose doors were chalked with the words *Vive le roi*, until it was finally poured out on his royal successor. To whom did *le roi* refer? To the dead king or to the new king, his successor? Perhaps the phrase was deliberately ambiguous like the version 'The King is Dead, Long Live the King.' The old King is dead but his spirit will pass into his successor, the new King and long may he live before his spirit too will pass over to his successor.

Glancing at another feature of the Wren Rite, we become

aware of what must have been a dominant concept in the megalithic and later eras, conscious as they must have been of the
shortness and fragility of life. This is the concept of nature, from
which we have received everything and which, at some time or
other, but with certainty, will recall the debt we owe to her. Dr
Sylvie Muller, mentioned above, lays great stress on this vital notion: 'To Pay or not to Pay the Debt of Nature'.

CHAPTER NINE

Man and Nature

Quoting the work of the French anthropologist, Roberte Hamayon, which discusses the ideology of some Siberian hunters and food collectors in connection with nature, which they regard as the supplier of food, the theory behind the practice becomes clearer:

> For these people, human flesh is given back to nature in return for all the animal flesh which has been taken from nature. After death, the hunter's body is thus exposed in the forest to be eaten by wild beasts. Therefore, nature feeds man as long as it can feed on him in return. In other words, death, his own death (and his diseases), is the price man has to pay to nature for enjoying life (and health). Furthermore, this means that man can induce nature to feed him even better by symbolically and ritually feeding it in advance with human flesh. The tales and epic poems recited by Siberian hunters before each hunting expedition, seem to serve that very purpose, for in them, the hero's only role is to die, be exposed and be eaten by nature ... In reality, then, the hunter is free to kill because he has symbolically paid the debt of nature in advance (1997, 149).

In this very, very ancient practice, belonging we may assume to the pre-megalithic people of hunter-gatherer societies, there is an understanding between man and nature and an arrangement between them in which nature feeds man by supplying him with the flesh of animals as well as fruit, roots and berries and medicinal herbs with the understanding that man at his death would willingly give himself to nature. This is reflected in the much later Celtic arrangement of the Irish with the Tuatha Dé Danann deities living underground in the sacred hollow hills – the Sí. The Tuatha Dé Danann would give good growth to the crops and give an

abundant harvest, but the Celts on the surface of the land were expected to show their appreciation by making offerings to the
Tuatha Dé Danann at certain times such as Samhain, respect their
sacred dwellings and customs. In both cases a very serious religious understanding was involved. Man understood his position
before nature as that of dependance, and expressed this truth in
his readiness to commit himself into the hands of nature willingly
when the time came.

The idea is curiously reminiscent of the last words of Christ on
the cross: 'Father, into your hands I commit my spirit' (Luke 23:
46) Omitting the word 'Father' it is a quotation from Psalm 31:5
which is a prayer in time of ordeal when the person praying is
being attacked by his enemies:

> Draw me out of the net they have spread for me,
> for you are my refuge;
> to your hands I commit my spirit,
> by you I have been redeemed.

The psalm ends with a ring of confidence:

> Love Yahweh, all his faithful;
> Yahweh protects his loyal servants,
> but he repays the arrogant
> with interest.
> Be brave, take heart,
> all who put your hope in Yahweh (Ps 31:23-24).

Perhaps it was in this mood that the sacred King, at the end of his
reign, handed himself over to Mother Nature, confident that his
spirit would be transmitted to his successor for the welfare of the
kingdom.

Again, there is a curious likeness between this archaic custom
and the words of Our Lord relating to his own death and resurrection, his descent into the tomb to be reborn from the womb of the
earth in a different form as the glorious Risen Christ, the Alpha
and the Omega, the beginning and the end.

St John records Our Lord's words regarding his passage from
the conditions of this world to the conditions of eternity:

> The Father loves me, because I lay down my life in order to take it up again. No one takes it from me; I lay it down of my own free will, and as it is in my power to lay it down, so it is in my power to take it up again (John 10; 17-18).

Here Our Lord establishes his identity as being the same before and after the resurrection. Before his passion he is the lowly selected victim due to suffer the most outrageous suffering and torture and die a human death on the cross. But after three days in the tomb he will rise again from the dead with a glorified body, immortal, transfigured, no longer subject to mortal conditions. His appearances to Mary Magdalen, the *Apostolorum Apostola* (Apostle to the Apostles) and his other appearances, sudden and bewildering, through closed doors as recorded in the gospels and especially in Chapter 24 of St Luke, all testify to this marvellous transformation and ascension to a higher form of life. There is, indeed, a kind of pre-presentation of this new state in the story of his transfiguration on the mountain where 'his clothes became dazzlingly white', whiter than any earthly bleacher could make them' and a voice from a covering cloud said: 'This is my Son, the Beloved. Listen to him' (Mark 9:2-9).

It is unfortunate that this great feast of the transfiguration (6 August) is so little esteemed in the West in contrast to the Eastern Rites where it is celebrated with great solemnity, as it should be, considering that it gives us an insight into the glory of heaven and the life of the world to come.

The *Troparion of the Divine Liturgy* (Mass) of the Byzantine Rite proclaims:

> At the time of the transfiguration on the Mount, O Christ our God, thou didst show to thy disciples as much of thy glory as they could behold: let also thine eternal light shine upon us sinners, through the prayers of the Mother of God. O thou giver of Light, glory be to thee' (*Byzantine Missal*, Birmingham, Alabama, 1958, 354)

Considering that this great Feast coincides with the Festival of Lughnasa – in which we celebrate the first fruits of the earthly harvest in Celtic tradition – surely a parallel can be drawn between the two, for in this glance into the otherworld of glory into which Christ has entered we see the first fruits of the spiritual harvest. He is the first glorified one but his faithful followers are on the way, following him. In the tradition of Lughnasa, the first ripened sheaf of wheat or barley is placed high on the Lughnasa Hill with the understanding that the rest of the corn will ripen in its turn. Sadly, the Ember Days of the Tridentine Rite have, for all practical purposes disappeared from the *Missale Romanum* of 1970. The meaningful liturgy of the 'Ember Saturday of Pentecost' in the old missal, was that of a 'First fruits' celebration corresponding to Lughnasa though occurring earlier, in May or June, to correspond to the wheat harvest in Italy which would be about two months earlier than in Ireland. We might say that the beginning of the wheat harvest occurred in Italy at Bealtaine and in Ireland at Lughnasa. What an extraordinarily casual approach to the Liturgy of the Church it was that, throughout the centuries, the Ember Days were not adjusted to the climatic conditions of each area.

Having reached and established himself in the Otherworld, the Risen Christ sends back the Holy Spirit on his followers to gradually change them as iron is changed in fire. This is expressed in the wonderful Collect of Ember Saturday after Pentecost:

> *Illo nos igne, quaesumus, Domine, Spiritus Sanctus inflammet; quem Dominus noster Jesus Christus misit in terrram, et voluit vehementer accendi* (May the Holy Spirit, we beseech Thee, O Lord, kindle in us that same fire which our Lord Jesus Christ sent down upon earth, earnestly desiring that it should burn mightily.)

In other words, the Holy Spirit, sent back by Christ after he had ascended into glory, would bring about a change of heart and attitude in his followers. As another prayer of Pentecost (Ember Saturday) puts it: 'Come, O Holy Spirit, fill the hearts of thy faithful; and kindle in them the fire of thy love.' The Spirit of the Risen Christ comes back under the image of fire, as in the tongues of fire at Pentecost, fire being the great element of transformation, and God became man in order to transform the world in mind and heart.

Perhaps, then, a certain link can be discerned joining ancient usages and recalling the great age of man on earth and his striving to make sense of the world in which he lives and unite himself with the divine, with what he, however dimly, recognises as the source of his being. If the thesis is correct and the 'Hunting of the Wren' a ritual expression of the burial of a dead king, the spirit of the dead king will return to vivify his successor, and as king succeeds king, a dynasty may be formed.

The Hunting of the Wren, then, when carried out properly, might have been a deeply religious experience, in which the ruling classes were brought into contact with ultimate reality and reminded of the temporary nature of office. The drinking and carousing which so often accompanied the performance of the Rite may not have been an abuse but may have been looked upon as a feature of the celebration, as it was of the 'Merry Wake'. If an ordinary person could be given 'a great send off', why not a king?

And what a wonderful thought it is to think of the people subscribing to 'bury the wren' as showing their loyalty to the dead king who had paid his 'debt to nature' in their name, and being aware that they too would pay their debt to the Great Mother when the time came.

The poor condition of the Rite as it is performed in some areas today obscures its deep significance. The Rite is clearly divided into two parts:

Part 1: The Hunting and Killing of the Wren;
Part 2: The Funeral and Burial of the Wren.

There is a tradition of using an effigy – a small bird carved out of wood or other material – instead of a real living wren, and the use of such a effigy obviates the necessity of killing a real bird (Danaher, 1972, 246). The actual 'Hunt' could be a mimed search for the artificial wren hidden in the hedges.

Traditionally, *Lucht an Dreoilín* (Wren Boys) are masked or have their faces blackened with soot, and wear pieces of skin from animals such as rabbits, or goats. They wore suits of straw and in this way the idea of animals and corn, the products of nature by which we live, are expressed. The mask is a traditional sign of the supernatural appearing among mankind, the visiting god arrives disguised. In this case, it is nature in her mysterious forces who is involved. It is a sobering thought that even in our modern sophisticated life style, famine and death will result if these basic things, the products and fruits of the earth symbolised in the Rite, are removed.

In modern performances, outlandish dress is sometimes worn and lots of coloured ribbons are used. Sometimes, the 'Captain' or leader wears military uniform of a spectacular kind. At least one man of the group dresses as a woman. This 'cross-dressing' is a well-known feature of Mummers' Plays also.

Musicians generally form part of the group and play various instruments, the bagpipes and bodhrán being particularly suitable for outdoor performances.

The wren is carried from house to house in different ways. Sometimes in a wren-box with glass sides so that he can be seen within.

Or, he can be tied by a leg to a holly bush carried by *Buachaill an Dreoilín* and people do a little dance around him. An interesting drawing from S. C. Hall's *Ireland* (London 1841, 24) shows the Wren Boys progressing through the city, presumably Cork, c. 1840, and stopping outside a house. Children, inside, peer through the large window and an excited group of men, women and children surround *Buachaill an Dreoilín* as he holds up a large beribboned holly bush. One woman points out the wren hidden in the bush to another woman. People make sure that the wren is there before they make their contribution to his funeral expenses and, since the bird is so small, it is sometimes difficult to see him through the greenery.

The picture captures the joyful, vigorous mood of the crowd of participants as the cortege moves slowly through the streets. In some versions of the rhyme recited outside the various houses visited, the hunt aspect of the rite was stressed and the trouble involved to the Wren Boys. No doubt, this prompted the householders to be generous in their contributions:

We're hunting this wren all day
Through muddy water and yellow clay,
From bush to bush and from tree to tree

And at Shroneburee he broke his knee (Muller, 1996-7, 144).

Another way of carrying the wren in the funeral procession is found in the Isle of Man and this form of presentation may have interesting connotations.

Two hoops, set at right angles to each other, are attached to the top of a pole so that a globe or sphere is formed. Then the hoops are decorated with evergreens and ribbons. The dead wren is hung from this framework so that he hangs from the centre of the globe (Killip, 1986, 184-185). This must have been a very impressive arti-fact with the spherical ball of greenery on top of the pole and the sacrificial bird at its centre and, no doubt, provided an awesome sight when carried by *Buachaill an Dreoilín* at the head of a proces-sion of disguised musicians and a group wearing animal heads.

The globe is symbolic of the world, and the sacrificed victim at its centre represents the cosmic effects of his offering of himself in death.

Something similar is seen in the Liturgy of the Catholic Church in the Procession of Palms on Palm Sunday. This Sunday com-memorates Our Lord's entrance into Jerusalem at the beginning of Holy Week, the week that will end with his death and resurrec-tion. Leading the procession in which the faithful carry palm branches, is the Crossbearer. He carries the long processional cross, and on Palm Sunday the figure of Christ on the Cross is sur-rounded by a circle of palms fastened by ribbons. The evergreens suggest the idea of immortality, just as the yew trees in cemeteries do, and Christ as the sacrificial victim on the Cross will be crowned with the palm of victory over death on Easter Sunday.

The *Láir Bhán, Mari Lwyd* in Wales, featured in the *Dreoilín* of Dingle, but this was unusual.

The *Láir Bhán* (white mare) is an artificial horse made of wood and covered with a white sheet, which is taken around in the pro-cession. Its jaws can be manipulated by strings operated by the 'rider' and snaps at those who are slow in handing over their money. The *Láir Bhán/Mari Lwyd* was well-known in seasonal rituals and mummers' plays. Her origins are uncertain; she could poss-ibly represent the Celtic horse-goddess Epona who is sometimes depicted riding her horse while a foal follows on behind. The

Romans stole her from the Celts and had her statue erected in their stables. She may correspond to Macha in Ireland who raced against the horses of King Conchur Mac Neasa and after whom *Ard Macha* (Armagh) is named.

Or, it may be a Scandinavian goddess. At any rate, a difficulty arises concerning the presence of a horse in the Rite. For if the *Dreoilín* is as archaic as it appears to be and belongs to the 'hunter-gatherer' and megalithic periods, then the presence of the horse would be anachronistic, for the horse is associated with the Celts and belongs to a much later period. In the case of Dingle, one is tempted to say: 'Restore the wren and get rid of the horse.' However, from the hard lessons learned from the reform of the liturgy in the Catholic Church, we are increasingly aware of the danger of tampering with ancient ritual elements on the grounds that they may not conform to historical data. The *Láir Bhán* is an exotic feature which brings wonderment and excitement to the celebration.

Nowadays, in many places, the *Dreoilín* has a social and charitable function. Money donated goes to support some worthy cause and the wren-boys are welcomed in hospitals and old peoples' homes. The patients look forward to their colourful visits which make them aware that they, in their somewhat isolated condition, are still part of the local community.

In some places, as in the mummers' plays, space for the dancers and musicians is maintained by a wren-boy carrying a balloon at the end of a stick. He strikes with the balloon those who approach too near and impede the performers of the Rite.

The cross-dressing in which a man wears a woman's clothes is a marked feature of the *Dreoilín* in some places, as it is in the mummers' plays. It seems to be a very ancient element and may not entirely, as is sometimes said, date from a period when patriarchy was becoming dominant. It may be seen as an insight into the nature of the ultimate Deity, transcending gender and embracing both the masculine and the feminine.

Usually, a few days after the actual performance of the Rite, a Wren Dance or Wren Wake is held. Dr Muller discusses the significance of this:

The function of this dance seems to have been to bring unmarried people (including , of course, the bachelor wren boys) together in order that they might find partners, marry and procreate. Down to the last detail, therefore, it would appear that this ritual seems to have been designed to promote the notion of successful reproduction in nature and human society (*Béaloideas* 1996-1997, 145).

We have seen, then, that the Winter Solstice, when the sun is at its lowest point of decrease but is on the point of turning and increasing in power, with a corresponding lengthening of daylight, is very well marked in Ireland, especially in the spectacular event at Newgrange where a ray of light from the rising sun makes its way through a long passage to the inner chamber of the cairn.

At the well-preserved, and excavated, *Drom Beag* (Drombeg) stone circle, near Rosscarbery in West Cork, the alignment 'is towards the winter solstice sunset which sets in a cleft of the hill to the south-west' (Roberts, J., *Exploring West Cork*, Clonakilty, 1989, 49.

Similarly, Martin Brennan comments on the case of Dowth, also in Brú na Bóinne:

On the day of winter solstice the sun projects its rays into Newgrange at dawn and into Dowth at sunset. The passage and chamber at Dowth are about half the size of their Newgrange counterparts, but the projected light beam is much larger, and it remains in the chamber for a longer period of time, creating an even more dramatic spectacle (*The Stones of Time*, Rochester 1994, 82).

We have seen also the archaic ritual of Hunting the Wren to mark the Winter Solstice, so that it is celebrated both in architecture and ritual and the peculiar behaviour of the sun itself in its annual course.

While alignments towards the rising sun at the Summer Solstice (21 June) do not appear to be as frequent as towards the Winter Solstice, the lighting of bonfires at the Summer Solstice, or St John' Eve was, as we have seen, enormously widespread and is still celebrated in many places in Ireland.

This situation means that the solstices are the really decisive points of the sun's course, with profound repercussions on the life of vegetation.

One of the objections which might be made against the Hunting the Wren – kingship theory is that the Wren Rite occurs every year, whereas the king's term of office might be 7, 8, 9 years. However, the Winter Solstice, with the declining sun and its re-birth with a new sun, may mark, in a general way, a suitable time for the replacement of the old king with a new king. There is a hint of this process in the story *Oidhe Mhuircheartaigh Mhic Earca* where Muircheartach the king suffers the threefold death by wounding, drowning and burning at Samhain which might have taken the place of the Winter Solstice among the Celts. Bealtaine (1 May) shares the lighting of bonfires with the Summer Solstice. Climatic conditions and the requirements of agriculture might have influ-enced the Celts to put the two hinges of the year six weeks before the solar poles – the two solstices – Samhain six weeks before the Winter Solstice and Bealtaine six weeks before the Summer Solstice.

There is, of course, another consideration – the Calender itself. The solstices divide the year into two equal halves. The Winter Solstice stands at the beginning of the 'increasing light half' as the sun grows stronger and the days grow longer.

The second half begins with the Summer Solstice. From this on the power of the sun decreases and the days become shorter, so that the Summer Solstice begins the 'decreasing light half'.

Now, we have seen that the wren is killed at the Winter Solstice. The presumption is that he is killed at the end of his reign, and it would appear reasonable then to suppose that some other bird would stand for the Summer Solstice and suffer the same fate as the wren. In other words, can we surmise that the wren's reign began at the Summer Solstice and ended at the Winter Solstice when people celebrate his funeral? Here, the wren is king of the 'decreasing light half' of the year.

The question then arises, who was king of the 'increasing light half' of the year? Who was the wren's successor, and possibly killer, at the Winter Solstice? Who would replace the wren for the rest of the year, until he too met the same fate at the end of his reign at the Summer Solstice and the wren took over again?

A very obvious candidate is the Robin Redbreast. When we look at our Christmas cards, at the Winter Solstice, there he is, perched on a tree against a background of snow and snug thatched houses from which warm light emerges. Why shouldn't he preen himself as he proudly ascends the royal throne left vacant by his predecessor?

Traditionally, the robin is a sacred bird whom it is forbidden to kill. Christian folklore speaks of the robin as trying to pull out the thorns from the crown of thorns on Our Lord's head at the crucifixion to relieve his anguish. Some of the blood fell on the robin's breast leaving its mark on the bird to this day (Hole, C., Radford, E. M., *The Encyclopedia of Superstitions* (Oxford 1995, 282-284).

Liam Ó Dochartaigh points out the importance of this idea in the Gaelic tradition:

> *Níl aon amhras nach í 'An Choróin Spíona' an mhóitíf is coitianta in Éirinn le broinn dearg na spideoige a mhíniú.*
>
> *Is léir leis na daoine gur éan beannaithe í, agus is é an fáth sin mar go n-abraíodh na seandaoine gur fhéach sí leis na deilg a tharraingt as ceann Ár Slánaitheora nuair a cuireadh an choróin spíona ar a cheann. Tá sé ráite fosta gur dá thairbhe sin atá an bhroinn dhearg uirthi ó'n lá sin go dtí an lá inniu (Béaloideas 45-47; 1977-1979, 176)*
>
> (There is no doubt but that the motif of the Crown of Thorns is the most common one in Ireland as an explanation of the robin's red breast.
>
> It is obvious to the people that she is a blessed bird for the old people used to say that she made an effort to draw out the thorns from Our Saviour's head when the crown of thorns was put on him. It is also said that that is why she has a red breast from that day to this.)

Another tradition says that the robin got singed when bringing fire from Hell to mankind.

One would expect some kind of ritual, corresponding to Hunting the Wren, at the Summer Solstice, to mark the killing of the robin and the wren's accession to the kingship. However, there is no sign of such a rite.

Nevertheless, the wren and the robin are closely associated with each other as in the rhyme:

Robinets and Jenny Wrens
Are God Almighty's cocks and hens'
(Cooper, Q., and Sullivan, P., *Maypoles, Martyrs and Mayhem*, London 1994, 358).

The two are brought together again in the obscure rhyme used at the funeral procession of the wren in the Isle of Man:

We hunted the wren for Robin the Bobbin,
We hunted the wren for Jack of the Can,
We hunted the wren for Robin the Bobbin,
We hunted the wren for every one (Frazer, 1923, 537).

Again, the two birds are mentioned as being present together at the crucifixion but being on opposite sides:

Nuair a bhí Ár Slánaitheoir á chéasadh, bhí an spideog agus an dreolán (dreoilín) ag crann na croiche, agus nuair a chuir na hIúdais na tairní i n-a lámha agus in a chosa, bhí an spideog ag eiteall thart, agus nuair a fuair sí alt, thug sí iarraidh na tairní a tharraingt le n-a gob, ach níor éirigh léithi. I n-a áit sin, bhí an dreolán an deabhail ag iarraidh a bheith a' daingniú na ndealg a bhí ins an chóróin spíona isteach i n-a cheann. Is é sin an t-ábhar ariamh ó shin a bhfuil oiread droch-mheasa ag daoine ar an dreolán (Béaloideas 45-47; 1977-1979, 176). (When Our Saviour was being crucified, the robin and wren were at the tree of the hanging, and when the Jews put nails into his hands and feet, the robin was flying around, and when she got a chance she tried to pull out the nails with her beak but she didn't succeed. On the other hand, the wren, the devil, was trying to embed the thorns of the Crown of Thorns more firmly in his head. This is the reason why people have such a poor opinion of the wren.)

Here the conflict between the wren and the robin is clearly seen.

It is, however, in a different context that a clue may be perceived regarding the robin's connection with the Summer Solstice A film called *The Kinkisha* was produced by Tomás Mac Ardghail in 1977. The subject was based on a tradition found in Co Monaghan, and in other places also, but not always involving the robin – it could be other small creatures. The tradition is that of the *Cincíseach* (from *Cincís* – Pentecost). The belief was that a baby born on Pentecost Sunday (Whit Sunday) inherited a peculiar and unfortunate destiny – he would murder or be murdered. The idea is reminiscent of the *Rex Nemorensis* – the king-priest of the grove of Nemi who guarded Diana's sacred tree with his life, and when his would-be successor came along, he would have to kill or be killed. Liam Ó Dochartaigh quotes the vivid account of the film *The Kinkisha* given by Elgy Gillespie:

> When their baby is born on Whit Sunday the old curse of the Kinkisha is declared by the mother; a cure must be made to eradicate the ill-fortune brought by its date of birth.
>
> We see the young wife desperately trying to trap a robin; for the mother insists that only by choking it in the baby's hand and letting the blood run into it will the curse be lifted (*Béaloideas* 45-47; 1977-1979, 193).

Pentecost is a moveable feast, depending of the date of Easter which occurs on the First Sunday after the First Full Moon after the Spring Equinox. Pentecost Sunday, then, commemorating the descent of the Holy Spirit on the Apostles (Acts 2:1-11) falls roughly from mid-May to mid-June, anticipating the Summer Solstice slightly. Could it be that there is here a vague folk-memory of an ancient usage connected with the succession of kings, and involving the shedding of blood at this time of the year? As the wren, having killed the robin at the Summer Solstice, began his reign immediately, so he was in turn killed by the robin at the Winter Solstice. In our Christmas cards we see him beginning his reign as king of the 'increasing light half' of the year. But his reign will be short, ending at the Summer Solstice when he, the slayer, will himself be slain.

From the point of view of the Liturgical Calendar of the Catholic Church, we can discern a somewhat similar design respecting the solstices. This is very clear in the case of the Feast of Our Lord's Birth at the Winter Solstice and the birth of St John the Baptist at the Summer Solstice.

As we have seen, Pentecost Sunday may be connected to the

Summer Solstice by way of anticipation, as it could be said that the Season of Advent, beginning four weeks before Christmas (the Winter Solstice) prepares for Christmas.

Christmas celebrates the incarnation when God became man and lived among us, and from Christmas to Pentecost (or from the Winter Solstice to the Summer Solstice), the 'increasing light half of the year' the story of Our Lord's life on earth unfolds, his miracles, his teaching, his going about doing good, his preparation of his disciples for the world-changing event of his death and resurrection with its repercussions of the final destiny of the human race. Then, his ascension into heaven to begin a glorious, spiritualised existence at the right hand of God, and his sending of the Holy Spirit on his apostles to spread the work our redemption which he had accomplished, and to draw us after him into the Kingdom of Light. This is beautifully set out in the Fourth Eucharistic Prayer:

> Father, you so loved the world that in the fullness of time you sent your only Son to be our Saviour. He was conceived through the power of the Holy Spirit, and born of the Virgin Mary, a man like us in all things but sin. To the poor he proclaimed the good news of salvation, to prisoners, freedom, and to those in sorrow, joy. In fulfilment of your will he gave himself up to death; but by rising from the dead, he destroyed death and restored life. And that we may live no longer for ourselves but for him, he sent the Holy Spirit from you, Father, as his first gift to those who believe, to complete his work on earth and bring us the fullness of grace (*The Sunday Missal*, London 1975; 45-46)

The presentation of the work of our redemption in the Liturgical Year concentrates on the life of Our Lord while he was on earth during the Winter Solstice to the Summer Solstice period, while the second part of the year from the Summer Solstice to the Winter Solstice is concerned with the sanctifying work of the Holy Spirit in the church.

This may have been expressed more clearly in the old liturgy (Tridentine Rite) than in the new reformed Rite. The old *Missale*

Romanum gave great prominence to the work of the Pentecostal Event through having a whole series of Sundays named 'Sundays after Pentecost'. Depending on the date of Easter, by which the Feast of Pentecost was determined, there could be as many as 24 Sundays after Pentecost, running from Pentecost until the First Sunday of Advent – in other words almost half the year – the period from the Summer Solstice to the Winter Solstice. The numbering of the Sundays in the new Missal as 'Sundays of the Year' – the 'Eighteenth Sunday of the Year' – and so forth, does not appear to carry the same weight of symbolism as the old method. It does not lead the minds of the faithful back to the transforming event of Pentecost when the apostles, in fear and trembling, were hiding behind closed doors and the Holy Spirit descended upon them. Then these intimidated men were suddenly transformed by the fire of the Holy Spirit into fearless preachers of the gospel who went out among their enemies, indifferent as to the consequences. Transformation of mind and heart is the great message of Pentecost and the successive Sundays after Pentecost were a re-minder of the continual operation of the Holy Spirit in the life of the church. The numbering of the Sundays as Sundays of the Year appears to have little religious significance, and if the 'Reform of the Reform' so devoutly wished for by some liturgists ever comes our way, it is hoped that there will be a return to the system of the old *Missale Romanum*. In the recent reform of the Syro-Maronite Rite, the traditional method has been retained: 'Thirteenth Week of Pentecost', etc. (Qurbono, *The Book of Offerings; The Service of the Holy Mysteries; According to the Antiochean Syriac Maronite Church*, New York 1994)

In the *Anaphora of Saint John*, the apostle, of the same Rite, this theme of transformation or change brought about by the Holy Spirit is clearly expressed. Firstly, there is the changing of the bread and wine into the Body and Blood of Christ and then the transformative effect of this on the faithful who participate in these mysteries:

Deacon: 'How awesome is this moment, O my beloved.
The Holy Spirit will descend from heaven
and overshadow this offering,

prepared for our sanctification.'

Priest: 'Through his overshadowing, may the Spirit make this + bread the body of Christ our God.'

Congregation: 'Amen.'

Priest: 'And make the mixture in this + cup the blood of Christ our God.'

Congregation: 'Amen.'

Priest: 'May these Mysteries sanctify the bodies and souls of those who participate in them, for the purity of their hearts, the cleansing of their thoughts, the holiness of their souls, and as a pledge of the heavenly kingdom and a new life, for ever.'

Congregation: 'Amen'

This is, as it were, the Pentecostal programme of the Holy Spirit which is emphasised in this period of the year from the Summer Solstice to the Winter Solstice. We find it again, magnificently set out, in the great hymn of Pentecost in the *Missale Romanum*:

> *O lux beatissima,*
> *Reple cordis intima,*
> *Tuorum fidelium.*
>
> *Lava quod est sordid um,*
> *Riga quod est aridum,*
> *Sana quod est saucium.*
>
> *Flecte quod et rigidum,*
> *Fove quod est frigidum,*
> *Rege quod est devium.*

(O most blessed light, fill the inner hearts of your faithful people. Cleanse what is stained, moisten that which is arid, heal what is hurt. Bend what is rigid, warm that which is frigid, rectify that which has gone astray.)

Here we have the Holy Spirit described as operating on the deviant hearts of humans to transform them and lead them to God. This aspect of the work of our redemption is emphasised during the second half of the year, the Pentecostal part or 'Wren-Reign

Half' from the Summer Solstice to the Winter Solstice when the 'Robin-Reign Half' begins, which, in the liturgy emphasises the redemptive life of Christ on earth. To tabulate it as follows:

From Winter Solstice to Summer Solstice = 'Increasing-Light Half' = 'Robin-Reign Half' – liturgical emphasis on life of Christ on earth.

From Summer Solstice to Winter Solstice = 'Decreasing-Light Half' – 'Wren-Reign Half' – emphasis on transforming work of Holy Spirit.

At Christmas, then, the Robin Redbreast in the Christmas card is a reminder that a new king has been installed and the citizens of Carcassone in the South of France, as we saw, were very aware of this when they saw the new year's date and *Vive le Roi* chalked on their doors after the Wren Boys had passed by.

But King Robin must know, as the human king whom he represents knows, that his reign is of short duration. The time will come when he has to give back to nature the life he has received from her. He must pay his debt to nature.

And if, at the end of his reign he gives back his life to nature, willingly and with good grace, aware that all he is giving back is what he has received, then, nature will be generous to his successor in the kingship and will bless his reign with peace and prosperity.

So, it was important for the human king to accept his fate willingly at the end of his period of office, to pay his debt to nature graciously, on behalf of his people, in the same spirit as, on their behalf, he had signed agreements and official documents of state.

The willingness of the sacrificial victim to surrender and hand back the life he had received from nature was touchingly expressed in the rite of sacrifice among the Romans:

It was a good sign if it went willingly to the slaughter. Juvenal, for instance, speaks admiringly of his ox as tugging at its rope to get to the priest's knife. If, on the other hand, it struggled and tried to run away, it was evidently an inauspicious animal which would not find favour with the gods. He would have to sell it back, buy another and start again (Ogilvie, R., *The Romans and their Gods*, London 1969, 44).

How reminiscent this is of the Christian tradition as expressed in Eucharistic Prayer II:

> Before he was given up to death
> a death he freely accepted
> (*Qui cum Passioni voluntarie traderetur.*)

Similarly, in the Liturgy of the Word on Good Friday, the words of the Prophet Isaiah are quoted:

> Harshly dealt with, he bore it humbly, he never opened his mouth, like a lamb that is led to the slaughter-house, like a sheep that is dumb before its shearers, never opening his mouth.

Both the pre-Christian and Christian traditions speak of the way of surrender at the end of life; they show us the way to die.

Considering then the tradition of the bipartite division of the year among the Celts – from Samhain to Bealtaine – the dark half, and from Bealtaine to Samhain – the bright half, it would seem that somewhat the same system was in use among the megalithic people who preceded the Celts. They, however, used the two Solstices as markers – from the Winter Solstice to the Summer Solstice and from the Summer Solstice to the Winter Solstice.

This consideration brings us back again for another glance at the superb phenomenon of the entrance of the rising sun through the long passageway into the chamber of Newgrange at the Winter Solstice.

This extraordinary phenomenon has given rise to widespread attention and people from far and near arrive at Brú na Bóinne to witness the event, though only a small number can be accommodated within the chamber.

There is little doubt but that this is the well-known archaic ritual of what was known among the Irish Celts as the *Banais Rí* – the Wedding of the King to the goddess of the land to promote the fertility of the earth; the *hieros gamos* of the Greeks; the sacred marriage of the Sky God to the Earth Mother.

The background is well presented by Chevalier, J., and Gheerbrant:

> Identified with the mother, earth is the symbol of fertility and

regeneration. She gave birth to all things, nourished them and then took from them the fertile seed once more. According to Hesiod, she (*Gaia*) even gave birth to heaven (*Ouranos*) who then had to impregnate her to give birth to all the gods. The latter copied this first sacred marriage to produce mankind and animal creation, the earth thus being the source of all life and in consequence being given the title of 'Great Mother' ... The waters were also at the beginning of the world and they are distinguished from earth in that they preceded the ordering of the cosmos, while earth produced all living things. The waters stand for undifferentiated mass; earth for the seeds of those differences ... On the one hand she is the Bountiful Mother, allowing mankind to live from the plants she bears; on the other hand she demands the bodies of the dead for her own nourishment and is in this sense, a destroyer (*Symbols*, London 1996, 332-333).

The awesome mystery of creation, destruction, death, resurrection, continuation of life belong to the Great Mother, the *Magna Mater*, the Earth Mother from whom all come and to whom all return. The faithful, receiving the ashes on their forehead at the liturgy of Ash Wednesday, are confronted with the unpalatable but undeniable formula: 'Remember, man you are dust and to dust you will return.' The agricultural setting from which the formula is taken is well expressed in the Book of Genesis (3:19):

By the sweat of your face will you earn your food, until you return to the ground, as you were taken from it. For dust you are and to dust you shall return.

In the revised liturgy of the Roman Rite, an alternative to the age-old formula 'Remember man you are dust and to dust you will return' is given, and this may be used by the priest if he so wishes. The alternative formula for the imposition of the ashes on the forehead is:

Turn away from sin and be faithful to the gospel (Mark 1:15).

It would be interesting to know what percentage of priests use this latter formula rather than the traditional one. Though both formulae are taken from scripture, the emphasis is different. The latter is gentler, more moralistic, more evolved, more concerned with the person's acceptance of the gospel. The 'Remember man …' formula is more primitive, more basic, more expressive of the fundamental condition of mankind since the world began irrespective of later religious formulations. It can fit easily into the categories of the Old Religion of the goddess.

CHAPTER TEN

The Cosmic Wedding

The issues raised by Newgrange are of the deepest kind and have been expressed with great intensity by different scholars:

> Originally, comedy was the ritual of life directed to making the crops grow and produce providential abundance; tragedy was the ritual of death and decay alike in nature and in human existence. Taken together they portray the passage from life through death to life in greater abundance, be it in the processes of vegetation or in the earthly pilgrimage of man. So they give expression to the most fundamental religious emotion – the sense of dependence on a transcendent Providence – and the deepest human needs – the promotion and conservation of life, summed up, as Miss Jane Harrison says, in the ancient formula, 'out with famine, in with health and wealth'.

> 'To live and to cause to live, to eat food and to beget children, these', in the words of Sir James Frazer, 'were the primary wants of man in the past, and they will be the primary wants of man in the future so long as the world lasts. Other things may be added to enrich and beautify human life, but unless these wants are first satisfied, humanity itself must cease to exist. These two things, therefore, food and children, were what men chiefly sought to procure by the performance of magical rites for the regulation of the seasons' (James, E. O., *The Beginnings of Religion*, London 1958, 40).

If we picture a twenty-first century man sitting by the fireside, surrounded by his wife and children, having eaten a substantial supper, and then picture a megalithic man, sitting by the fireside, surrounded by his wife and children, having eaten a substantial supper, we can say that there is fundamentally little difference between them. They are both happy men, as well they might be, considering that both have the two basic requirements – food by which the individual lives and children by which the community lives. While the twenty-first century man may wish for a new car and the megalithic man may wish for a new axe – these are only secondary considerations. So that the archaic monuments and rituals of ancient people must be considered in terms of the continuity of life, and when it comes to the elemental things, modern man and archaic man are not so far apart.

Taking the idea of the 'Continuation of Life' as a basic philosophy of the earliest period of mankind, we can see the area of Brú na Bóinne as a wooded area upon which no monuments have yet appeared. This is the earliest period – the era of the 'hunter-gatherer people' when people lived by the animals they killed in the hunt and the plants, berries, fruits and nuts provided by the earth for food, medicine and clothing. Some would say that from the religious point of view – the relationship between man and the deity – that this was the Golden Age in which mankind saw itself as utterly dependent on nature, the Great Earth-Mother who supplied all their basic necessities. It was obvious that it was the female who produced offspring, who contributed directly to the 'Continuation of Life'. The earth too, was obviously female. It produced the grass for the cattle, plants and fruits and later corn for man. Early man must have been dumbfounded by the awesome power of the female.

Then, the era of the hunter-gatherer was gradually superceded by the discovery of cereals and the domestication of animals, cattle, sheep, pigs, goats. This was an enormous step forward (although some would say it was a step backward) for it gave people a certain independence from nature. Food production could be organised and food stored and a more sedentary form of life introduced. This was the period of the megaliths when humans were getting more control over nature and the role of the male was better understood in the cycle of production. The food surplus that emerged from the new agricultural way of life allowed leisure for the undertaking of massive construction projects such as those in the Boyne Valley at Knowth, Newgrange and Dowth, and others on a lesser scale throughout the country.

As already discussed, the building of these enormous mounds demanded immense motivation, labour, knowledge and organisation.

There is little doubt, but that it was all connected to the fertility of the land, of animals, of humans, to ensure that the seasons of the year came and went in their due order and with them the correct changes in vegetation to ensure an abundant harvest and the arrangement of animal husbandry. The *Buaile* of Irish tradition may go back a long time before the Celts, that is the custom of taking the cows up to the hills for summer grazing at Bealtaine (1 May) and bringing them down to the sheltered areas at Samhain (1 November). This custom is intimately connected to the changing seasons and it may be significant that when the cows (*Tréad*, herd) are on the hills, the *Pleiades* (*Treidín*, little herd) are below the horizon, and when the cows are below the Pleiades are visible in the sky. This is the type of cosmic arrangement one expects to find in the megalithic period. In short, what is involved in the megaliths is the principle of the 'Continuation of Life'; the flow of Life, like a great river meandering on and on for ever and ever like the Boyne itself, the *Bó fhinn* the white cow, like the Egyptian cow-goddess Hathor, the symbol of enduring life. One wonders if the common depiction of the 'meander' and 'chevrons' in the art of the Boyne Valley, so like the patterns of the rippling river itself, are not symbolic of the flow of life. Is that the great and universal message of Brú na Bóinne for us today – the value of life?

One way of looking at the great mound of Newgrange is to envision it as a theatre. A theatre, especially designed for the annual performance of a great drama – the Sacred Marriage of the Sky-God with the Earth-Mother, at the Winter Solstice.

As in the case of other megalithic monuments throughout the country, Newgrange can be seen as gynaecomorphic – woman-shaped – in a highly stylised form to emphasise the maternal organs, vagina, womb, belly. As in the case of very ancient statuettes of the mother-goddess, the principle of *pars pro toto* (a part for the whole) is involved, in other words, head and limbs are omitted or downgraded so that all the emphasis is on the reproductive organs, and these statuettes such as the 'Venus of Willendorf' (c.

30,000 BC) and the 'Venus of Laussel' (c. 15,000 BC) show that this principle was known from the most remote period (Pollack, R., *The Body of the Goddess*, London 2003, Pls 8 and 9)

E. C. Krupp sees the Newgrange phenomenon of the Winter Solstice firstly as the renewal of the life of vegetation at the turning of the sun:

> Winter is the death of the earth, but when the sun changes course at winter solstice, death is on the way out and making room for the springtime revival that always emerges from the body of Mother Earth. In that sense the year is reborn at winter solstice, and the day is certainly reborn at sunrise. When the sun comes up in front of Newgrange, it pumps life back into the tomb as if it were fertilising Mother Earth (*Skywatchers, Shamans and Kings*, New York 1997, 140).

Attention has been drawn to the *Banais Rí* (woman-sleeping of the king) in its later Irish form by the great Celtic Scholar Professor Proinsias Mac Cana, and his elaboration of the idea helps to an understanding of the earlier phenomenon at Newgrange:

> The sacral king is the spouse of his kingdom and his inauguration ceremony is known as *banais righi* (wedding-feast of kingship): in other words, he is then ritually united with the sovereignty of the territory over which he rules' ... 'The wedding ritual of the *banais righi* evidently comprised two main elements, a libation offered by the bride to her partner and the coition. The sexual element is almost always present, whether explicitly or by implication, and one of the normal ways of reporting the inauguration of a king is to say that he was wedded to (literally 'slept with') his kingdom' (*Celtic Mythology*, London 1970, 120)

In short, the territorial goddess Méadhbh (the Intoxicating One), of the Provence of Connaught, or Mór Mumhan of Munster, for instance, handed a goblet of liquor to the candidate for kingship and then had sex with him. The goddess was represented by the queen or, perhaps, by a druidess.

The transforming effect of the *Banais Rí* on both the hero and the goddess is clearly expressed in the ancient story *Eachtra Mac Eachach Muigmedóin* which tells of the five sons of King Eochaidh. They are out hunting and get very thirsty. Each of the sons sets out in turn to get some water. But the well is guarded by *Cailleach an Tobair* – an ugly emaciated hag who will only give them water on condition that they kiss her. They all refuse except Niall who embraces her, and when he looks again he sees that she has been transformed into the most beautiful woman in the world. She gives him the water and declares that she is *flaitheas Éireann*, the sovereignty of Ireland and on him she has bestowed the kingship. In the ritual handing of the drink to the candidate for kingship by the goddess, there may be a subtle pun or play of words. *Flaith* means kingdom / sovereignty and *Laith* means liquor / drink. So, when the goddess gave the *laith* to the candidate she gave him the *flaith*. 'The theme of sovereignty tales is that the hero must sleep with the earth goddess, for unless he does he shall not be king of Ireland' (Smyth, D., *A Guide to Irish Mythology*, Dublin 1988, 113).

Notice, in this story from *Leabhar Buí Leacáin*, the profound changes that take place in both the hero and the goddess as a result of the *Banais Rí*, the Sacred Marriage.

From being a lesser son and an unknown hunter, Niall is raised to the new status of king.

The goddess, too, is changed from her barren, emaciated winter aspect of *cailleach* (hag) to her fertile summer aspect of *babóg* (young woman / doll). It is the transition from winter to summer, from Samhain to Bealtaine.

Returning to Newgrange, we see that after the *Banais Rí* or *hieros gamos* has taken place at the Winter Solstice, the rejuvenation of nature is on the way. The period of new growth has begun though it is still in its infancy and very weak. This new movement of growth of vegetation is primarily concerned with the goddess.

In the story of Niall Naoi nGiallach, as we have seen, the goddess herself underwent a radical change through intercourse with the appropriate spouse, and the appearance of new growth in vegetation will reflect this in Brú na Bóinne and throughout the country.

But what of the other partner of the sacred marriage – the sun itself? As Niall was transformed from hero to king through the *Banais Rí,* did something analogous happen to the sun at Brú na Bóinne at the Winter Solstice? Did the sun undergo a radical change also?

We, today, know, as the brilliant engineers who constructed Newgrange knew, that the sun, after the Winter Solstice, turns back, as it were, and begins to rise further to the north each day, so that from the Winter Solstice on, the days are getting longer and the nights shorter, so that we have entered the half-year period of increasing light. This is the period from the Winter Solstice (21 December) to the Summer Solstice (21 June).

From the Winter Solstice on, as the days grew longer and light increased, the megalithic people must have experienced an immense feeling of relief. For months, the sun's power had been declining, the days were getting shorter, the nights longer. The sun appeared to be fighting a losing battle against the dragon of darkness. They knew, from former years, that the sun recovered from the dragon's clutches after the Winter Solstice, but could one be certain of this turning? If the weakening sun did not recover, then the days would grow shorter and shorter and the nights longer and longer until eventually there would be no day, only perpetual night, no plants would grow, there would be intense cold and life would perish from the earth. This period of the year, corresponding to the Advent Season of preparation for Christmas in the liturgy of the Catholic Church, must have been a period of intense anxiety and this apprehension is actually reflected in the liturgy with its violet vestments and penitential character. When the sun recovered at the Winter Solstice, the Romans of a later time were so relieved that they instituted the great Feast of *Sol Invictus* – the Unconquered Sun. Life would continue for another year. From this was chosen the date of Christ's birth. The real date was unknown and so the Winter Solstice was chosen for symbolic reasons. He had said: 'I am the light of the world; anyone who follows me will not be walking in the dark; he will have the light of life' (John 8:12).

This is also the feast of the god Mithra whose cult, especially among the Roman soldiers, was extremely popular and a serious rival of Christianity. It may be wondered if there is any connection between him and the Irish god Midir of Brí Léith (Co Longford) who features in the story *Tochmarc Étaíne* from *Leabhar na hUidhre* and *Leabhar Buí Leacáin* – a story which may cast some light on the Winter Solstice event at Newgrange. Although this mysteriously haunting Celtic tale comes from a period about 4,000 years after the foundation of Newgrange, could it be that some long-lasting folk-memory endured to give a clue as to what was happening at Brú na Bóinne?

In any event, the story opens by telling us that there was once a famous king of the divine race – the Tuatha Dé Danann (peoples of the goddess Dana) in Ireland. He was named *An Daghdha* (the good god) and Eochaidh Ollathair (the horseman, the universal father) and he had control over the seasons and the harvest. Ealcmar was lord of Brú na Bóinne and he was married to Eithne, also called Boand (*Bófhinn* – the white cow), the goddess of the Boyne. An Daghdha wanted to sleep with Bófhinn, and she was quite willing, but she was afraid of Ealcmar. An Daghdha, however, got over this difficulty by arranging some important diplomatic mission for Ealcmar which would keep him out of Brú na Bóinne for some time. This 'when the cat's away the mice will play' plan worked well. When leaving, Ealcmar assured An Daghdha that the mission wouldn't take very long – that he would be back by nightfall. However, An Daghdha cast great magical spells on him, so that Ealcmar was away for over nine months, but he didn't notice the changing of the seasons or the days and nights and he returned to Brú na Bóinne thinking that he had only been away one day.

Meanwhile, in Ealcmar's absence, An Daghdha slept with Bófhinn and she produced a son whom they called Aonghus. By the time Ealcmar had returned she had fully recovered, so that he had no idea that she had slept with An Daghdha. The child, Aonghus, had been given to the god Midir of Brí Léith to be fostered by him. Aonghus was called *An Mac Óg*, the young son, for his mother had said, in reference to Ealcmar's belief: 'Young is the son who is conceived at dawn and born before dusk.' He is also known as 'Aonghus Óg'.

Because of his associations with Brú na Bóinne, Aonghus was known as *Aonghus an Bhrogha* and he probably corresponds to

Mabon of Wales and British *Maponos* who was identified with classical *Apollo,* the sun god. The name Aonghus means something
like 'Unique Vigour' and he stands for the concept of 'Youth'.
Later, in the story *Tochmarc Étaíne* (*Ériu* 12), Midir of Brí Léith
(Ardagh Hill, Co Longford) fosters Aonghus Óg for nine years.
Aonghus is a champion hurler and leader of the group of boys in
fosterage. He eventually finds out that his real father is An
Daghdha, who instructs him by means of a complicated legal trick
involving nights and days, how to take over Brú na Bóinne from
Ealcmar, who is given Cletach, on the Boyne, in exchange. In an-
other version, it is An Daghdha himself that Aonghus replaces (Ó
hÓgáin, D., *Myth, Legend and Romance,* New York 1991, 38-41).

It will be noticed, however, that in the story of Aonghus Óg,
three elements are prominent – youth; replacement of one character by another; day and night as a significant unit.

Strangely, in the tale *Altram Tige dá Medar,* it is Aonghus, also,
at the prompting of the sea-god Manannán Mac Lir, who reluctantly banishes Ealcmar from Brú na Bóinne. In this case it is not
days and nights that is involved but a powerful 'Banishing Spell'
or Exorcism, which according to Manannán, was employed by
God to drive the rebellious angels out of heaven. Then it was employed by the Tuatha Dé Danann to drive out the Fir Bholg from
their territories and after that employed by Clann Mhíle to drive
out the Tuatha Dé Danann themselves, and now it is being employed to expel Ealcmar from Brú na Bóinne. When Ealcmar had
been expelled, the stewardship of Brú na Bóinne was given to
Dichu (*Ériu,* XI-Part 11) This idea of the replacement of the old by
the new is a recurring theme in these stories connected with
Aonghus Óg and Brú na Bóinne and it is likely that they have a
calendrical significance.

This megalithic sanctuary is where the action takes place, although it is the Celtic gods and goddesses, An Daghdha, Bófhinn /
Eithne, Midir, Ealcmar, who are involved. Even this looks like a
replacement in which gods of the Celts occupy a sacred site erected
by the megalithic peoples thousands of years before the Celts
arrived and intended for their own religious rites.

However, considering Newgrange as the stylised body of the

goddess of fertility and taking into account the enormous prestige of the goddess among the Irish Celts, whether she is known as the MórRíoghan (the great queen), Éire, Banbha, Fodhla, Cailleach Bhéarra Boi, Badhbh, Dana, or more localised names which many women bear today – Meadhbh, Aoibhinn, Úna, Clíodhna, Áine, Doireann, Eithne and others – the religious differences between the two cultures may not have been so great. The Celts would probably have placed greater emphasis on male gods. Nevertheless, the king, representing the male god, was only the consort of the goddess of the land as was dramatically expressed in the rite of the *Banais Rí*. Had the megalithic monuments become disused by the time the Celts arrived about 500 BC? Had the megalithic people themselves become extinct by that late period? If not, had the Celts intermarried with them? What language did the megalithic people speak? If intermarriage took place what effect had it on the linguistic, religious and social affairs of the dominant Celts? The rationale of even simple, well-known customs often remain obscure. The *Bean Rua* or red-haired woman is believed to bring bad luck to the Connemara fisherman if he meets her on his way to work. He may as well turn back as he will catch nothing that day. Why should this be? Could it be that the Celtic aristocrats in Gaul (France), who were supposed to be red-haired, were feared by the megalithic or Bronze Age people? Could the *Bean Rua* have represented the conquering race? Similarly, young men, when passing a *Sí* or sacred hollow hill of the Tuatha Dé Danann (*Aos Sí*) at Samhain, carried the *Scian Coise Duibhe* – a black-handled knife – for the Tuatha Dé Danann feared iron and would not try to lure the man into the Otherworld. Why should they fear iron? Perhaps, it was because the Stone Age people recollected that they had been overcome by the iron weapons of the invading Celts. These and a multitude of other similar questions can be proposed but the answers are few and uncertain. This period, between the late neolithic and the early Celtic, is the 'twilight zone' where mists of uncertainty abound. One picks up a clue here and a clue there and puts them together to try to build up a picture of what happened, as the police do in a murder case. After all, a murderer does not go to the police station and tell them politely that it was he who murdered so and so. No, he makes them earn it.

In a discussion of the Winter Solstice Event at Newgrange it appears that the *Banais Rí* or wedding of the king to the goddess of the land was a key notion. Professor Myles Dillon speaks at some length on this matter in the later Celtic period in Ireland:

> Kingship in general, and Irish and Indian kingship in particular, have been discussed by many scholars recently, and there seems to be agreement that among most peoples whose beliefs are known the king was a sacred person and often a priest, usually descended from a divine ancestor ... O'Rahilly, in his great book on *Irish Mythology and History*, had a good deal to say about the King-God, although he is more interested in gods than in kings. He showed that Conn and Eogan were ancestor-gods of the Connachta and the Eoganachta respectively, and that Labhraid was the ancestor-god of the Lagin. Daire was the ancestor-god of the Erainn (*Celtica* 10, 1).

Apart from the Indian-Irish connection, Professor Wagner discusses the Sumerian tradition of Mesopotamia with regard to the *Banais Rí*. It is commonly believed that it was here, between the two rivers Tigris and Euphrates, that civilisation began:

> Our inquiry leads to the conclusion that the *ban-fheis rig* (woman-sleeping of the king) rite depicted in Irish literature derives from the Istar/Tammuz-rite practised in Mesopotamia and in other parts of the Mediterranean world since (at least) the middle of the third millenium BC. Eastern religion could have reached the Celtic world either from the Southwest (Massilia?) or from the Southeast via Asia Minor and Thrace. A similar origin has been suggested by Weisweiler for the 'cult of the divine bull' reflected in the Ulster cycle and in Continental Celtic art (cf the stone-altars of Notre-Dame-de-Paris). The chronological gap between Sumerian and Celtic literary traditions becomes less significant if we bear in mind that ancient Mesopotamian beliefs, shaped in the third millenium, were carried deep into the first millenium BC.

The festival of the *Hieros Gamos* (holy wedding) between the earth-goddess (Inanna) and the king marked the beginning of the New Year in Mesopotamia.

In Ireland the New Year (ie the Year of Growth) begins with 'Beltine' 'Mayday', one of the three great festivals of the year (*Ériu* 26, 1975, 15-16)

It would seem then, that the Celts had obtained the rite of the *Banais Rí* from Mesopotamia and had brought it to Ireland with them, though it may well have been the case that it was reinforced by the occurrence of the same or a similar custom among the megalithic people whom they found there before them.

Professor E. O. James describes in some detail what is known of the rite:

> That such sacred nuptials were held at the end of the Babylonian Akitu Festival is suggested by the king and queen repairing to a chamber called 'gigunu' decorated with greenery situated it would seem on one of the stages of the 'ziqqurat' … the newly reinstated king cohabited with his spouse to engage in a ritual marital intercourse symbolising the union of the Goddess with the Young God to reinforce the creative powers of spring in nature, the flocks and mankind. It was in such a 'gigunu' as 'the seat of joy' that the nuptials of Enlil took place for this purpose, and the adornment with greenery enhanced the efficacy of the rite and warded off evil influences. Therefore, the sacral king enacted the role of the divine bridegroom in the seclusion of the 'gigunu' with all its safeguards to renew vegetation as the culmination of the Akitu Festival (*Seasonal Feasts and Festivals*, London 1961, 87-88).

Here, in this incredibly ancient rite, it is human actors, the king and queen, or in other cases the king/hero and a priestess/druidess, who impersonate the god and the goddess.

If the theory is correct that the Newgrange Event at the Winter Solstice is really the *Banais Rí* or *hieros gamos*, it is on a more than human level, for the goddess earth is herself there in the mound and the god is himself there in the sun. This is the cosmic union of earth-mother and sky-father with no intermediary and, without doubt, this is the great archetypal act which gives origin and effect to all others.

If then, following this cosmic action, there occurred a communal mating among the people, as is hinted at in later literature in the case of Bealtaine, then nine months later, at the Autumn Equinox (c 21 September) many children would have been born at the time of the corn harvest.

If the insular Celtic system were followed, however, with Bealtaine as the time of communal sex, then nine months later, Imbolc (*Lá 'le Bríde*, 1 February, Feast of St Brigid) would be the birth time, and St Brigid is the patron of childbirth. Her fame was so great that, according to tradition, she was transported by Angels to Palestine to assist the Virgin Mary herself with the birth of Christ. This must have been the goddess Brigit, of course, as historically the saint didn't arrive on the scene until several centuries later.

If on the other hand, as seems likely, Samhain were an alternative, then the time of birth would be Lughnasa (c 1 August) – again corresponding to the grain harvest.

In any case, the idea of human fertility being brought into harmony with other expressions of it in nature may be indicated.

The passages at the great mound of Knowth are aligned to the rising and setting sun at the Spring and Autumn Equinoxes.

Newgrange is aligned to the rising sun at the Winter Solstice.

Dowth is aligned to the setting sun at the Winter Solstice.

The absence of an alignment to the Summer Solstice (21 June) at Brú na Bóinne is puzzling. Could it be that it is concealed in the great mound of Dowth (*Dubhadh*) which, as yet, is not fully excavated? There must be some explanation for the absence of this major feast still celebrated with bonfires right to the present day, as we have seen, and celebrated in the liturgical rites of the Eastern and Western churches as the Feast of St John the Baptist. He is intimately connected with the Summer Solstice by his saying: 'I must decrease' – the sun having reached its climax at the Summer Solstice is now beginning to decrease in light and strength – 'and he (Christ) must increase' (John 3:30)– at the Winter Solstice (Christmas) the sun is at its lowest strength but is now beginning to increase in strength and light of day. The Feasts of Our Lord and St John the Baptist, then, stand at the pivotal points of the solar and megalithic year – at the Winter and Summer Solstices.

It does seem odd, then, that so archaic and venerable a tradition as the Summer Solstice does not appear to find a place in the Brú na Bóinne complex.

One may wonder if it were actually marked but in a way which is less obvious to us today. Very highly decorated stones seem to be chosen as markers for a passage, and a fine example of this is, of course, the magnificently carved entrance stone at Newgrange (K1) itself, leading into the passageway to the central chamber.

Straight across the mound from this is the highly decorated Kerb Stone (K52). However, when this area was excavated no passageway was discovered. This is at the northwest of the mound.

Not far from this, on the northeast side, is another highly decorated stone with its double spiral or S-Spiral engraving (K67).

Unfortunately, most of the great monoliths of the stone circle surrounding the mound have disappeared. The two decorated kerb-stones mentioned seem to occupy a place close to the position of the rising and setting sun at the Summer Solstice. If the great monoliths of the circle had been preserved, is it possible that two of them could have thrown shadows on these engraved stones at the Summer Solstice? No doubt, these possibilities have been considered already by professional archeologists employing compasses and computers to recreate Brú na Bóinne of 5000 years ago. But this alluringly magnificent site is in no hurry to reveal all its mysteries.

It would be fulfilling, however, if the whole calendar were included in Brú na Bóinne, while it is recognised, of course, that the complex is much more than an indicator of the four stations of the sun. These could be indicated just as effectively by much simpler methods. Leaving aside such matters as the moon and Venus and concentrating only on the entrance of a ray of sunshine into the mound of Newgrange at the Winter Solstice, the likelihood is that this was the well-known *Banais Rí* or *hieros gam*os of ancient cultures, but on a massive planetary scale, the union of the Sky-Father and the Earth-Mother; in Celtic terms, An Daghdha and Bófhinn (MórRíoghan). A similar episode describes An Daghdha and MórRíoghan uniting at the river Unshin (Co Sligo) at Samhain and the place was named *Luí na Lanúine* (bed of the couple) after the event (Gray, E., *Cath Maige Tuiread*, Dublin 1982, 44-45).

At a later stage, the question of death symbolism at Newgrange will be discussed, as indeed the site is often referred to as a tomb and a small amount of cremated human remains were found in the central area. This, however, does not indicate that Newgrange was a huge communal graveyard. In concrete remains, this is a surprisingly small feature, but one which may be of great significance in the overall meaning of the site. The anthropologists Dr Caroline Humphrey and Dr Piers Vitebsky of Cambridge University unite these two ideas of death and rebirth in their discussion of Newgrange:

> The design of some tombs clearly link astronomy to rebirth. The passage-grave resembles a vagina leading into the womb and some tombs have entrances shaped very clearly like a vulva. This interpretation is borne out by the facing of the burial mound at Newgrange with white quartz, making the tomb resemble an egg. In many religions today the tomb is also a place of regeneration and rebirth, and it seems likely that this was also the case for many neolithic peoples. At Newgrange at the winter solstice, the rays of the rising sun penetrate nearly 100 feet (30 metres) along the passage to the back wall. This was very carefully calculated, as the uphill gradient of the passage was compensated for by a tiny opening in a 'roof box' which let in the sunlight. It was as if the deceased, just like the dying year, will be reborn at the touch of the returning sun (*Sacred Architecture*, London 1997, 85)

So, the indications are that Newgrange was a sanctuary in which the rite of the *Banais Rí* was performed on an interplanetary scale at the Winter Solstice to renew the face of the earth. On a tiny scale, in a suburban garden, lush vegetation can be seen to shoot up from the moist earth when the sun shines down on it. So that the idea of the *Banais Rí* is rooted in nature itself, and the performance of the rite was not just a commemoration, a mental act of recalling something that happened in the past, but rather an act that brought about what it symbolised, namely, the fertility of the land and the growth of crops.

Now, it seems possible from a reading of Celtic mythology that a certain personal note was introduced into the overall agricultural 'greening of the land' scene.

We have already seen in the story *Oídhe Mhuircheartaigh Mhic Earca* that the goddess of the well was dramatically transformed from *Cailleach* or 'Old Hag' winter form to *Babóg* or 'Beautiful Young Woman' summer form through union with the hero Niall. Niall himself also undergoes transformation – from hero to king. So that transformation occurs in the case of both parties. In the Ritual Calendar of Duhallow as already mentioned the *Cailleach Bhéarra Buí* of the Samhain (winter site) changes into *Babóg* or summer form at Bealtaine and is known as *Iníon Bhuí* (Daughter of *Buí/Boi/Baoi*). The road joining both sites is Boherbue – in all probability *Bóthar Buí/Boi/Baoi*, the road which the Hag traverses to regain her youth in six months. She becomes her own daughter *Iníon Bhoi*, the *Babóg na Bealtaine*. Iníon Bhoí is regarded as one of the three great saints of Duhallow and large crowds of pilgrims flock to her Holy Well at Drom Tairbh at the beginning of May (Bealtaine). The *Cailleach Bhéarra Boí* is connected to the Bearre Peninsula, with landscape formations and megalithic tombs: '... and is represented as even constituting, corporally, the very fabric of landscape in the identification of physical features with aspects of her body: the Paps of Anu, *Dhá chíoch Anann* (a mountain range in Kerry); Brú na Bóinne? *Cnogba*, Newgrange and Knowth burial chambers (the latter being 'the telluric womb' of the goddess in the words of Tomás Ó Cathasaigh (Ó Crualaíoch, G., *The Book of the Cailleach*, Cork 2003, 89-90).

After the Winter Solstice, as the days lengthen and buds appear on the trees, and green grass begins to make its appearance, the transformation of the goddess occurs.

But what about the sun? Does that also undergo a transformation? Of course it does, and it is more immediately observable than in the case of the Earth-Mother, though it does take some time to realise fully that there is a lengthening of the days.

It is here that we are reminded of the strange episode in *Tochmarc Étaíne*, already mentioned, in the incident of Aonghus Óg being conceived and born in one day.

Could this be a folk-memory, or an ancient interpretation of the Winter Solstice, going back to a remote period parallel to the folk-memory of the local farmers of Brú na Bóinne regarding the entrance of the sunlight into the mound at a certain day of the year?

If the Winter Solstice (21 December) is the shortest day of the year then, theoretically, the next day (22 December) (although this is not quite accurate) will be the turning point. The sun will rise a little further to the north, so that this day will be a little longer than yesterday and the sun has recovered. In practice, the sun seems to stop for a little while, but theoretically, the next day after the solstice, the sun will rise a little earlier, so that 22 December is really New Year's Day.

Could it be, that it is this phenomenon that is expressed in the *Tochmarc Étaíne* story, and that the sacred mound of Newgrange is personified as Bófhinn / Eithne / MórRíoghan, while the sun is personified as An Daghdha? In human terms, if the theory is correct, the visitors to Newgrange at the Winter Solstice come to attend the wedding of An Daghdha and Bófhinn.

In discussing the ancient rite of *An Dreoilín* (Hunting the Wren), we have seen the division of the year into two halves – from the Winter Solstice to the Summer Solstice presided over by the Robin King, and from the Summer Solstice to the Winter Solstice presided over by the Wren King. A similar arrangement is the Celtic system of the dark half of the year from Samhain to Bealtaine and the bright half from Bealtaine to Samhain.

This system of dividing the year into two halves, presided over by two different personalities, must have been well-known and widespread in antiquity since it left its mark on the ordering of the Christian Liturgical Calendar at the beginning of Christianity. Here, the feast of the birth of St John the Baptist is assigned to the Summer Solstice and the feast of the birth of Christ to the Winter Solstice.

Could it be then, that a 'Half-Year Unit' was part of an ancient tradition and that it sprang, naturally enough, from the solstices which so accurately divided the year into two equal halves?

To return, then, to *Tochmarc Étaíne* and *An Daghdha*.

An Daghdha can be seen as a sun god. He is *Eochaidh Ollathair* (horseman, universal father) – the horse in some traditions pulls the sun-disc around the sky. He is *Ruadh Ró-Fheasa* (lord of great knowledge) and, indeed, someone who looks down from the sky and watches the antics of the human race would be expected to be a being of great knowledge. He is *Deirgderc* (red-eye/sight), the sun. He drags around a huge club, with wheels to facilitate transport, as with a modern suitcase. By striking somebody with one end of the club he kills him, and by striking the dead man with the other end of the club he brings him back to life. Perhaps this symbolises the deadly power of the sun around the Summer Solstice and the 'Dog-Days' which destroy vegetation, and then the gentle, weepy sun which revives and nurtures it.

Taking into account the two great divine characters associated with Brú na Bóinne' – An Daghdha and his son Aonghus Óg/An Mac Óg, we examine for a moment how it would be possible to relate them to the progress of the sun around the earth in the course of a year.

However, as Autumn and Winter approached, it became increasingly clear that the days were actually getting shorter and the nights longer, and as already said, people became anxious as to the future of the sun. If the sun continued to lose energy, would it eventually be swallowed up by the great dragon of darkness and shine no more, bringing death and destruction to the world?

The Liturgy of Advent, although serving a different purpose – preparation for the coming of Christ at Christmas – may echo the anxiety of this winter period and introduce the element of Christian hope.

Some random texts may illustrate the idea:

'See, the king, the Lord of the world, will come. He will free us from the yoke of our bondage.'

'And all mankind shall see the salvation of God.'

'The Lord is my light and my help; whom shall I fear?'

'Behold, our Lord will come with power and will enlighten the eyes of his servants.'

'He has rejoiced as a giant to run the course; his going out is from the end of heaven and his circuit even to its end.'

The most remarkable of these texts is the 'O Antiphon' for 21 December, the Winter Solstice. The 'O Antiphons' are short texts, based on the Bible, which form part to the Office of Vespers (Evening Prayer) in the Roman Rite, for 17 to 23 December. As an example, I give here the 'O Antiphon' for 23 December:

> O Emmanuel, our King and Lawgiver, the expected one of the nations and their saviour, come to save us, O Lord our God.

Here, and in the other Antiphons, there is a clear calling on God to come and save people who are engulfed in some kind of trouble from which they cannot escape without the intervention of an outside agent. The origin of these Antiphons is obscure, but they are thought to be Gallican and to be about 1000 years old. They are sung with great solemnity, to an elaborate Plain Chant melody, in Benedictine Monasteries to herald the coming of Christ the Saviour at Christmas. They may to some extent retain echoes of the Roman *Saturnalia*: 'The year ended, as the modern year ends, with a great holiday of peace and goodwill. Indeed the customs of Christians are directly derived from the ancient festival of the *Saturnalia*, originally confined to 17 December but later extending over several days' (Ogilvie, R. M., *The Romans and their Gods*, London, 1986, 98). Ogilvie goes on to describe the parties, presents, paper hats and Mock Kings, which perhaps echoes the idea of a change of Kings at the Winter Solstice.

The 'O Antiphon' for 21 December, although it is now sung at Vespers in the evening rather than in the morning, bears an uncanny echo of the Newgrange scene at the Winter Solstice:

> *O Oriens, splendor lucis aeternae, et sol justitiae; veni et illumina sedentes in tenebris , et umbra mortis.*
> (O Dawn of the East, brightness of everlasting light and Sun of Justice, come and enlighten those that sit in darkness and in the shadow of death.)

'O Oriens' may be interpreted in this context as referring to Christ, who is like the rising sun at dawn, bringing light to the darkness of the night: 'I am the light of the world, anyone who follows me will not be walking in the dark; he will have the light of life' (John 8:12)

In the phrase 'brightness of everlasting light and Sun of Justice' we see the preoccupation with the idea of light, and Christ as revealing the divine, everlasting light/life of God. As the sun is the greatest source of light of which we have knowledge, the comparison to the sun is natural. 'Sun of Justice' may refer to Mt 5:45: 'he (God) causes his sun to rise on bad men as well as good', so that the idea of harmony is presented.

The phrase 'come and enlighten those who sit in darkness and in the shadow of death' has precedents in other parts of scripture. St Luke's gospel sees John the Baptist as a prophet who will prepare the way for the coming of Christ: '... because of the faithful love of our God in which the rising Sun has come from on high to visit us, to give light to those who live in darkness and the shadow dark as death, and to guide our feet into the way of peace' (Luke 1:78-79)

An antecedent to the phrase occurs earlier in the Prophet Isaiah (9:1): 'The people who walked in darkness have seen a great light, on the inhabitants of a country in shadow dark as death light has blazed forth.'

This last phrase could be seen as operating on two levels. Firstly, on the ordinary everyday level with the turning of the sun and the increasing light dissipating the darkness of winter.

On the second level, it is reminiscent of the ray of light penetrating to the inner chamber of Newgrange to light up the ashes of the dead. We will see more of this aspect of the tomb later. While it must be remembered that the Newgrange event is several thousand years earlier than the biblical texts, nevertheless, Psalm 19 (18) gives a fine description of the glory of the sky:

In making the sky, he (God) has pitched a tent for the sun
who leaves his pavilion like a bridegroom,
like a champion enjoying the race to be run.
Rising on the one horizon,
he runs his arc to the other,
and nothing can escape his heat.

Similarly with the well-known Antiphon of Advent: *Rorate caeli desuper, et nubes pluant justum; aperiatur terrra, et germinet*

Salvatorem (Let the clouds rain down the Just One, and the earth bring forth as Saviour). Here, in this obvious reference to the mystery of the incarnation, the sky and the earth are the polarities mentioned.

The remarkable 'O Antiphons' are now sung at Vespers in the evening. In many churches, however, they were sung in the morning at the Office of Lauds, to accompany the *Benedictus* canticle which speaks of St John the Baptist as coming to prepare the way of the Lord. All this takes place on the last days before the Winter Solstice and the people call on the promised Saviour to come and set them free with a mixture of anxiety and confidence. These may well reflect the emotions of ancient peoples as they waited expectantly for the turning of the sun at the Winter Solstice, counting the days, as it were. In the 'O Antiphons', Christ, the promised Saviour, is addressed by various titles: *O Sapientia* (O Wisdom); *O Adonai* (O Lord); *O Radix Jesse* (O Root of Jesse); *O Clavis David* (O Key of David); *O Oriens* (O Rising Sun); *O Rex Gentium* (O King of the Peoples); *O Emmanuel* (O God with us). This is the order in which the antiphons are sung, one for each day from 17 to 23 December. Then the Winter Solstice occurs on 21 December. Now, liturgists have called attention to a peculiarity of this order of the titles. If you take the first letter of each title and begin at the end you get: E,R,O,C,R,A,S. Then proceed to separate O from C. This gives you 'ERO CRAS', meaning 'I will be here tomorrow.' For each of seven days, the people have been making a request to Christ to come and save them while addressing him by different titles. They, then, look back at their requests and they find that he has actually enclosed a coded message in answer to their prayers: 'I will be with you tomorrow.'

An ancient Roman antiphonary prescribed the use of the 'O Antiphons' from the Feast of St Nicholas (6 December) to the Feast of St Lucy (13 December). This shows the connection with the Winter Solstice which, according to an alternative calendar, fell on St Lucy's Day, while accordingly the Summer Solstice fell on the Feast of St Barnabas (11 June).

The dates could be easily memorised from the rhyme:

Lucy light, Lucy light,
shortest day and longest night.

Barnaby bright, Barnaby bright,
longest day and shortest night.

Considerable flexibility prevailed and a very widespread date was 6 January which became to some extent the real Feast of Christmas in the East and especially among Christians of the Armenian Rite. The 'Twelve Days of Christmas' from 25 December to 6 January became a sacred interval in the year to celebrate the Birth of Christ and the Winter Solstice.

The 'O Antiphons', then, although belonging firmly to the biblical tradition, with their emotional appeal, sacred chant, the ringing of church bells, incensation of altars proclaim the arrival of a turning point in the year when supernatural forces visit the earth (cf Knoblach, T., 'The "O" Antiphons', *Ephemerides Liturgicae*, 1992, 177–204)

A widespread custom in Catholic churches today is the 'Advent Wreath' made in the form of a ring with four candles. The candles stand for the four weeks of Advent and one is lighted each Sunday, so that when Christmas comes all the candles are lighting and a large Christmas Candle is put in the centre. This is a simple way of building up our expectancy of the coming of Christ at the end of the dark period of the year.

One could imagine the custom taking a different form. For instance, at the beginning of Advent, all four candles could be lighted. Then, as the weeks progressed, the candles could be gradually quenched to reflect the increasing darkness as we approach the Winter Solstice, the darkest day of the year. Then, when all is blackness and Christmas arrives a brilliant shower of candles could be lighted to celebrate the event so long desired.

With regard to the division of the year into two equal halves a pattern can be seen in the two periods provided by the two solstices; by the two periods governed by Samhain and Bealtaine; the two periods provided by the wren and the robin; by John the Baptist and Christ; by the Summer grazing and the Winter feeding.

An Daghdha, then, may be visualised as the Lord of the Sun's Course through the heavens in the space of a year. Setting out on his half-year's reign along with King Robin at the Summer Solstice, he makes his blazing path through the sky growing weaker, gradually, from his effort, and failing as the shortening of the days and increasing darkness indicate. At last, at the Winter Solstice, the shortest day of the year, he, An Daghdha, mates with the Earth Goddess (Bófhinn/MórRíoghan/Boí) and overnight a son is conceived and born. He is called Aonghus Óg (young Aonghus) and he is the re-incarnation of An Daghdha who has been re-born in his son Aonghus Óg. Aonghus Óg is the new sun in the sky. He is still only a child and is still very weak, but gradually his youthful energy will show in the increasing length of the day. Before the Winter Solstice, the weakening sun in the sky that you see is 'An Daghdha,' but after the Winter Solstice, it is the young energetic sun you see – Aonghus Óg.

Aonghus Óg continues his triumphant path through the heavens pouring out his heat on the earth to make the crops grow and warm the hearts of humankind.

But eventually, the Summer Solstice (21 June) arrives, and young Aonghus realises that he is no longer young. He is no longer Aonghus Óg but has become the father figure, An Daghdha. As An Daghdha, he begins his downward course from the Summer Solstice cheered by the bonfires and good wishes of the earth-dwellers who want to keep him at full strength and energy to ripen their harvests of wheat, oats and barley.

But, inevitably, the old sun-god An Daghdha reaches his final day, the Winter Solstice. He mates with Bófhinn and overnight they have a son called Aonghus Óg – the young sun of the New Year – and he runs his course in the sky until reaching his highest point at the Summer Solstice. He undergoes metamorphosis and becomes An Daghdha – and so the process of alternation proceeds for ever and ever – 'The Myth of the Eternal Return'.

One can well imagine what an overpowering ethos this mighty cosmic play engendered among the Stone Age inhabitants of Brú na Bóinne and beyond, who had provided, with immense labour and intellectual ability, a noble theatre for the performance of a ritual drama whose major actors were the sky and the earth and whose effect was to provide the fertility of the land upon which human life depends.

So far, our attention has been focused on the living and on the fertility of the land which sustains them in that condition in this world. But this is a temporary state, as everybody knows, and the day comes when we have to make our departure. So, is Brú na Bóinne involved, in some way, in an Afterlife of some kind for human beings when our earthly life is over? To clarify the issue, we look first at the magnificent classical formulation of the doctrine of death and afterlife in the Preface for the Dead in the Liturgy of the Catholic Church:

> ... *per Christum Dominum nostrum. In quo nobis spes beatae resurrectionis effulsit, ut, quos constristat certa moriendi conditio, eosdem consoletur futurae immortalitatis promissio.*
>
> *Tuis enim fidelibus, Domine, vita mutatur, non tollitur; et dissoluta terrestris hujus incolatus domo, aeterna in caelis habitatio comporatur.*
>
> (... through Christ our Lord. In him (Christ), for us, the hope of a blessed resurrection has shone out, so that they who are saddened by the certain lot of dying, are comforted by the promise of future immortality. Indeed, for your faithful people, O Lord, life is changed, not taken away, and when this temporary earthly home of ours is destroyed, an everlasting dwelling-place is provided in heaven.)

This piece is not only a gem of literary Latin but a masterly exposition of Christian doctrine with regard to death and to what happens after it.

Christ, risen from the dead, is the model for the dying. As he rose from the dead in a transformed, spiritualised body, so will his followers. The scriptures show him, in his resurrected state, suddenly appearing among his disciples and just as suddenly disappearing. As already said, the scene of the transfiguration of Christ on the mountain, when 'his face shone like the sun and his clothes became as white as the light' (Mt 17), even though taking place before the resurrection, was as it were, a foreshowing of the form his Risen Body would take. The Feast of the Transfiguration (6 August), falling at the time of the Celtic Harvest Festival of Lughnasa, can be seen as the feast of Christ, risen from the dead and presenting himself in his glorified state as the First Ripened

Sheaf of the harvest. The rest of the corn will also turn golden in its turn, modelled on the First Sheaf which in Gaelic tradition the farmer cut and placed on a hill with a wish that the rest of the field would ripen also.

So, Christ, risen from the dead, with a glorified, spiritualised body, no longer subject to death or decay, is the model for his followers. What happened to him will happen to them, and while their mortal bodies will be destroyed, they will acquire spiritual bodies adapted to a different type of existence. The Preface for the Dead leaves many details unexplained and unexamined, but it does give a basic exposition of the final destiny of man and attempts an answer to the great mysterious puzzle which has confronted humankind since the world began.

CHAPTER ELEVEN

Brú na Bóinne and the Ancestors

With regard to the lot of the dead in the megalithic period of Brú na Bóinne we are faced at once with a difficulty.

It cannot be considered as a general graveyard where all the local people are buried in the fashion of today, but there is a tradition of the kings of Tara being buried there, and in the beautifully restored Knowth what are called 'satellite tombs' are arranged around the main mound. Nevertheless, these would only constitute a small select burial ground as can be seen from the actual site. Again, only a few human remains were found within the mound at Newgrange. While in common speech, Newgrange is often referred to as a tomb, this is not entirely accurate. A great medieval cathedral is not referred to as a tomb even though several bishops are buried there. Everybody understands that the cathedral is used for many other purposes: baptisms, weddings, funerals, the celebration of the Eucharist, Divine Office, blessings, etc.

If Brú na Bóinne, were an ordinary graveyard, as understood today, it would have to be very extensive to accommodate burials over thousands of years. So, the idea of a communal graveyard can be ruled out. It is difficult to know what happened the dead in this populous and prosperous area. One thinks immediately of cremation, which would have left little or no trace.

The scarcity of bodies in Newgrange and other megalithic 'tombs' is quite a puzzle along with so many other aspects of this ancient civilization. We are forced to the conclusion that the few people buried in Newgrange formed a special group, an elite.

But what kind of an elite? It is most likely, as already discussed, these would have been the Blessed Ancestors who, when they lived had been, perhaps, the founding fathers of the local community, the inspired few who had organised the people in making the land suitable for agriculture, constructing the great monuments themselves, leaders and fathers of their people. When these men died, their bodies would, presumably, have been interred within the megalithic mounds with special honour.

As already explained in the quotation from Rundle Clarke, the Ancestors were the guardians of the source of life and vigour, sustenance and growth, the fertility of the land, increase of herds, the well-being of the local community. These powerful Ancestors dwelt in the megalithic tomb and this was the centre from which their power emanated. Without the tomb, life on earth would be miserable, perhaps impossible. One notices, on occasion, that megalithic monuments are situated on the brow of a hill – not on the top. Perhaps the local inhabitants imagined the power of the Ancestors inhabiting the tomb as floating down the hill on to the level agricultural land below as in the case of the well-preserved Court Tomb of Shanballyedmond in Co Tipperary and in Lough Gur, Co Limerick, where the power might descend to the lake below to give an abundance of fish.

In these prehistoric shrines, some of which may have been pilgrimage sites catering for more than the local community, ambiguity exists as to how the Ancestors lived in them so that they could be points of contact between the needy humans and the powerful denizens of the Otherworld. Were they in the bones or ashes in the fashion of a consecrated altar in the Catholic Church where small pieces of the bones of the saints are contained in the small *Sepulchrum* or cavity in the marble altar, or, are they 'enstoned' – literally present in the stone of the tomb, stone being a hard and endureable medium worthy of the everlasting Ancestors themselves? And, if present, in bone or stone, were the Ancestors present all the time, or only on special occasions when the tomb was 'charged' by the performance of ritual dances, circumambulation, or other forms of ritual, when the whole sacred site became activated? The Winter Solstice would be one of those occasions.

With regard to Newgrange, we saw that folk memory retained a vague notion of a ray of sunshine entering into the mound at some time of the year. Once the hint had been given, it was easy enough to deduce the date of the event for the passage was aligned to the south-east, the portion of the sky where the sun would rise during the winter. The Winter Solstice, as the big event at that time of the year, would immediately come to mind.

But the important point is that the hint or clue to this extraordinary phenomenon was given by the local farmers. It was the farmers who told Professor O'Kelly, not Professor O'Kelly who told the farmers. Here, surely, is a supreme example of folk-memory persisting over a period of thousands of years.

This folk memory concerned the entry of the light into the mound. But could there possibly be other folk-memories which might illustrate other aspects of the site?

I think that one such possibility may exist in the well-known story *Toraíocht Dhiarmada agus Ghráinne* (The Pursuit of Diarmaid and Gráinne). While the manuscripts are late, nevertheless there are indications that they contain some archaic elements. A critical edition of the story: *Toraíocht Dhiarmada agus Ghráinne* (Baile Átha Cliath, 1971) has been produced by Nessa Ní Shé.

In this romantic story belonging to the Fenian Cycle of tales, Fionn Mac Cumhaill, the great hero and leader of Fianna Éireann (the heroic warrior band charged with safeguarding the country from foreign invasion) is engaged to be married to Gráinne, daughter of the High King Cormac Mac Airt.

Gráinne, however, is in love with the young handsome hero Diarmaid Ó Duibhne, the darling of many women. At the wedding feast in Tara, Gráinne arranges that drugged drink be given to all the guests except Diarmaid and a chosen few. All fall asleep and Gráinne puts Diarmaid *faoi gheasa* – a kind of magical obligation, to elope with her. On account of his loyalty to Fionn, his Captain, Diarmaid is a reluctant lover. The story relates their wanderings throughout the country in their flight from Fionn Mac Cumhaill who pursues them relentlessly from place to place. To this day, numerous megalithic tombs are known as *Leaba Dhiarmada agus Ghráinne* (Bed of Diarmaid and Gráinne). The pair slept here and in folk-tradition these are considered to be places where a woman might conceive more easily. Whether this was because they were looked upon as 'waiting rooms' in which souls of the dead waited to be re-incarnated is uncertain or, perhaps, it was due to the powers of fertility of the archetypal couple.

Professor Dáithí Ó hÓgáin points out certain similarities between Diarmaid and Adonis in classical mythology. Adonis, like Diarmaid, was killed by a wild boar (*Myth, Legend and Romance*, New York, 1991, 161-162).

After many singular exploits, and the defeat of Fionn on many occasions, Diarmaid's great friend and fosterer the Tuatha Dé Danann god of the Boyne, Aonghus Óg, managed to negotiate a peace agreement between the two, and Diarmaid and Gráinne and their children settled down to normal life on their estate.

Diarmaid, then, is connected to megalithic Brú na Bóinne through his friend Aonghus Óg who comes to his aid frequently.

It was prophesied that Diarmaid would have the same length of life as the magic *Torc Binne Gulbán*, the wild boar of Ben Bulban, Co Sligo.

Then, at last, the pig went on the rampage and Diarmaid went off to hunt him. In a ferocious encounter, the boar killed Diarmaid, but at the last moment Diarmaid killed the boar and so both died together and had the same length of life, as had been destined. The origin of the situation was that Donn, the father of Diarmaid, had killed the only son of the *reachtaire* or director of Brú na Bóinne. The *reachtaire* had seized a magic wand, struck his dead son with it and turned him into the wild boar of Beann Gulban and decreed that it was by him that Diarmaid would eventually fall. The stark primitive character of the event is conveyed in the *reachtaire*'s dramatic pronouncement: '*Cuirimse faoi gheasa thú gurb ionann saol duit agus do Dhiarmaid Ó Duibhne agus gurb leat thitfeas fá dheireadh*' (Ní Shé, 1971, 61) (I put you under 'geasa' that you and Diarmaid Ó Duibhne will have the same length of life and that it will be by you that he will die at last.)

Again, the megalithic connection may be noticed. It is the son of the director of Brú na Bóinne who is killed and it is the director who is responsible for the wild boar of Beann Gulban and his destiny and that of Diarmaid Ó Duibhne.

The introduction of the magic boar into the story is not only reminiscent of the Adonis cult but of a usage in the island of Malekula in the New Hebrides and surrounding islands. This area is of immense importance to us as it continued a megalithic culture until fairly recently and some of its megalithic monuments, recently erected, might easily be mistaken for some in Ireland erected thousands of years ago. A marvellously detailed study of this culture has been made by Dr John Layard and published as *Stone Men of Malekula* (London 1942) as well as other publications.

In these Malekulian islands in the Pacific the natives say that the megalithic culture was introduced by maritime immigrants from outside. These spread over a large part of the globe in late neolithic or early Bronze Age times and fused with pre-existing cultures.

'In South West Bay these immigrants are said to have been white-skinned, with aquiline noses. Their chief – for the immigrants had chiefs, whereas the present inhabitants have none – is said to be buried sitting on a stone seat in a stone chamber. This chamber was covered with a mound of loose stones and earth. In Europe we should call this a tumulus or round barrow. The body of this chief is said to be incorruptible. In the fertility rite, on which the health and survival of the people are said to depend, the main observance consists of displaying images of his body and that of his wife, and in reanimating them by ritually washing them. The chief's ten grandsons are said to have been incarnated in stones, which still exist and serve as seats for the heads of the ten families of which the clan consists to sit on during their assemblies' (Layard, J., *Spiritual Disciplines*, Bollinger Series XXX, 1960, 118)

Here, in this immensely complex culture, we can detect certain echoes of the neolithic in Ireland. One of the frustrating elements in the study of this subject is the variety of usages in a small area which makes it difficult to make broad general statements. Malekula is only about 60 miles long but something like 200 languages are spoken in it. The indications are that in many parts of the ancient world, small groups predominated, and because of their isolation and lack of contact with other groups, developed in somewhat different ways so that 'localisation' may be a key factor in a study of neolithic and even later cultures.

At any rate, one of the strange coincidences between the story of Diarmaid and Malekulian usage concerns the boar who had the same life-span as Diarmaid.

The Melekulian custom was that, at birth, a special boar was given to a child and it had a special relationship with him from then on. When the person died, his relatives or friends killed the pig in sacrifice on his behalf, so that the boar and the person had the same length of life as in the case of Diarmaid.

The thinking behind this observance was connected with the Journey of the Dead in Melanesian Malekula. When a person died, the passage of his soul to the Otherworld, to the Land of the Dead, was not so straightforward. The passageway to the Otherworld was through a cave and this was guarded by the terrible Female Devouring Ghost known as Le-hev-hev. Firstly, his friends had to sacrifice his boar on his behalf and Le-hev-hev was satisfied to devour the soul of the boar instead of the dead man's soul and so allow him to pass through to the Otherworld. But this was not all. There was another condition in the form of an entrance test.

Le-hev-hev stationed herself in front of the entrance to the cave, and on the ground she drew a labyrinthine design. Then, as the soul of the dead man seeking entrance approached, she blotted out one half of the elaborate design. The soul, or ghost, had to complete the figure on the ground accurately, otherwise *Le-hev-hev* would devour him on the spot and his chances of arriving in the Land of the Dead were gone for ever.

Now, how could he do this? The solution lay in the Ritual Dances which formed a major part of Malekulian life. It appears that the designs on the sand at the cave entrance represented the elaborate steps of the dances, and if the soul/ghost were well versed in the Ritual Dances through a lifetime of performance, then he would be able to complete the design from memory, and the Female Devouring Ghost would allow him to enter the cave and make his way to the Land of the Dead.

One is immediately struck by certain similarities between the Malekulan death rituals and the account of Diarmaid and the boar of Beann Gulbán. In both accounts the man and the boar have the same span of life and they both die together. The Malekulan account gives and explanation for the killing of the tusked boar – it is a sacrificial offering to the Devouring Female Ghost, *Le-hev-hev*, who accepts the boar's soul in place of that of the human. Was there something of this sacrificial idea also in the case of Diarmaid Ó Duibhne, and could the terrible *Badhbh* – the goddess of war who flew screeching over the battlefield avaricious for blood – be the Irish equivalent of the Female Devouring Ghost of Malekula but who was placated by the sacrifice of *Torc Binne Gulbán* so that Diarmaid was permitted to proceed to the Otherworld? And could the elaborate designs on the massive entrance stone at Newgrange echo the designs at the cave entrance in Malekula?

The dead man, having got past Le-hev-hev, makes his solitary way down the coast of Malekula and at a certain point lights a bonfire. This attracts the attention of the Ferryman on the volcanic island of Ambrym in the distance – the Land of the Dead. The Ferryman comes to collect him in his ghost-canoe and takes him to the Land of the Dead where he joins his ancestors. Here, they dance all night and sleep all day.

As regards the *Badhbh*, in Irish tradition this fearsome 'female battle demon usually appears in the form of a crow, inciting warriors to do battle against one another and rejoicing over the corpses of the fallen' (Maier, B., *Dictionary of Celtic Religion and Culture*, Woodbridge, 2000, 38).

When looking at some of the 'Portal Tombs' such as Brownshill, Co Carlow; Kilmogue, Co Kilkenny; Timony, Co Derry; Aannaghmore, Co Leitrim; Ballykeel, Co Armagh, one is struck by the strange phenomenon that the huge table-stone resting on smaller standing stones is not flat like a table, as you would expect, but sloping upwards. Unlike a cow grazing beside it, whose back is flat and parallel to the ground, the stone slopes upwards at one end, exactly resembling the stance of a bird. Perhaps this was a deliberate attempt to portray the *Badhbh*, the devouring female goddess in stone, as a wooden figure of a hawk surmounted some megalithic monuments in Malekula. This was the dark side of the goddess, portrayed as a bird of prey.

Excellent photographs of these sloping Portal Tombs may be seen in Carleton Jones' book *Temples of Stone*, Cork 2007.

By the killing of the boar of Beann Gulbán, Diarmaid Ó Duibhne had paid his debts to the *MórRíon/Badhbh/Macha* or by whatever name she was known.

The narrative of the *Toraíocht* describes the aftermath of the death of Diarmaid on the mountainside of Beann Gulbán. Gráinne's people arrive from nearby Rath Ghráinne and so does Aonghus Óg, the god of Brú na Bóinne, with his retinue. They show the rough side of their shields to each other to announce that they come in peace.

Then they join together in raising '*trí tromghartha adhbhal-mhóra uafásacha ós corp Dhiarmada, ionas gur chlos i néalaibh neimhe, agus i bhfrithibh na firmiminte aerga, agus i mbeanna sléibhe, agus in oileánaibh mara, agus i gcúigí Éireann, mar an gcéanna*' (three heavy shouts, mighty, terrible, over the body of Diarmaid, and these were heard in the clouds of the sky, and in the wild places of the firmament of the air, and in the summits of mountains, and in the islands of the sea and likewise in the provinces of Ireland).

Gráinne's people say that they have come for Diarmaid's body to take it to Rath Ghráinne but Aonghus Óg will not allow this: '*Adúirt Aonghus nach ligfeadh corp Dhiarmada leo, agus go mbéaradh féin leis é do Bhrú ós Bóinn, "agus ó nach féidir liom á athbheochan arís, cuirfead anam aerga ann ar chor go mbia ag labhairt liom gach lá".*' (Aonghus said that he would not allow them to take Diarmaid's body; he would himself take it to the mansion above the Boyne (Brú na Bóinne), and, "since I am unable to restore him to life again, I will put an aireal / spiritual soul in him so that he will be speaking to me every day".'

'*As a haithle sin cuireas Aongus iomchur fán gcorp i n-eileatram orga, agus a shleá os a chionn inairde, agus do ghluais roimhe go ráinig Brú na Bóinne.*' (After this, Aonghus put transport under the body by way of a golden bier, and his spear on high before him and went ahead until he reached Brú na Bóinne).

This funeral scene is strangely reminiscent of the procession of the Holy Grail.

In some manuscripts the story ends here, in others there is a short description of Gráinne's arrangements with her sons as to how to wreak vengeance on Fionn Mac Chumhaill; in others, she returns to Fionn amidst much mockery from the Fianna. What concerns us is the funeral of Diarmaid and the connection with Brú na Bóinne.

We have seen that, as the body of Diarmaid lay on the mountainside of Beann Gulbán, Aonghus Óg and his retinue of three hundred arrived from Brú na Bóinne and took possession of the body.

Then Aonghus announces that he cannot re-vivify (*ath-bheochan*) Diarmaid. Presumably, this means that he is unable to restore him to his ordinary human life, to the condition he was in before the boar killed him.

But, instead, he will put an *anam aerga* into Diarmaid – an 'airy, ethereal soul' – so that Diarmaid will be speaking to him every day. This seems to mean that Diarmaid, though dead in human terms, will be alive in some other form in which he will speak to Aonghus, the god of Brú na Bóinne, every day. This seems to be a kind of 'transfiguration scene' in which Diarmaid has lost his human, this-world form and has been changed into a form in which he can converse with the immortal gods.

In other words, in Brú na Bóinne, to which his body is transferred, is Diarmaid, the great hero and performer of mighty deeds, to be raised up to the status of Ancestor and numbered among the powerful deities of the Otherworld? Was Brú na Bóinne a centre for the creation of the Ancestor Class?

In describing the hunt of the boar of Beann Gulbán, the various versions of the story tell of how Diarmaid was awakened from his sleep three times by the barking of hounds. He is persuaded to go back to sleep twice by Gráinne, but in the early morning he sets out to see what is happening on the mountain, not knowing the destiny which awaits him there that day.

The phrase is used of this night *i gceann na bliana* and *an oíche dhéanach don (den) bhliain* –'at the head of the year' and 'the last night of the year'. Whatever the phrase may mean in exact calendrical terms, it represented the ending of the old year. Presumably the New Year began on the day after the Winter Solstice. At the Winter Solstice, 21 December, the shortest day of the year, the ray of the rising sun enters Newgrange. In theory, for it takes some days before any visible change is noticed in the length of the days, New Year's Day is 22 December when the sun turns. In fact, our present system of the New Year beginning on 1 January is quite a close approximation to the Winter Solstice system and the great Liturgical Feast of the Epiphany (6 January), the manifestation of Christ's Divinity, is also a traditional date for the Winter Solstice. This is the end of that ambiguous period which we call 'The Twelve Days of Christmas', and on 'Plough Monday', the Monday after the Epiphany, with the ritual blessing of the plough, the agricultural cycle of the new year begins again.

Obviously, a difficulty presents itself here as to what calender they were using. In a story from the Fiannaíocht Cycle of tales, it would be normal to expect the use of the insular Celtic Calendar with its four great Feasts of Samhain, Imbolg, Bealtaine and Lughnasa. But, considering that Aonghus Óg and Brú na Bóinne are so heavily involved in this story and that the great mound of Newgrange has been registering the Winter Solstice for 5000 years, it is more likely that it is the Winter Solstice, not Samhain, that is meant as the marker for the New Year, and that the calendar they were using is what we may for convenience call the megalithic calendar with its two Solstices and two Equinoxes.

The corpse of Diarmaid, then, is placed on a golden bier, with his spear raised up before him and the bearers begin the long funeral procession from Beann Gulban to Brú na Bóinne. This is probably accomplished magically on a parallel with Aonghus and his retinue's arrival at the mountain from Brú na Bóinne for *do ghluais i gcomaoin na gaoithe glan-fhuaire go ráinig Beann Gulbán* (he travelled with the favour of the clean cold wind until he reached Beann Gulbán).

The funeral, having arrived very quickly at Brú na Bóinne, perhaps the body of Diarmaid was hastily cremated or taken into the mound of Newgrange as it was, as the *Caoineadh* or funeral lament was sung.

Then, the remains of Diarmaid lay in the dark mysterious chamber of Brú na Bóinne, at rest at last, after a life of great anxiety and mighty deeds, to be celebrated by poets and storytellers for ages yet to come.

And then morning came, the morning of the Winter Solstice; the sun rose slowly above the neighbouring hill and, suddenly, shone into the tomb, and in a blaze of glory lifted Diarmaid up into the Otherworld to begin his new life among the gods and ancestors.

What I am suggesting here is that the entrance of the beam of sunlight into Newgrange at the Winter Solstice was not only the *hieros gamos* or sacred marriage of the Sky God with the Earth Mother resulting in the fertility of the land, but that it also served another purpose – the creation of Ancestors. These would of necessity be a tiny elite group who in this life had been outstanding members of society or famous heroes. When raised to the level of the immortal gods they would become beings of power for the continual benefit of mankind.

This consideration brings us to the question of the transforming character of fire, of fire from the sun. What is in question here is fire as the instrument which transfers the dead man to the realm of the immortal.

In ancient India, cremation came to be thought of as a transition to immortality. The Indian fire god Agni, himself immortal, confers immortality and guides the deceased to the celestial world ... the ascetic Sarabhanga, who has nothing more to gain from terrestrial life, wishes to leave his limbs, like the snake wriggling out of its old skin. He lights a fire, sacrifices butter while uttering the appropriate formulas, and steps into the fire. It then consumes his hair, his old skin, bones, flesh and blood. A youth, the fire's counterpart, arises shining and wanders through the world of the gods to the highest heaven. (Eliade, M., (ed), *The Encyclopedia of Religion*, New York 1987, Vol 5, Art: Fire).

The 'youth' in this story from the Indian epic *Ramayana* is no other than the old ascetic Sarabhanga transfigured, rejuvenated, made immortal, transferred to the realm of the gods by the action of the fire god Agni. Similarly, in the case of Herakles, his death on the funeral pyre frees him from the poisoned mantle of Nessus but also confers immortality upon him among the gods of Olympus.

Perhaps the golden coffin which transferred the body of Diarmaid from the mountain to the grave was itself symbolic of the ray of sunshine at the Winter Solstice conveying his soul to the Otherworld. At any rate, we may well surmise that this extraordinary event of the sun's visitation on the shortest day of the year, united with Aonghus Óg's remark about equipping Diarmaid with an 'aerial soul' so that he 'may be able to speak to me each day' is connected with the rejuvenation of the hero and his entrance into the world of the Ancestors.

There is a marked similarity between the later Indian and Classical examples cited. If anything, the Newgrange event is more strikingly spiritual, in the sense that it is the sun which is involved from the beginning in a most spectacular manner. In the Indian and Greek examples, the cremation fire was probably provided by the ancient method of fire sticks, in which two pieces of wood were rubbed vigorously together to produce sparks to ignite combustible material. In the case of Diarmaid, however, fire came directly from the sun and shone on him. This would seem to be the fulfilment of Aonghus Óg's statement of giving him an 'aerial soul'. The fiery ray of the sun descending on him was the 'aerial soul' which would make him a fellow-citizen of the gods and ancestors. From this on, his place was among the deities.

Something of a parallel to this is found in the largely uncharted territory of the Liturgy of the Catholic Church. This is not to say of course that there is any derivation of one from the other, but who is to say that certain common mind-patterns may not have been operating and prevalent in both the ancient and the medieval world.

On the Feast of Pentecost, the Holy Spirit descends on the apostles in the form of tongues of fire, and these fear-filled men, hidden away behind locked doors, are suddenly transformed into fearless preachers of the gospel.

The Collect or Opening Prayer of the Mass for Ember Saturday after Pentecost (Tridentine Rite) also speaks of this transforming fire:

Illo nos igne, quaesumus Domine, Spiritus Sanctus inflammet: quem Dominus noster Jesus Christus misit in terram, et voluit vehementer accendi (May the Holy Spirit, we beseech you, O Lord, kindle in us that same fire which our Lord Jesus Christ sent down upon earth, earnestly desiring that it should burn mightily).

This concise but complex text recalls Christ's words: 'I have come to bring fire to the earth, and how I wish it were blazing already' (Luke 12:49) The fire is the intervention of God in history in the incarnation, when God became man in Jesus Christ. It is present in the world of men but it is the Holy Spirit who will actually enkindle it in each individual person. So, we who are saying the prayer ask God the Father that the Holy Spirit may inflame us / set us on fire / enlighten us with the fire which Christ brought to earth. The text is concerned with transformation, with change of form brought about by fire, and God wants to lift us up and give us a share in his own fiery nature as he had shared our human nature when he became man. For fire is the great symbol of God.

After the Winter Solstice the sun begins to strengthen and the lengthening days proclaim his victory over the dark forces of chaos. This is an appropriate time for the making of Ancestors and the beam of light shining on the relics of the dead may indicate their deification.

The concept is clearly portrayed on the *ikonostasis* or ikon-screen in a church of the Byzantine Rite. The screen, with three doors, separates the nave or body of the church where the people are, from the sanctuary reserved to the priest and sacred ministers. Ikons of the saints adorn the ikonostasis and walls of the church and the people kiss them and light candles before them while the priest in magnificent vestments emerges from behind the screen to offer incense to them at several points during the liturgy. This is a familiar and moving example in our own day of the veneration of the Ancestors in a Christian form, preserved in that masterpiece of worship the great Byzantine Rite.

In a less spectacular way, in the Roman Rite, the faithful show their respect for the spiritual ancestors by lighting candles before shrines and by pilgrimages to sacred places.

In the Catholic and Orthodox Churches, obviously, Christ and the twelve apostles are the foundation of the church and this is shown in the Byzantine Rite by the ikons of the Last Supper and the twelve apostles high on the ikonostasis.

Nevertheless, throughout the centuries, what we call Spiritual Ancestors, or saints, may be added on in the process of canonisation. These are people of outstanding holiness, charity, zealous in following Christ, exemplary Christians who are recognised as such after extremely careful examination.

In the case of the neolithic, can we assume that a similar development took place and that, from time to time, some outstanding persons could be added to the original group of Ancestors? It is very likely that here also, as in the ancient churches, development could take place and the addition of new members to the group of original Ancestors could, perhaps, explain changes and additions of stones to the original monument. We may be considering a dynamic rather than a static reality.

If this is so, then the question of raising Diarmaid Ó Duibhne to the status of Ancestor as hinted in *Toraíocht Dhiarmada agus Ghráinne* is a distinct possibility. As to the eligibility of Diarmaid for such an honour, there is the remarkable account of his heroic actions on behalf of Fionn Mac Cumhaill and the Fianna given by himself in his dying moments. On a heroic scale, Diarmaid was a worthy candidate for ancestral status.

The argument is, then, that *Toraíocht Dhiarmada agus Ghráinne*, late though it be, may contain a folk-memory of a practice of Ancestor creation among the megalithic people of Brú na Bóinne, somewhat parallel to canonisation in the ancient churches of Christendom.

Another possibility occurs when we consider what we have called 'the funeral of Diarmaid', the procession from Beann Gulbán to Brú na Bóinne, the corpse being borne on a golden bier. Presumably, on arrival, the body was cremated or prepared in some way for burial and taken inside the chamber at Newgrange to await the shaft of light from the rising sun at the Winter Solstice which would awaken Diarmaid to a new life in the Otherworld among the gods and ancestors.

From this we turn to one of the most remarkable and elaborate of all Christian liturgies – the Consecration/Dedication of a Church – to see if there is any parallel.

In the Roman Rite, until drastically shortened and simplified after Vatican II, this was an extremely long and elaborate ceremony. It involved the local bishop and numerous clergy, who by the use of rituals drawn from both Roman and Gallican sources took possession of the new building for the religious use of the local Christians.

Some of the symbolic ritual was based on the Sacrament of Baptism: just as a person was introduced into membership of the Christian community by the water and anointing with oil in baptism, so there took place an elaborate sprinkling with holy water of the walls of the building, followed by anointing with oil. Another part of the ritual is claimed to come from Celtic sources. This was the writing of the alphabet in Latin and Greek on the floor of the church which had been strewed with ashes. This probably explains St Patrick's practice of 'writing alphabets' mentioned in early writings – he was consecrating new churches.

Apart from the elaborate sprinkling, anointing and writing of the Latin and Greek alphabet on the ashes on the floor of the new church, a most important and vital part of the rite was the transfer of relics of the saints from their former resting place into the altar of the new church where a small *sepulchrum* or burial chamber had been prepared for them. A cavity was cut out in the marble altar and the relics – small pieces of bone – were put into this tiny 'grave'. A stone cover, sealed with cement, completed the interment. It is this 'Transfer of Relics' which is the main point of comparison with the '*Toraíocht* – Brú na Bóinne event'. It may be significant that the Rite of Dedication of a Church owes much to Gaul where megaliths are well-known, especially in Brittany.

The Rite of the Consecration of a Church in the *Pontificale Romanum* places great emphasis on this 'Transfer of Relics' and, indeed, it was remembered at all Masses in the Tridentine Rite. At the very beginning, the priest ascended the altar and kissed the altar-stone containing the relics, saying: 'We beseech you, O Lord, by the merits of your saints whose relics are here, and of all the saints, that you may forgive me all my sins.'

In practice, it means that small portions of bone from the body of a saint are taken from his/her grave, or these relics may be preserved already in a shrine kept in a church. At any rate, these

relics, usually kept in a small, rich, ornamental casket or reli-
quary, are brought to a building very close to the church to be consecrated. In this temporary abode, they are treated with great honour and surrounded by many candles. On the night before the
Consecration/Dedication of the new church, an all-night Vigil is
held in this temporary oratory where the priests recite the Hours
of Matins and Lauds of the Divine Office in the presence of the
relics. This must be an extremely archaic custom. In Benedictine
monasteries today, when a death occurs in the community, members take it in turns to recite the psalms, verse by verse, throughout the night, in the presence of the body. That this is not an entirely
monastic tradition is indicated by the fact that the priestly stole is
put on over the monastic cowl for the occasion. When in search of
the archaic it is expedient to examine closely those ceremonial
procedures which are associated with birth, marriage and death.
In these basic events of human experience, archaic features tend
to be preserved, even though they have vanished from normal
everyday life.

In the Consecration of a Church, then, in the morning when the
new building has been duly prepared, the bishop and his assistants go to the oratory where the relics are. An ornamental reli-
quary or casket containing them is placed on a bier placed on the
shoulders of four priests dressed in red vestments. A procession
to the new church sets out with torches and incense preceding the
bier as at a funeral. During the procession, Antiphons are sung:

> With joy may you appear and go forward with rejoicing, for
> even the mountains and hills themselves leap with joy as they
> await your coming.

> Rise up, O Saints of God from your dwellings, sanctify these
> places, bless the people and preserve us sinners in peace.

When the procession arrives at the new church it does not
enter but makes a circuit of the building, proceeding *tuathal* (anticlockwise) until it arrives back at the door. During the circumambulation with the relics, *Kyrie eleison* (Lord have mercy) is said
continuously. Even to this day, in some parts of the country, the
coffin is carried around the graveyard before it is brought in for

burial, as if the dead man first honours the resident dead by the ancient practice of circumambulation before joining their ranks. It may be noted that the Irish practice is to go *deiseal* (clockwise), keeping the sacred object – holy well, church, fire, etc. – at one's right hand, following the course of the sun, whereas the ecclesiastical custom is different.

After the circumambulation of the church, the relics are brought in and the bishop places them in the small sepulchre prepared for them in the altar. They are covered with a little stone slab which is firmly cemented in place and, now, the saints have taken up their new abode where they will listen to the local people's prayers and attend to their spiritual and temporal needs: as the Antiphon of the interment puts it:

> Under the altar of God you have accepted a dwelling-place, O Saints of God; intercede for us to Our Lord Jesus Christ. The Saints will rejoice in glory and rejoice in their beds.

The saints are seen as inhabiting the two worlds of heaven and earth and acting as intermediaries between them. The saints, whose relics are being transferred to their new home, are addressed directly and the reason for their transferral is indicated.

Being a tale belonging to the late *Fiannaíocht* Cycle, *Toraíocht Dhiaramada agus Ghráinne* would normally be expected to use the 'Samhain, Imbolg, Bealtaine, Lughnasa' calendar. If, then, the transfer of the body from Beann Gulban to Brú na Bóinne took place at Samhain, there would be an interval of six weeks between it and the Winter Solstice (21 December).

Now, might it not be, that this six weeks interval served a ritual purpose?

This would have been the well-known practice of 'Excarnation' described by Andrew Collins:

> This is the process whereby human remains are denuded by scavenger birds, vultures in particular, before the remaining bones are gathered up and deposited in a disarticulated state within what is known as a secondary burial. This was a regular practice in Neolithic times, and has also been carried out in recent times by various indigenous peoples. For example, such

burials form part of the funerary practices of various American tribes, and to this day Tibetans still practise 'sky burial' as they call it, indeed, like their cousins the Zoro-astrians of Iran, the Mandaeans also once practised excarn-ation, linking them directly with the Neolithic cult of the dead (*The Cygnus Mystery*, London, 2008, 18).

This may be another version of the hunter-gatherer custom of leaving the body of the hunter exposed in the woods to be the prey of wild birds and beasts – a form of paying back to nature the debt it owed to nature for the gift of life and sustenance, as we saw it dramatised in the rite of 'Hunting the Wren'.

The dead may have been exposed to the *Badhbh* or scavenger crow on a wooden platform at the centre of a circle of wooden posts following the indications of such features at Knowth and at Ballynahatty, Co Down. Such a structure could have served as a ritual site for circumambulations and the disarticulation of the skeleton in preparation for the second part of the funeral – the de-position of the bones in the megalithic tomb. The six week interval between Samhain and the Winter Solstice might have served as the excarnation period before what remained was taken inside the tomb for the Winter Solstice event, which would proclaim the assumption of the hero to the divine status.

In this matter of the ritual use of Brú na Bóinne, what I have been doing is searching for clues as to what might have taken place there and the conclusion reached is that the site was connected to two vital operations, firstly, the Sacred Marriage (*Banais Rí*) – the marriage of the Sky-God to the Earth-Mother to guarantee the fertility of the land – and secondly, a centre for the inauguration of Ancestors, again bound up with the welfare of the community and bearing some resemblance to the canonisation of saints in the Catholic Church.

Since there are no written documents from this remote period of 5,000 years ago, all we can do is to gather what may be clues to primitive observance from folk-memories and the ritual customs of indigenous peoples, as well as from seasonal folk-dramas, mummers' plays and children's plays. This is no place for 'infallib-ility' but, on the grounds that it is better to have some theory rather than none, we piece together what we have and try to form some kind of picture of what may have happened in this far away past.

I have brought to the reader's attention two ancient stories *Tochmarc Étaíne* and *Toraíocht Dhiarmada agus Ghráinne* as well as the *Rite of Consecration of a Church*, on the grounds that I suspect that these contain some very archaic ritual elements which might give some clues to the mysteries of Brú na Bóinne.

CHAPTER TWELVE

The Constellation of the Swan

In his outstanding work of research *The Cygnus Mystery* (London, 2008), Andrew Collins has brought together a large collection of sources relative to the importance of the northern sky in ancient thought and to the orientation of temples towards the north, rather than towards the east, at a very early period. This is the area of the North Pole – Polaris as we know it today, but due to the changes in the earth's axis over the millennia this was not always so. The great constellation Cygnus (the Swan) or Northern Cross in the Milky Way became the centre around which the circumpolar stars rotated creating the idea of stability, order, rest, eternity in the heavens, in contrast to the wandering habits of other stars which appeared and disappeared at different seasons of the year. Cygnus is in fact one of the few constellations which closely resembles its designation for it very obviously looks like a swan with outstretched wings in full flight. It is marked by the intensely bright star Deneb. Collins develops his thought on the mystique of the swan in folklore and in such an ancient tale as *Aisling Aonghusa* in which the god of Brú na Bóinne falls hopelessly in love with the 'Swan-Maiden', *Caor Iúbharmhéith*.

She alternates annually between woman and swan. After much searching , he eventually finds her at the lake of *Loch Bhéal Dragain* (lake of the dragon's mouth) in present Co Tipperary, at Samhain, along with 150 companion swans, each pair joined with a silver chain.

Here Aonghus meets Caor who is in the form of a swan. They fly around the lake three times and then set out for Brú na Bóinne. On arrival, the lovers sing and the people of the Brú fall asleep for three days and three nights. The girl remained with Aonghus after that. Could there be some obscure reference here to an archaic period when the Constellation of the Swan (Cygnus) was an important feature in the astronomy of the Bend of the Boyne? And is it significant that the lake mentioned in the story is Loch Bhéal Dragain (the lake of the dragon's mouth) considering that Cygnus lies very close to the Constellation of Draco (the dragon) in the northern sky?

Collins comments briefly on the vast array of references to the mystique of the Swan:

> Today we can accept that there was once a worldwide proliferation of interest in Cygnus as a symbol of cosmic life and death. What is more, situated at the northern extreme of the Milky Way – universally seen as an astral road or river to the sky world – it marked the entrance to the realms of light, the abode of the gods and the place of the afterlife, a belief that could well go back to paleolithic times (90).

This area of Cygnus (Northern Cross), as a place of stellar stability, may have been considered as the area of creation, the area of 'the unmoved mover' from which the scattered elements of the created elements of the visible world emanated and to which, in due time, they would return to 'rest in peace'.

Strangely, a similar idea is found in the *Hymn to a Confessor Bishop* in the *Monastic Breviary*:

> *Sit salus illi, decus atque virtus,*
> *Qui supra caeli residens cacumen,*
> *Totius mundi machinam gubernat,*
> *Trinus et unus.*
>
> (To the Three in One be respect, honour and greeting. The Trinity lives above the highest point of the heavens and controls the machinery (workings) of the whole world.)

The phrases *caeli cacumen* and *regna polorum* in official ecclesiastical texts seem to indicate an interest in the circumpolar region of the sky, well in accord with the most ancient traditions of man as he stands in awe before the night sky and the ordered 'machinery' of the heavens as it rolls on eternally.

Emerging from the idea of the Constellation Cygnus (Swan) as the area of creation and the place to which people's souls return after they die comes the mystique of the swan.

Three recent authors have done a great deal of research on this highly complex matter and have thrown light on a remarkably obscure subject. These are Anthony Murphy and Richard Moore in their book, *Island of the Setting Sun; In Search of Ireland's Ancient Astronomers* and Andrew Collins in *The Cygnus Mystery*.

Apart from the wealth of myth and folklore associated with this majestic bird, Newgrange is a very important wintering ground for whooper swans coming from breeding grounds in Iceland and this may have been a feature of this part of the country since the construction of the monuments of Brú na Bóinne.

It is suggested, for instance, that the internal plan of Newgrange forms a cross or cruciform shape like the Christian Cross but also the shape of the Constellation Cygnus (the Swan) which again is in the shape of a swan in flight. The long passageway into the mound suggests the long straight neck of the swan, the two sidechambers represent the outstretched wings and the back chamber represents the tail, while the body of the swan is represented by the large central chamber of Newgrange. The egg-shaped form of some monuments as well as creation-myths involving the world-egg further suggests a connection with the swan or the goose. This swan connection also involves the idea of re-birth, re-creation as the phenomenon of the penetration of light into the chamber at the Winter Solstice heralds the birth of the sun of the new year.

As already explained, the role the Constellation Cygnus was of immense importance in former ages as being the Polar Region (*Regna polorum*) from which life emerged and returned.

This *emergence* and *return*, Creation and Dissolution, can be seen as the archetypal birth and death.

Folklore frequently describes the newly-born baby as having been brought by the stork/swan from the otherworld and presented to the new mother and similarly, at death, the soul is often depicted as making its exit from the mouth of the dying person as a bird and taking off on its flight to the Otherworld.

In the neolithic context in Ireland, however, it appears that the strange habit of the swan's emigration to Iceland and her later return to Ireland may have been seen as the occasion of the swan's acting as ferryman of the sky to transfer the souls of the deceased to the region of the polar stars and later to bring them back again to this world to be reincarnated in newly-born infants and live a human life all over again, while not perhaps having any recollection of their former human existence. It may be that some of these souls who had been transferred to the starry realms did not wish to return but perhaps some did. In the story of Oisín the great warrior of the Fianna, he has been taken to Tír na nÓg, the Land of Youth, by the goddess Niamh Chinn Óir, of the golden hair, and for 300 years, according to human reckoning, has lived in the greatest state of happiness and luxury. Yet, he feels a longing to return to see his old friends and experience the old life, simple and primitive as it may have been and no match for the glories of Tír na nÓg. In the story, Niamh reluctantly allowed him to return to this world for a brief visit to renew old acquaintances, as it were, but warned him on no account to touch the soil of Ireland. He did indeed return, but everything had changed, his old friends were gone and new people had taken their place. Then he fell off his magic horse on the soil of Ireland and immediately became an old man weighed down by the years that had passed, while the horse turned around and galloped back to Tír na nÓg. This was a sad return from the Otherworld and here there was no question of reincarnation.

On the other hand, in the story of Mongán, king of part of Ulster, it becomes known that even though he is reigning happily and successfully as king, he is, in fact, a reincarnation of Fionn Mac Cumhaill, the Chief of Fianna Éireann in a former existence and he is aware of historical occurrences which he couldn't have known about unless he had been around at a previous time.

In view of the long *Leaba Dhiarmada agus Ghráinne* tradition which held that the great megalithic tombs throughout the country, in which Diarmaid and Gráinne slept on their flight from Fionn, were centres of fertility where women could easily become pregnant, could the thought have been that these monuments were places where the carrier-swans, returning from the polar stars, deposited the souls of those who wished to be reincarnated? Here, the returned souls may have waited until a pregnant woman came along and then became reincarnated in her, so that the soul of the embryo was in fact the soul of somebody who had previously lived on earth, and who later on in life may show certain characteristics of his former existence. Hindus make jokes about over-friendly, gregarious individuals by saying that they were politicians in a former life.

The swan, then, may be considered as a 'Psychopomp' from the Greek *Psyche* (soul) and *pompos* (conductor) – a conductor of souls to and from the Otherworld in the region of the polar stars. The swan differs from the great Christian Psychopomp, St Michael the Archangel, who leads souls into heaven. In so far as this is a one-way traffic operation, he deposits the souls in heaven and leaves them there. The Christian belief is that the souls in heaven are enjoying the Beatific Vision or consciousness of God to a supreme degree and are so preoccupied and charmed by the revelation of God's nature in its infinite variety that they feel no longing to return to earth.

The swan tradition, however, seems to operate on a different system, transporting souls to and from the circumpolar stars.

What a strange phenomenon it is that, even today, the supreme ambition of so many young women is to become 'a Star', to be numbered among the 'Stars of the Silver Screen'. One wonders if this vocabulary is derived from an age-old consciousness of the glory and eternity of the starry sky and its link with the destiny of the person.

At any rate, the emphasis on the Constellation of the Swan along with its folkloric associations with birth may give a clue to a basic neolithic belief that the final resting place of the soul of human beings was among the stars in the northern realm in the Milky Way associated with Cygnus.

This belief appears to have differed from the typical Christian belief in the permanent residence of the soul in the Otherworld for the corporeal or earthly swan, who was a figure of the astral swan, (Cygnus) operated as a psychopomp or soul-carrier in two directions.

On this basis, we can well speculate on what an 'Otherworldly' religion the neolithic system of belief must have been, with its

constant looking towards the Northern Stars shining brilliantly in
the night sky and wondering in which part of it one's humanly
dead but astrally alive relatives were living, or perhaps wondering if they had actually left the place and been reincarnated, so
that the possibility of meeting one of them in this world, without
recognising him, could not be excluded. The situation certainly
led to exciting possibilities. Examining the night-sky must have
been a great act of religion, something like a traditional 'Retreat' in
the Catholic Church where the retreatants are encouraged to leave
aside worldly affairs for a little while and direct their thoughts to
the purpose of life: death, eternity and life in the world to come.
Indeed, Christians could do worse than gaze reflectively at the
starry sky and be filled with awe at the mighty expanse of the
heavens and the incomprehensible distance between the heavenly
bodies, which scientists calculate in terms of light-years. Psalm 19
(18) discusses the phenomenon of the heavens:

> The night-sky proclaims the glory of God,
> the day-sky, his creative skill;
> day after day, this is re-attested,
> night after night, this is reaffirmed.

> Not by speaking, not by talking,
> Not by any sound that can be heard,
> But, by spanning the whole earth,
> This message reaches the entire world.

Star-gazing must have been a feature of life from the earliest times,
engendering a feeling of wonder and awe at the vast expanse of
the sky with its multitude of stars. Perhaps no other exercise can
arouse such a feeling of the littleness of man in face of such a vast
panorama of celestial lights. This too, at a later date, must have
been part of what the Christian Celts called the *Reacht Aiceanta* –
the law of nature – the revelation of God in nature previous to and
independent of the written revelation of the Bible.

It would seem, then, that orientation towards some particular
point in the heavens or earth has been a feature of human behaviour from a very early period. This point, however, varied
according to different peoples or periods and was looked upon as

a centre of great sanctity: if on earth, a place of pilgrimage for the faithful where new life, energy and inspiration was available from the Deity; if in the heavens, a place for the dead, the ancestors and the gods themselves and perhaps some sacred sanctuaries gathered all together – the dead, the ancestors, the deities and the living humans in one great gathering place for one overwhelming religious experience.

Today, Christians turn to the east for prayer; Muslims turn towards Mecca, Christian Celts turn to the east (*cosa an mhairbh soir*) while Pagan Celts turn to the west, to *Tech nDoinn* and the region of the setting sun. It would seem that in the remote past when the Constellation of Cygnus marked the area of the circumpolar stars, people turned to this region of the Swan and the Milky Way, the north, a custom still maintained by the Mandeans.

While the direction might vary according to the underlying particular philosophy, the system of orientation served to direct the individual human person outside of himself and connected him to the awesome cosmos of which he was a part. Was the 'Primordial Vision' of the Ancients, in which they saw themselves as integral parts of the vast complex of the Universe, the great 'Health Design' now threatened by 'Alienation' in which man feels himself alone in the world, cut off from people and from nature?

In the thought of the great nineteenth-century German theologian Schleiermacher, religion, properly understood, was intrinsic to human nature, the highest expression of self-consciousness, which at its best is also God consciousness. Redemption, in the Christian sense, embracing the death and resurrection of Christ, is necessary because man in his weakness and imperfection has lost his consciousness, awareness, of God and his attention has wandered off to dwell on material things and diverse preoccupations. As a result, man's sense of the infinite is obscured. As a consequence, his life has become fragmented and disoriented, having no central focus.

> Christianity is unique and universally valid because it is the only religion to make redemption central. Christ is unique because he had a perfect, uninterrupted God consciousness, and

because he had no need of redemption himself (which distinguishes him from other founders of religions). Rather he was the initiator and mediator of man's redemption. We receive the effects of his life and work through participation in the life of the Spirit in the church, the redemptive community. Redemption means the fulfilment of true humanity as intended by God, and men are so constituted that no individual can be completely fulfilled until all are brought into harmonious and loving relationship with each other in the kingdom of God (Wiest, W. E., *New Catholic Encyclopedia*, Art: Scleiermacher).

It appears that in his theological thinking Schleiermacher is giving expression to the link between the mankind's primal vision of being one with God and the rest of creation and the recovery of this lost or obscured vision through the work of Christ. Christ was the total embodiment of the primal vision for he was totally absorbed in his consciousness of God. This is reminiscent of the folk-story regarding St Brigid's uninterrupted awareness of God in contrast to St Brendan's wayward orientations between God and temporal affairs. The effect of the story is amplified by the introduction of the lowly whale who was able to distinguish precisely who was totally absorbed in God and who was not.

Christ, then, is the 'Totally Aware of God One'. He has the Divine vision. He comes among those who have lost this vision and leads them back to the primal vision. Here all are seen, united in God. This is universal harmony.

Perhaps Emily Bronte, in her poem 'No coward soul is mine' which in its elemental expression resembles her great novel *Wuthering Heights*, is in some way reflecting on the theological viewpoints of Schleiermacher.

O God within my breast,
Almighty, ever-present Deity.
Life, that in me hast rest,
As I, Undying Life, have power in Thee.

With wide-embracing love
Thy spirit animates eternal years,

Pervades and broods above,
Changes, sustains, dissolves, creates and rears.

Though earth and moon were gone,
And suns and universes ceased to be,
And Thou were left alone,
Every existence would exist in Thee.

There is not room for Death,
Nor atom that his might could render void,
Since Thou art being and breath,
And what Thou art may never be destroyed.

In this extraordinary exposition of Emily Bronte's personal religion, one senses an affinity with the stark 'nature-utterances' of
early Celtic religious pronouncements such as the *Song of Amergin*
the druid as he placed his right foot for the first time on the earth of
Ireland:

Is gaoth ar muir mé; Is loch i maigh mé; Is fuaim mara mé.' (I am the
wind on the sea; I am a lake in a plain; I am the sound of the sea, etc.)
(Macalister, R., *Lebor Gabala Erenn*, Dublin 1956, V, 110-111).

Some would look for a Celtic influence on the genius-author
of *Wuthering Heights* in the wild raw expression of nature in the
Yorkshire Moors, while others would look to her Ulster ancestry
especially in the person of Pádraig Ó Pronntaigh who wrote the
early novel of Celtic mythology and adventure *Eachtra na gCuradh*
(Eagarthoir: Ní Chléirigh, Meadhbh, Baile Átha Cliath, 1941). At
the end of the book the author signs himself:

Finis air *Eachtra na cCuradh* airna sgríobhadh le Pádhruig Ua
Pronntaigh chum úsáide gach léightheora ... An ceathramh lá
déag don Mí October, anno Domini 1761. Guidhim beannacht
gach léightheora a n-onóir na Trionóide (End of *Eachtra na
gCuradh* –Adventure of the Heroes –for the use of each reader,
14 October 1761. I ask the blessing of each reader in honour of
the Trinity).

The theologian Huston Smith concludes his book, *The World's
Religions* (San Francisco, 1991, 382) by quoting John Collier, one
time United States Commissioner of Indian Affairs:

They had what the world has lost; the ancient lost reverence and passion for human personality joined with the ancient lost reverence and passion for the earth and its web of life. Since before the Stone Age they have tended that passion as a central sacred fire. It should be our long hope to renew it in us all.

By drawing on such ancient sources as those of India and the Native Americans as living examples of a philosophical system in which matter is considered to be penetrated by spirit, we can get some idea of an alternative worldview whose loss may lead to ecological disaster on a massive scale. The prevailing mindset tends to see man as the master of creation which he can adapt or control as he finds convenient. The other paradigm is that of man as a partner in creation in which man may alter aspects of creation slightly and gently, while seeing himself as a part of the vast panorama of the Universe. These are sometimes referred to as the 'Master and Partner Paradigms'. The biblical account of the Creation states: 'Yahweh God took the man and settled him in the garden of Eden to cultivate and take care of it' (Gen 2:15). This, however, is often taken as meaning that man has utter control of the earth and can use it as he wishes, as God also said to Adam and Eve: 'Be fruitful, multiply, fill the earth and subdue it. Be masters of the fish of the sea, the birds of heaven, and all the living creatures that move on earth' (Gen 1:28).

As we have already seen, man must have been in very close partnership with creation during the 'hunter-gatherer' period of society, but with the more settled and agricultural forms of the neolithic period mankind was already slipping away from this close embrace of nature and securing more control over his environment and activities. Nevertheless, despite all the marvellous scientific advances, climate change, tsunamis, tornadoes and the like make it extremely clear that man's control of nature is quite limited.

Now, in terms of theology, we can look on God from two basic points of view, both of which are correct.

God is 'transcendent'. This means that God is beyond anything which we can visualise or imagine. While man is made in the image of God, God is more unlike man than like him. In the liturgical texts God is addressed as 'All-powerful and ever-living God';

'God, all-powerful Father'; 'Almighty God'; 'God, our Father'; 'All-powerful, Eternal God'; 'Father of everlasting goodness.' These terms try to express the mystery of God, but those who use these terms know perfectly well that these terms are inadequate in describing God. God is infinite, without beginning or end, and the best we can do is to use finite terms containing the notion of 'distance' and 'height' to give some idea of his divine nature.

But God is not only 'transcendent' and infinitely distant from us, he is also 'immanent' – very near us, he inhabits everything, he is in the trees, he is in the rivers, he is in all the forms of nature, he is in ourselves.

Now, it appears that the Church, while accepting that God was also immanent, tended to emphasise the transcendence of God, the Distant God. Since the desire of man's heart is to be united with God as his final end and fulfilment, the provision of a hierarchy to lead the person gradually to this distant God, is important.

On the other hand, the Celts and other ancient peoples seem to emphasise the immanence of God – the idea that God was very near, surrounding us on all sides. With this mentality, the person seeking God and realising that God was very near, tried to build up in himself an awareness of the divine presence and immanence. So that progress in holiness would consist of developing, to a high level, an awareness or consciousness of God. He would see the various phenomena of life, the trees, the earth, the rocks, the rivers, the birds and animals, etc, as manifestations of the Divine – God was sending out his *neart* or 'life-force' from himself to take on these various forms temporarily. This makes one very conscious of the great mystery of creation, for one is aware that the most ordinary walk in the countryside is an 'Epiphany' – a 'manifestation' of God expressing himself in various ways in the different types of vegetation, animals, birds, clouds, that one encounters on the way. Everything is more than it appears to be, filling one with a feeling of awe and wonderment like a mother looking at her baby.

In a remarkable verse, the poet Elizabeth Browning expresses the great mystery of creation in terms of the immanence of God while referring back to the biblical story of the Burning Bush:

Earth is crammed with heaven,
and every common bush afire with God;
but only he who sees
takes off his shoes.

The poet is expressing the ancient feeling of awe of creation as she realises that the external form of the tree is not all that is. The bush contains the *neart* or life-force which only the initiated see. The original account of the Burning Bush gives powerful expression to the worshipful awe which ancient man felt in the presence of the great phenomena of nature:

> The angel of Yahweh appeared to him (Moses) in a flame blazing from the middle of a bush. Moses looked; there was the bush blazing, but the bush was not being burnt up. Moses said 'I must go across and see this strange sight, and why the bush is not being burnt up.' When Yahweh saw him going across to look, God called to him from the middle of the bush. 'Moses, Moses' he said. 'Here I am', he answered. 'Come no nearer' he said. 'Take off your sandals, for the place where you are standing is holy ground. I am the God of your ancestors' he said, 'the God of Abraham, the God of Isaac and the God of Jacob.' At this Moses covered his face, for he was afraid to look at God. (Exodus 3:2-6)

What a wonderful guide to worship this biblical episode is. Moses covers his face for he was afraid of God revealing himself so openly, considering what would happen to him if he gazed directly at God, just as we are wary of looking directly at the sun when it shines intensely. Moses is told to take off his shoes in this special place made holy by the manifestation of God. This is a gesture to be seen still at the Divine Liturgy (Mass) in the Coptic Rite when the people take off their shoes when approaching to receive Holy Communion.

The appearance of God in the form of fire in the incident of the Burning Bush is exceptional in the sense that the *neart* or dynamic life force emanating from God is capable of being seen. But it is there just as really when it is not seen, so that to the Celts and other ancient societies every bush was a burning bush 'afire with God'.

They had the awareness, the 'Awen' or supernatural insight, and so they treated the earth with care, for it was holy ground. Like the Burning Bush the earth was *Ardens sed Virens* (burning but green).

There is a marked likeness between this expression of the immanence of God and St Paul's speech before the council of the Areopagus as recorded in the Acts of the Apostles: 'And he (God) did this (created the world) so that they (people) might seek the deity and by feeling their way towards him, succeed in finding him; and indeed he is not far from any of us, since it is in him that we live, and move, and exist, as indeed some of your own writers have said' (Acts 17:27-28). A note in *The New Jerusalem Bible* remarks that this phrase ' in him we live, and move, and exist' is an expression suggested by the poet Epimenides of Cnossos, sixth century BC. It may come as a surprise to some that St Paul should quote this pre-Christian Greek poet with approval.

In the *Roman Missal* (1974), in the Preface of the Mass for Sundays in Ordinary time, VI, the same phrase, 'In you we live and move and have our being', receives highly theological development:

> In you we live and move and have our being. Each day you show us a Father's love; your Holy Spirit, dwelling within us, gives us on earth the hope of unending joy.
>
> Your gift of the Spirit, who raised Jesus from the dead, is the foretaste and promise of the paschal feast of heaven.

The text connects two worlds: firstly, this present world in which we experience the initial presence of the Spirit. But this Spirit which we now have, at least in some initial way, is, as it were, the first-fruits, it is pointing to a greater abundance of the Spirit in the next and everlasting world, just as a farmer looking at his field of wheat notices that some patches of corn are already ripe, and he knows that the rest of the corn will soon turn golden as well. We might think of Christ being led by the Spirit into the desert after his baptism, on one hand, and then, on the other hand, the abundance of the Spirit poured out on him at the resurrection/ transfiguration. This could mean that the presence of the Spirit was manifested in different degrees on different occasions. One wonders, however, was St Paul superimposing his own ideas of the Holy Spirit, the third Person of the Blessed Trinity, on the foundation of the pagan poet's concept of *neart* or the animating 'life-force' common to many peoples from remote ages.

The unifying function of the spirit or life-force is well expressed in a text from the West Indian tradition:

> From Wakan Tanka, the Great Spirit, came a great unifying life-force that flowed through all things, the flowers of the plains, blowing winds, trees, birds and animals, and was the same force that had been breathed into the first man. Thus all things were kindred and were all brought together by the one mystery (Luther Standing Bear, *Laxoto: A Natural Education*, Summerton 1944, 14).

A more specific and elaborate expression of this unifying life-force is found, however, in many forms and in many parts of the world and seems to be a significant part of the Celtic understanding of creation. This is the Purusa Myth and it explains many obscure points, particularly relating to sacrifice. In Indian tradition Purusa is the primordial man whom the gods dismember, and the various parts of his dismembered body become the diverse parts of the Universe.

Firstly, the dismemberment of Purusa results in the formation of the four groups of Indian society:

> His mouth became the Brahmin; his arms were made into the Warrior, his thighs the People, and from his feet the Servants were born (O'Flaherty, W. (trs), *The Rig Vega*, Penguin 1981, 31).

From this, the myth moves on to the creation of man: 'The moon was born from his mind; from his eye the sun was born … and from his vital breath the wind was born.'

There are many different versions of the Purusa Creation Formula and they can be tabulated conveniently as follows:

From his Head comes the Sky;
From his Brain comes the Clouds;
From his Eyes comes the Sun;
From his Mind comes the Moon;

From his Flesh comes the Earth;
From his Hair comes Vegetation;
From his Breath comes the Wind;
From his Blood comes the Water.

It is obvious that this creation myth is very different from the familiar story from the Bible on the creation of the world out of nothing, in six days. Here the world is not created from nothing but from the dismembered body of Purusa, so that the Creator is inside his creation rather than outside of it.

It can be seen also that there is a certain likeness between the parts of Purusa's body and the allo-forms, the correspondences in the created world. Even today, a highly intelligent but not very practical academic is spoken of as 'having his head in the clouds'. In chemists' shops 'mud-packs' are on sale as an aid to keeping the flesh fresh and healthy, and here the correspondence of flesh and earth is clearly seen. It was an old custom in some places that after a haircut, the hair was buried under a sod. The presumption apparently was that medicinal herbs might grow from the severed hair which (herbs) could be used as 'Herbal Shampoo' to improve the condition of the hair. In this way the idea of a cosmic circle was established.

In Egypt there was the custom of making a cloth image of the murdered and dismembered god Osiris and filling it with sand and fertile clay in which corn was sown. When watered and exposed to the sun, the corn sprouted and sprang up through the mummy-like image. The wheat grew from the body of the god.

Similarly, in the case of the Indonesian goddess Hainuwele, a spiral dance is being performed and Hainuwele is being pushed into the centre by the movement of the dancers. There she is thrown into a pit and sacrificed. Then her body is dismembered and the pieces are taken around and buried in various places in the island of Ceram. From these pieces, various types of plants grow and these produce different types of food upon which the people live. In other words, Hainuwele, sacrificed and dismembered, becomes the sustaining food of the population.

The great mythologist Joseph Campbell sees this ritual formula as being of basic importance and central to ancient thought:

The underlying myth is of a divine being, slain, cut up, and the parts buried, which thereupon turn into the food plants on which the community lives; and the leading theme, as I have said in my earlier work, is the coming of death into the world; the particular point being that it comes by way of murder. The second point is that the food plants on which man lives derive from that death. And finally, the sexual organs, according to this mythology, appeared at the time of that coming of death; for reproduction without death would have been a calamity, as would death without reproduction. Hence, we may state now, once again, 'that the interdependence of death and sex, their import as the complementary aspects of a single state of being, and the necessity of killing – killing and eating – for the continuance of this state of being, which is that of man on earth, and of all things on earth, the animals, birds, and fish, as well as man – this deeply moving, emotionally disturbing glimpse of death as the life of the living is the fundamental motivation supporting the rites around which the social structure of the early planting villages was composed.' And it was also, we have now to add, the fundamental motive out of which the entire mythology, civilisation, and philosophy of India has grown. (*Oriental Mythology*, 164)

Peter O'Connor remarks: 'This type of belief persists to the present day in the Catholic practice of taking the host to be the body of Christ' (*Beyond the Mist*, London 2000, 202).

Another formulation of the 'Purusa/Hainuwele Myth' describes the Polynesian Ulu returning from the temple and telling his wife that the god Mo'o has made known to him that he will die tonight, and he instructs her on what to do with his dead body.

She is to bury his head carefully near their spring of running water and his heart near the door of the house. His feet, legs and arms are to be buried in the same way. Having given these instructions, Ulu fell on his face and died.

His wife sang the traditional lament for the dead and carried out his instructions precisely.

In the morning, the house was surrounded by vegetation which had grown from the various parts of Ulu's body. From his heart had grown the great bread-fruit tree and this was called 'Ulu' in his remembrance. Near the well the banana tree grew and all around were sugar-cane and yams and sundry other plants which supply healthy food for the area (Campbell, 1976, 200-201).

In the story, Ulu is not 'murdered', that is ritually slain as a re-enactment of the 'murder' of Purusa or Hainuwele, but he is told of imminent death by the voice of a god and his wife carries out the *Sparagmos* or dismemberment and burial precisely as instructed. While the myth concentrates on food production, the idea of health-producing plants is present also as the story tells of the little son of the couple who is sickly but, having eaten the plants, becomes extremely healthy and ends up as a famous warrior. In this, the story reiterates the motif of the health-restoring herbs which grew from the body of Miach in the Irish myth of Dian Cecht and Airme where 365 herbs grew from the body of the murdered Miach, one for each of the 365 diseases with which humans are afflicted. Airme, Miach's sister, had spread her cloak at the side of his grave and had begun to lay out the herbs on it in the order in which they grew on the body – the herb which grew from his forehead would cure headache, that from his heart would cure heart disease, and so on – but before she had time to memorise the exact layout of the herbs her father, Dian Cecht, who had murdered Miach, arrived and snatching up the cloak scattered the herbs in all directions, so that we no longer know which herb will cure which disease.

Joseph Campbell explains with great perception (*Primitive Mythology*, 181-182) that the sacrifice of life involved, as in Miach, Ulu, Hainuwele, are not *Do ut des* (I give so that you may give back) sacrifices in which an offerer gives a gift to the god to induce him to do him some favour – as for instance when a Catholic woman prays and lights a candle before a statue of the Blessed Virgin Mary so that her daughter may get a job. The Purusa sacrifice and dismemberment is different. It belongs, rather, to the category of mimesis, imitation, re-enactment of what has happened to the god himself:

> These are not gifts, bribes, or dues rendered to God, but fresh enactments, here and now, of the god's own sacrifice in the

beginning, through which he, she, or it became incarnate in the world process. Moreover, all the ritual acts around which the village community is organised, and through which its identity is maintained, are functions and partial revelations of this immortal sacrifice.

Campbell points to the similarity of the Purusa myth to the Christian myth while noting the stress on the guilt-aspect in the latter case:

Something of the sort can be felt in the Christian myth of the killed, buried, resurrected, and eaten Jesus, whose mystery is the ritual of the altar and communion rail. But here the ultimate monstrosity of the divine drama is not stressed so much as the guilt of man in having brought it about; and we are asked to look forward to a last day, when the run of this cosmic tragedy of crime and punishment will be terminated and the kingdom of God realised on earth, as it is now in heaven (*Primitive Mythology*, 182-183).

The 'ultimate monstrosity' is the killing and dismemberment of the god for the creation of the universe, but Christianity tends to stress the guilt of mankind for the death of Christ, whereas the pagan view stresses the act itself which resulted in providing food and medicine.

Perhaps the killing and dismemberment of Purusa resulted, in the first place, in the production of the four elements – earth, air, fire and water, which then, in different combinations, proceeded to form the diverse phenomena of the world.

As we have seen, the myth had very wide distribution and occurs in a variety of versions. One of these is the hilarious English Folk Drama 'The Old Tup' or 'The Derby Ram' from Nottinghamshire performed by about six men with blackened faces at Christmas time, the Winter Solstice. The players, like the *Dreoilín* (Wren Hunt) in Ireland, went from house to house to perform the play carrying a Tup – an artificial ram. Outside the door they sang:

There is a little tup,
and he's standing at your door;
And if you'll have him in, Sir,

He'll please you more and more.

Those inside sing: 'Bring him in, bring him in.'

They all troop in; the man playing the part of 'tup' has a home-made ram's head, with a cloth covering the rest of his body. He is led in, prancing, on a rope. Then the Otherworldly characteristics of the ram are chanted:

The very first day that tup was born,
He cut some funny capers.
He ate a field of turnip tops,
And fourteen tons of taters,
Bailey, Bailey, laddie-fer-lairey-aye.

The wool that grew (up) on his back, Sir,
It grew so mighty long,
The eagles built their nests in it,
I heard the young ones' song,
Bailey ...

They horns that grew up on his head,
They grew so mighty high,
That every time he shook his head,
They rattled against the sky,
Bailey ...

They then call for a butcher; he enters, and with a knife, proceeds to 'kill' the ram who collapses on the ground.

The remaining verses describe the uses made of the dismembered body of the ram;

All the women in Derby
Came begging for his hide,
To make some leather aprons
To last them all their lives,
Bailey ...

All the young lads in Derby
Came begging for his eyes
To kick them up and down the street
For footballs and bulls-eyes,
Bailey ...

All the ringers in Derby
Came ringing for his tail,
To ring the Derby passing-bell
That hangs upon the wall, Bailey ...

This concludes the play. A collection is held and cakes and ale are distributed (Abrahams, R., 'Folk Arts; Folk Drama', in Dorson, R., (ed), *Folklore and Folklife – An Introduction*, Chicago 1972, 355-357).

What a marvellous piece of folk-drama this is. The giant ram represents Purusa in his vastness. He is killed and dismembered. The severed parts of his body are not, in this case, used for food or medicine but for the daily purposes of country life – leather aprons, footballs, and ropes. One wonders if the phrase 'Bailey,Bailey, laddie-fer-lairey-aye' is a 'nonsense-rhyme' or if it is a remnant of some phrase in a long-forgotten language from the remote past to match the sacred time element of the Winter Solstice. In any case, this is a fascinating example of a local folk-drama preserving and expressing the great international myth of Purusa.

It does seem that the Purusa Myth may be recognised in the last dramatic episode of the renowned Celtic saga *Táin Bó Cuailnge*, the Cattle Raid of Cooley, Co Louth. This is the most famous of this type of story and is found in *The Book of Leinster* (12th century) but in some form it may go back to a much earlier period. It gives a long complex account of Meadhbh, Queen of Connacht, raising an army and invading the province of Ulster to secure a famous bull, *Donn Cuailnge*, the brown bull of Cooley, so that she can be on equal terms with her husband Ailill who already has a renowned bull *Fionnbheannach*, the white-horned one.

The time is well chosen, for the Ulstermen are deprived of their martial vigour through the curse of the goddess Macha and are unable to fight. The great hero Cú Chulainn has alone escaped the curse and he has to defend Ulster on his own against the massive might of Meadhbh's army. At the end of a long campaign of great slaughter, Meadhbh succeed in securing the Ulster bull and bringing him home to Cruachú, the royal site of Connacht. At last the two great bulls, *Fionnbheannach* of Connacht and *Donn Cuailnge* of

Ulster meet and they paw the ground viciously as they prepare to fight each other to the death:

> The Donn Cuailnge arrived. He turned his right side to Cruachú and left there a heap of the liver of the Fionnbheannach. From this comes the placename Cruachna Ae (hill of the liver).
>
> He came forward to the brink of Áth Mór and there he left the loin of the Fionnbheannach. Whence the name Áth Luain (ford of the loin) Athlone (O Rahilly, C., (ed), *Táin Bó Cualgne*, Dublin 1967, 272).
>
> *Chuir sé a láirg de go Port Láirge. Chuir sé a chliabhrach uaidh go Duibhlinn ar a dtugtar Áth Cliath* (Ó Loinsigh, E., (eag), *An Táin*, Baile Atha Cliath 1989, 163) (He sent his thigh flying to Port Lairge (place of the thigh) Waterford. He sent his rib-cage to Dublin (black pool), now called Áth Cliath (the ford of the wicker-frame).

In the bull-fight, the Fionnbheannach, the Connacht bull, is the victim. He is Purusa, while Donn Chuailnge, even though he later dies from his wounds, is the slayer. The various pieces of Fionnbheannach are falling off as the bulls chase each other all over the country and they give their names to the areas in which they fall. Could there be a suggestion here that, as in the case of Miach, the herbs which grew from these dismemberments had a specific use as a cure for a specific ailment? In the Miach story, no clue survived as to the curative connection between a particular herb and a particular disease, and so the story was of little value in the practice of medicine.

The Miach account is found in the ancient story *Cath Maighe Tuireadh*.

But supposing, for instance, that it was noticed that in the area of Cruachú Ae (the high place of the liver) in Co Roscommon, where Fionnbheannach's liver fell out, there was a preponderance of a specific species of herb, then could it be presumed that this type of herb contained a cure for liver complaints on a universal scale, so that the account in *Táin Bó Cuailnge* is in the category of revelation? Similarly for the other areas. Botanists might pinpoint the occurrence of a type of herb prevalent in the Áth Cliath (ford of the rib/wattle frame) area, for instance, and *Táin Bó Cuailnge* may, in this respect, be performing two functions: firstly, presenting the Purusa Myth in a very clear form in which the place of Purusa and his slayer are in animal shapes with human understanding, as the two bulls were originally men but have been transformed, and secondly, as providing medical material for the welfare of humans, as well as giving hints as to where the herbal remedies may be found. Was Áth Cliath, for instance, the place to find a cure for a chesty cough?

Turning, then, to the ecclesiastical scene in Ireland, we encounter a remarkable Old-Irish tract illustrating the rite of Mass, more or less as it is found in the 8th-9th century Stowe Missal.

In the tract, considerable attention is given to the *Fractio Panis*, the breaking of the bread and the arrangement of the pieces of eucharistic bread on the paten or plate. The form differed according to the feast being celebrated – a simple formation of the pieces on ordinary days and a more complex arrangement on important feastdays such as Easter and Christmas. In parts, the tract is strikingly reminiscent of the Purusa Myth in terms of the passion of Christ:

> The Host upon the paten, the Body of Christ upon the tree of the Cross. The fraction upon the paten, the Body of Christ being broken with nails upon the Cross. The meeting whereby the two halves come together after the fraction, a figure of the integrity of the Body of Christ after Resurrection (*Ind oblae forsin meis, coland Crist hi crann cruche. A combag forsin meis, Corp Crist do chombag co cloaib forsin croich. In comrac conrecatar in da leth iarsin chombug, figor oge chuirp Crist iarn esergo*) (MacCarthy, B., 'On the Stowe Missal', *RIA*, Vol XXV11, 1886; 250-251).

We can distinguish three actions performed by the priest with the Host or Eucharistic Bread. Firstly, he lays the Host on the paten; this symbolises the laying of the Body of Christ upon the Cross. Secondly, the priest breaks the Bread; this represents the Body of Christ being broken by nails on the Cross; thirdly, the priest take the two parts of the Host into which it has been divided and places them together, re-unites them so that the loaf looks complete again. This is a symbol of the complete, resurrected, integrated Body of Christ as he appeared after his Resurrection.

The presentation here is reminiscent of the Purusa Myth in its various stages of killing, dismemberment, burial and transformation for the benefit of mankind.

In the present form of Mass in the Roman Rite, the ritual is much the same. The Host is lying on the paten, the celebrant takes it and breaks it in two halves, lays one half on the paten, breaks off a little piece of the other half and places it in the chalice saying: 'May this mingling of the body and blood of our Lord Jesus Christ bring eternal life to us who receive it.' However, the two parts of the Host are not placed together again as in the Celtic Rite though the same symbolism may be contained in the Roman commingling.

The Stowe Tract then goes ahead to describe the way in which parts of the Host are distributed or laid out on the paten which must have been a large dish as in the case of the Derrynaflan (Co Tipperary) paten. The ritual of the Breaking of the Bread presents a visionary view of Christ as the centre of the earthly and heavenly church:

> There are seven varieties of fraction of the Host: five parts of the ordinary Host to symbolise the senses of the soul; seven of the feasts of Confessors (saints) and Virgins, the chief saints excepted, in figure of the seven gifts of the Holy Ghost; eight of the feast of Martyrs in figure of the eight-fold New Testament; nine of Sunday in honour of the nine choirs of Heaven; eleven on the Feasts of Apostles to signify the incompleted college of the Apostles after the defection of Judas; twelve of Circumcision and of the Last Supper in remembrance of the complete apostolate, and thirteen of Low Sunday and of the Ascension, at first, although they are distributed more minutely afterwards in giving Communion in figure of Christ and his twelve Apostles. The 5, 7, 8, 9, 11, 12, 13 – they make 65 altogether, and that is the number of parts proper for the Feasts of Easter and Christmas and Pentecost. And all is arranged on the paten in the form of a Cross.

Moreover, certain particles are assigned to bishops, priests, married people, youths, penitents – all are included in this massive vision centred on Christ.

The Stowe Tract then goes on to describe how the particles are distributed or laid out on the paten in the form of the well-lnown Celtic Cross. On the 65-particle days (Easter, Christmas, Pentecost) 14 particles were in the stem of the Cross; 14 on the horizontal bar; 20 around the rim and 16 around the hub. This makes 64, so that the hub or centre itself contained the celebrant's part, thus making a total of 65, so that Christ at the centre contained in himself all the feasts of the year. Perhaps the best way today of getting a glimpse of this vision is to go into a church of the Byzantine Rite and see the majestic figure of Christ as *Pantokrator* overlooking all from the roof of the building and, seeing in the ikons below, the scenes of his own life, the lives of the different categories of saints, and the hosts of angels in the heavenly world into which he has entered and into which he draws us all after him.

In throwing out the statues of the saints and the general simplification of Catholic churches, what we might call the rationalistic modifications, after Vatican II, we may well wonder if a terrible mistake were made, resulting in continually diminishing congregations and a generalised apathy. It is doubtful if many Irish Catholics today see their church as a group of people with a vision of another world of everlasting life into which they are being led by Christ on a tortuous but challenging path, being attacked on all sides by human and demonic forces, but supported by the help and heroic example of the saints of old and those of modern times.

The arrangement of the particles on the paten in a specific order is not unknown elsewhere. In the Rite of Mass (Divine Liturgy) in the modern Byzantine Rite, for instance:

> The priest breaks the holy Bread into four parts, with great reverence and care, saying secretly: 'Broken and distributed is the Lamb of God, the Son of the Father; broken but not divided, ever-eaten but never consumed, the sanctifier of those who participate.'
>
> 'Then he arranges the fragments on the holy paten in this manner:

```
            IC
   NI              KA
            XC
```

(Jesus Christ conquers) (Raya, J., *Byzantine Missal*, Birmingham, Alabama, 1958).

According to the early Eastern theologian, Theodore of Mopsuestia, the breaking was meant to show how the Lord 'distributed' his presence among many (Kucharek, C., *The Byzantine-Slav Liturgy of St John Chrysostom*, Ontaria, 1971, 672).

Similarly, in the Mozarabic Rite of Spain, the particles are arranged on the paten in the form of a Cross and each bears the title of a mystery in the life of Our Lord:

	CORPORATIO	
MORS	NATIVITAS	RESURRECTIO
	CIRCUMCISIO	
	APPARITIO	GLORIA
	PASSIO	REGNUM

(King, A., *Liturgies of the Primatial Sees*, London 1957, 616).

The extraordinary liturgical tract attached to the Stowe Missal highlights the importance of 'The Breaking of Bread' as the rite by which the participants take the divine into their own bodies. While the tract itself is little known, attention was drawn to it by a lecture given by the antiquarian scholar Rev P. Power to the members of the Royal Irish Academy in 1939 and published by them that same year (*PRIA*, Vol XLV.) He had quite a remarkable story to tell. Canon Power described how, at a sale, he bought the upper part of a stone quern (*Bró uachtarach*), used from most ancient times to grind corn to make flour. The stone was about one and a half feet in diameter and was richly engraved in the form of a Celtic wheel cross with lots of small squares. At the centre is a hole into which the wheat was fed, and in the upper shaft of the Cross an aperture for the handle by which the *bró uachtarach* was rotated. This takes up the space of 3 squares. Canon Power surmised that the quern may have come from the great monastic site of Lismore.

At first, he thought that the engraving was mere decoration, but on reading the Stowe Tract and counting the small squares, it dawned on him that perhaps here was something more than decoration, for it seemed to illustrate in hard white sandstone, the layout of the Eucharistic particles on the paten, for the celebration of Mass in the Celtic Rite, as described in the Tract, but not in the Rite of Mass as it occurs in the Stowe Missal.

At any rate, Canon Power found that the engraving on the quern corresponded to the Tract. The main difficulty is that the 20 particles around the rim in the Tract are not found in the quern. There may be two reasons for this anomaly: the rim particles may have dropped out of use in the ritual or, due to the greater friction at the rim between the upper and lower stones, they just may have worn away. At any rate, it must be one of the most stunning 'finds' in the history of the Christian liturgy.

The reality of the divine presence of Christ is asserted clearly in the Stowe Missal in the antiphons said during the Fraction: 'They recognised the Lord in the Breaking of Bread' (Luke 24:35) and 'The bread which we break is the Body of Our Lord Jesus Christ; the chalice which we bless is the Blood of Our Lord Jesus Christ' (cf 1 Cor 10:16).

The stark, primitive, realism that we have encountered in discussing the Purusa Myth is found again in Christ's words to the people:

I tell you most solemnly, if you do not eat the flesh of the Son of Man and drink his blood, you will not have life in you. Anyone who does eat my flesh and drink my blood has eternal life and I will raise him up on the last day. For my flesh is real food and my blood is real drink. He who eats my flesh and drinks my blood lives in me and I live in him (John 6:53-56).

These are strong statements, and one can sympathise with the listening Jews as, with suggestions of cannibalism passing through their minds, they said to one another: 'How can this man give us his flesh to eat?' (John 6:52).

But while the reality remained the same, and the previous assertions clear and unmodified, it was revealed later, at the Last

Supper (Mark 14:22-25) that his Body and Blood would be made available to people in more socially acceptable forms, that is, under the appearances of the common food items of bread and wine.

CHAPTER THIRTEEN

Psychomachia, Spiritual War

We now turn to some early Irish texts which have proved difficult to interpret and seem to suggest the primordial vision, of which we have been speaking, as background.

One of these texts is the much-quoted *Lúireach Phádraig*, St Patrick's Breastplate which is thought to go back to the 8th century. The word *Lúireach* is a Gaelicisation of the Latin *Lorica* meaning the metal breastplate worn by Roman soldiers to protect themselves from sword-stabs, and this idea of protection, in a wide sense of defence against the attacks of spirits, demons, diseases, bad weather, denigration, disgrace and so forth, was very important in early Christian Ireland and it is generally held that the Irish had a greater number of protection prayers than any other area of Europe. The short, common phrase: *Dia idir sinn agus an t-olc* (God between us and all harm) gives the fundamental idea of God forming a protective circle (*caim*) around us to keep out the various inimical forces that are attacking us.

Within *Lúireach Phádraig* itself is a formula which, when re-arranged gives the four points of the compass, above, below, with and within:

> *Críost romham; Críost ar mo dheis; Críost i mo dhiaidh; Críost ar mo chlé; Críost os mo chionn; Críost fúm; Críost liom; Críost ionam* (May Christ be before me; at my right hand, behind me, at my left hand, above me, below me, with me, within me)

'Before me' means to the east of me, as one turns to the east when praying according to ancient Christian custom. Then, when facing east, your right hand is to the south, your back to the west and your left hand to the north. Then above and below. These six directions, though found here in a Christian prayer, appear to have quite a large cosmological significance for the Celts.

In an episode of *Táin Bó Cuailnge*, Cú Chulainn's father Sualdamh goes to Eamhain Macha, the capital of Ulster, to complain that his son is left to defend Ulster on his own. He rides into the royal court and shouts: 'Men are being wounded, women are being abducted, cattle are being stolen, and my son Cú Chulainn is left to defend Ulster on his own.' He rides into the banqueting hall and repeats his complaint.

Now, it is *geis* (taboo) to speak before the king has spoken and it is *geis* for the king to speak before the druid has spoken, and so Sualdamh has broken the *geis* and his doom is inevitable. His horse rears up, and the shield Sualdamh holds cuts off his head. The severed head shouts out the same formula. The king, Conchúr Mac Neasa, takes a mighty oath saying that the sky is above us, the earth underneath us, and the sea all around us, and unless the sky fall down on us, or the earth open up to swallow us or the great sea invade the land to drown us, then he will bring back every cow and every woman taken from Ulster.

Here, in this dramatic episode, is an example of Celtic cosmology. It was said of the Celts that they feared only three things – that the sky would fall down on them, or the earth open up under them, or the sea invade the land. The Celts, in their various areas of habitation, must have had first-hand experience of violent thunderstorms, earthquakes and extensive flooding. In other words, cosmic order was disturbed when one element invaded the area of another, as when the sea invades the land, and the idea was to ensure that each great force of the Universe stayed in its proper place and so maintained world harmony. In this sense, one can appreciate the Celtic tradition of fighting against the waves with swords and spears. This curious custom may have been provoked by the idea of a great dragon in the sea surrounding the land and sending destructive waves inwards, and the god Taranis, with his hammer, trying to keep the dragon at bay, assisted by his faithful followers.

The *Lúireach 'Críost/Dia romham'*, then, incorporates this cosmology of the sea all around, the sky above and the earth below. In a very simple, everyday occurrence, the idea can be seen in dressing against the cold. A man puts on his clothes, wraps himself around; his shoes and stockings protect him from the cold earth below; and his hat protects him from the freezing sky above. Wrapped up like this he sallies forth in defiance of the tempest.

The importance of the 'psychomachia' or spiritual warfare against the forces of evil obviously appealed to the warlike Celts, who as Christians, saw from the writings of St Paul (Eph 6:10-17) how the ideas of normal civic warfare could be transferred to the spiritual plain:

> Finally, grow strong in the Lord, with the strength of his power. Put God's armour on so as to be able to resist the devil's tactics. For it is not against human enemies that we have to struggle, but against the Sovereignties and the Powers who originate the darkness of this world, the spiritual army of evil in the heavens. That is why you must rely on God's armour, or you will not be able to put up any resistance when the worst happens, or have enough resources to hold your ground.
>
> So stand your ground, with truth *buckled* round your waist, and integrity for a *breastplate*, wearing for *shoes* on your feet the eagerness to spread the gospel of peace and always carrying the *shield* of faith so that you can use it to put out the burning *arrows* of the evil one. And then you must accept salvation from God to be your *helmet* and receive the word of God from the Spirit to use as a *sword*.

This Pauline text, with its insistence on an unseen, spiritual army of dark, evil beings on the march to attack the Christians, must have been the basis for the abundance of *Lúireacha* in Celtic spirituality.

St Paul enumerates the military equipment of a soldier of the Roman Empire at that period, buckler, breastplate, shoes, shield, arrows, helmet, sword, and gives their equivalent in the spiritual armour of the Christian soldier. The triple rejection of Satan and the forces of evil which takes place at the Easter Vigil, 'Do you reject Satan?, etc, is a remnant of this militaristic type of early Christianity, so different from the more domesticated form which followed it. It presumes, in a way uncommon today, the presence of unseen but powerful forces of evil whom the Christian has to contend with. Though unseen, those forces are real.

In the numerous 'Dragon-Fights' in which the Irish saint has to fight a dragon, the dragon represents the forces of evil. In overcoming the dragon, the saint is putting the victory of the Risen Christ over death into effect on the local scene.

Dragon-Fight and Lúireach are combined in the *Life of Mac Creiche*, a saint of Co Clare. In this picturesque tale, a fire-spitting dragon called Broicseach has been terrorising the people of the Shannon. The renowned dragon-fighter Mac Creiche is summoned from Loch Léin (Killarney) to get rid of him as the local saints Maeldála, Mac Aiblen and Blathmac have failed despite all their efforts and striking of bells and reliquaries with their pastoral staffs. Mac Creiche realises that he is in serious trouble as the dragon hurls balls of fire at him. He calls on Christ, the angels and saints to help and protect him in a typical protection prayer (*Lúireach*):

> '*Do neimh ar ccúl go ccuire Críst*': 'May Christ repel your venom; may he not allow it to reach me any more; O dumb Broicseach, though rough the encounter, I am to subdue you, trusting in holy Christ. The seven archangels from the fair city (heaven), God the Creator has ordained them to repel you from me; the four noble Evangelists shall lower your strength, Matthew and Mark, Luke and John.'

Fire shoots out from Mac Creiche's bell which sets the dragon's mouth on fire and he retires to the lake of Loch Broicsí. The people cheer the saint's victory, but too soon, for the dragon again emerges from the lake. Mac Creiche takes off his hat and flings it at the dragon. The hat assumes a hard metallic form, grows bigger and bigger, descends over the dragon's head forcing him under the water of Loch Broicsí where he remains to this day (Plummer, C., 'Life of Mac Creiche', *Miscellanea Hagiographica Hibernica*, Bruxelles, 1925).

This fantastic tale, of epic proportions, involves parts of Kerry, Clare and Shannonside. It includes crowds of the local people who by prayer, fasting, cheering and prostrations, not to mention the heavy monitory exactions of Mac Creiche, take part in the action. There is also the unseen presence of God, the angels and

the saints militarily engaged in fighting the forces of evil themselves, who are portrayed spectacularly in Broicseach, the fiery
dragon. He gives his name to the lake – Loch Broicsí (Loch Raha),
near Corofin, Co Clare.

The impression given is that of a wild, mad story, closely
bound up with a local landscape in which a local holy man, a
spiritual hero overcomes a monster who has been devastating the
countryside, and confines him to the depths of a lake from which
he may only emerge every seven years.

Similarly, in many places in medieval Europe, the dragon
formed part of the Rogation Procession on the Monday, Tuesday
and Wednesday before Ascension Thursday. It is in this ritual
context that the Broicseach Lake event should be situated.

Behind it is the eternal theme of the presence of evil, forces of
disintegration, return to chaos. The dark figures of the
Fomhóraigh, associated with the violent sea, precede the orderly
Tuatha Dé Danann and a constant battle goes on between those
forces which stand for integration and those representing chaos.
So, what we are trying to do is to keep creation in operation and
prevent it from falling back into the chaos from which it emerged.
Cosmos and chaos engage in an on-going contest: '*Mors et vita
duello, conflixerunt mirando, dux vitae mortuus regnat vivus*' (Easter
Sunday Hymn) (Death and life in a marvellous battle contended,
the Lord of Life, who died, reigns triumphant.) The rising up of
the dragon from the lake is a reminder of mankind's role in resist-
ing the pressures dragging us back into primeval chaos and
thwarting the ongoing task of building up a world of harmony,
where all the diverse pieces of creation fit together to provide a
comprehensive picture of the Universe. Like the builders of the
great medieval cathedrals who moulded the diverse pieces of
stone and wood with such immense labour, love and expertise to
construct these breath-taking masterpieces, so in a multitude of
ways people co-operate to continue the work of creation and
painfully drag the world out of the clutches of chaos, being aware,
all the while, of the dragon lurking in the lakeside reeds – the spec-
tre of war and world unrest ever threatening the forward movement of evolution. In the hymn *Urbs Jerusalem beata* of Vespers for

the Dedication of a Church, the new building is seen as a city designed in heaven and let down to earth to be constructed by architects, its stones moulded and arranged so that it becomes the New Jerusalem, the City of God.

A much neglected part of the Easter celebration is Christ's descent into hell. It is mentioned as one of the propositions in the Apostles' Creed, 'He descended into hell', and the theme received much elaboration in the early Apocryphal Gospel of Nicodemus. It was a popular idea among the Irish and manuscripts in Irish and Latin containing it are still extant. It may owe some of its popularity to its heroic character and warlike spirit and the fact that a category of story-telling in the native tradition, called *Orgna* (Destructions) already existed and these could be related to Christ's Destruction of Hell – *Argain Ifrinn*.

Basically, the idea is that in the period between the death and burial of Christ on Good Friday and his resurrection on Easter Sunday, while his body was in the tomb his soul paid a visit to hell, to those multitudes of people of olden times such as the Patriarchs of the Old Testament, King David, King Solomon, Adam and Eve, who were all imprisoned by Satan (the Dragon) and his demons in darkest hell for many centuries. There they lived on in strict confinement, yet they were not without hope, as it was known to them that some day a rescuer would arrive and set them free. Then, suddenly, one day, dark hell was lighted up and the prisoners knew that the day of destiny had come. A mighty voice was heard outside the gates of bronze demanding entrance, and then the gates come crashing down as Christ in glory makes his entrance surrounded by angels and saints. He overcomes Satan and ties him up in chains. The demons flee in terror. Then the glorious Christ takes Adam by the hand and drags him out of hell. Eve holds on to Adam, somebody else holds on to her and they are all rescued and released from their dark prison. Then they are handed over to St Michael the Archangel who leads them into paradise.

Several medieval pictures illustrate the *Descensus ad Inferos*. Some show hell as a highly fortified building and Satan as a giant with a horse's ears. He is firmly chained up and his assistant demons flee for their lives in all directions. Other pictures show Satan as a Dragon in whose belly the Old Testament saints are detained. Christ thrusts his bannered processional Cross into the Dragon's mouth forcing him to cough up his prisoners. Again, Christ takes Adam by the hand and leads him out, followed by all the others, while terrified demons flee.

The eighth century poet Blathmac described the scene: 'He (Christ) was victorious from fighting that, his battle with the Devil. Miserable Devil, his strength was crushed; a mighty prey was taken from him. It is your son, Jesus, who cast seven chains about his neck and bound him (no falsehood) in the depths of his dwelling' (Carney, J., The Poems of Blathmac Son of Cú Brettan, Dublin, 1964, 61).

This military encounter between the Risen Christ and the Dragon, showing considerable violence, has a very early prototype in the Easter Homily of Bishop Melito of Sardis in Asia Minor. According to Bishop Melito the Risen Christ boasts: 'Who shall contend with me? Let him stand up to face me. I have freed the condemned, brought the dead to life, raised up the buried. Who will speak against me? I am the Christ', he says, 'It is I who destroyed death, who triumphed over the enemy, who trampled the underworld underfoot, who bound up the strong one and snatched man away to the heights of heaven; I am the Christ' (The Divine Office, Liturgy of the Hours, 2, 367-368).

One is reminded of the celebrated passages in the story Scéla Mucce Meic Dathó where, at a feast, the great champion Ceat Mac Maghach sets out, as the greatest warrior present, to cut up the cooked pig according to the custom of the 'Curadhmhír' or 'Hero's Portion'. His supremacy is constantly being called in question by other warriors present and he has to continually boast of how he has defeated each one of them in turn.

In Ireland, as among the Celts in general, the tradition of the laoch, or hero was very strong and the heroic ideal as expressed by Cú Chulainn, 'I don't care if I live only a single day so long as my great deeds live on after me', received reiterated expression in literature and folklore throughout the centuries.

It is probable, then, that in Ireland the other aspects of the

Easter Mystery such as the 'Empty Tomb', the renewal of the human race, the taking on of a glorified, spiritualised body, were all subsumed by the idea of the Heroic Christ, the Champion who descended into the darkness of the underworld and fought a *comhrac aonair* – in single combat – with Satan, the Dragon, overcame him, tied him up and deposited him in the depths of hell. He liberated the Dragon's prisoners, and this implies that he is their guardian still.

A question remains to be asked. Why did Christ not destroy Satan/the Dragon, outright, and be finished with him, when he had the chance?

The answer is that the fight must go on. Otherwise the human race, with no call to arms, would settle down to a comfortable, lazy life from which progress would vanish. As St Columbanus remarked: 'If there is no opposition, there is no fight, and if there is no fight there is no victory.' So, the Dragon is subdued but not definitively conquered and it is our task to call on the protection of Christ and continue the war against him on all fronts.

An early modern Irish *Argain Ifrinn* or 'Harrowing of Hell' text (*Celtica* XIII, 1980, 40-50) demonstrates to quite an incredible extent the way in which the Irish could see the destruction of hell in terms of a violent encounter of two champions locked in deadly combat, as Cú Chulainn and Ferdia were in *Táin Bó Cuailnge*.

The scene describes Christ's arrival in hell with bombastic oratory and long lists of adjectives beginning with the same letter:

> *Is ann sin do éirigh an leomhan leadurthach laomdha lot,(ch). Agus do mhéadaigh a uaill agus a ardaigneadh ar faicsin a fhola 'na fhiadhnuise; agus do ghluais roimhe go h-uaillmhear, aghmhur, ionnsaightheach, dána, díoghuinn dasachtach, fíochdha, feargach, faidchémendach, crodha, cnestollach, comharthach d'argain Ifrinn iargcúlaigh iar sin …*
> (Then the rending, valiant, crimson-wounded lion arose and his mettle and his high spirit swelled on seeing his blood before him; and he moved forward, proud and lively, victorious, hostile, bold, stout and enraged, fuming, furious and far-stepping, hardy, pierced of skin, battle-marked, to harrow furthest hell forthwith, and it is related how he put his feet on the secure, firm heavy-valved strong door of cavernous-hot northern hell,

firmly and full fiercely, forcefully and imperiously; and the wearying, noisy-screaming, shadowy-deceptive denizens of upper hell scattered with a rush on seeing the brown-lashed, white-toothed glowing countenance of the Almighty coming to extirpate and swiftly scatter them. For he was a ruddy-flaming huge royal candle, and a red-seething mass of molten metal, ... And the saviour extended that long-fingered, noble right hand to the hard iron door, and shattered and violently broke it from its rude, thick, aboriginal hinges, ... so that he released the rich, fair victoriously-trumpeting, widely-descended, eager, well-born throng up from the stations and mansions of populous hell; for that is the Red Onslaught of the King of the Stars and of the Constellations after his resurrection from death and burial.)

In this short extract from the manuscript we have an example of the brilliantly bombastic oratorical style of the narrator recounting the *Eachtra* (adventure) of the Hero Christ in the underworld, his defeat of the forces of evil and his release of the captives. The cosmic overtones of the scene are apparent from the description of the Hero and his titles as 'King of the Stars and Constellations'.

Easter is linked to the dragon-fight in the liturgies of East and West though not quite in the wild, spectacular, outdoor forms of the Irish. A folktale concerning St Patrick unexpectedly provides a link between the two. According to the tale, St Patrick was travelling in the Sligo-Mayo area and noticed that, as night fell, the people shut their doors and pulled the blinds on their windows to block out all light. He was told that a serpent had invaded the area, and stood upright in a cave near Ballina every night holding a lighted candle in his mouth. Anybody who saw the light of the snake's candle dropped dead, hence the precautions taken by the local people.

On hearing this, St Patrick challenged the light-bearing snake by lighting his own huge candle and confronting him in his den. When the snake saw St Patrick's candle he dropped dead. This is a somewhat domesticated form of dragon-fight but still the element of fire is prominent and St Patrick is the champion.

Now, as regards the link with Easter in this story, the clue is in the candle-bearing snake. In the medieval celebration of Easter in the Rite of Braga (Portugal) and in Mozarabic Spain as well as other great cathedrals of Europe, at the Easter Vigil, the Easter fire was first lighted, and then the light from the fire had to be transferred to the large Paschal Candle. The priests and deacons did this by the use of a small candle and the candle was in the jaws of a wooden snake at the end of a long staff shaped like a curled snake standing on his tail. This was called the *Arundina Serpentina* or simply the *Serpentina*. The altar-boy who held the *Serpentina* when not in use, was called the 'Dragonifer' – 'the dragon-bearer'. Obviously, this is what is behind the popular tale of St Patrick's adventures in Ballina, but how it came from Toledo and Braga to Ireland remains unknown.

In all of this, the Christian saint is taking the place of the Risen conquering Christ, trampling the forces of darkness underfoot and liberating the enslaved, the idea lying at the very heart of the Mystery of Easter.

The opening or breaking down of the gates of hell so that the jail-breaker could get in to get the prisoners out is an obvious feature of plundering of hell. It is shown graphically in the Ikon for Easter in the Byzantine Rite showing Christ smashing the gates of hell and taking Adam by the hand to lead him and all his followers to freedom. The theme is easily dramatised by using a certain section of Psalm 24/23, the *Attollite portas* lines in which the Conquering Hero strikes on the door from outside to be answered from inside by the defenders:

'Gates, open on your own,
open up, you ancient doors,
and let the King of Glory in'.

'Who is the King of Glory?'

'The Lord, strong and victorious;
the Lord, victorious in war.'

'Gates, open on your own,
open up, you ancient doors,
and let the King of Glory in'

'Who is the King of Glory?'

'He is the Lord Sabbaoth,
he, the King of Glory.'

What appears to be the most complete expression of the *Argain Ifrinn* within the actual liturgical celebration, however, comes from the *Ordinale and Customary* of the Benedictine Nuns of Barking Abbey in Essex. This was destroyed after the Reformation and only the ruins now remain. The nuns had a very elaborate liturgy as described in the *Ordinale and Customary* which luckily survive. The 'Harrowing of Hell' took place within the huge monastic church after Matins on Easter Sunday morning, and it is explained that the Lady Abbess, Dame Katherine de Suttone (1358-1376) arranged it for this rather late hour so as to accommodate the faithful who wished to attend.

For the Rite itself, the Abbess and community of nuns left their choir stalls, and accompanied by some priests and clerics, all carrying palms and unlighted candles, proceeded to the Chapel of St Mary Magdalene and entered there, closing the doors behind them. They represented the souls of the Spiritual Ancestors detained by Satan in the underworld.

Then the Celebrant in full vestments, and accompanied by a deacon carrying the processional Cross and another carrying the smoking censer, with altar-boys carrying torches, arrives outside the closed door of the chapel and sings the *Tollite portas* while those inside answer him. The doors burst open and all are released while appropriate antiphons are sung. They light their candles and wave their palms in joy (Tolhurst, J., (ed), *The Ordinale and Customary of the Benedictine Nuns of Barking Abbey*, London, 1927, 106-108).

In this magnificent and moving piece of ritual, Christ's victory over Satan, the destruction of his stronghold and the release of his prisoners against his will, was spectacularly portrayed. The Kingdom of God had triumphed. Nothing would ever be the same again.

In the Barking Rite, the breaking down of the doors and the release of the prisoners are highlighted. Would it be possible to portray, in some symbolic way suitable for performance in church, the third element – the actual *Péistchomhrac* or Dragon-Fight?

Prompted by the *Serpentina story* that we have seen, one could visualize a form of 'Dragon-Fight' at the Easter Vigil in association with the Renewal of the Baptismal Promises.

A pole, shaped liked a snake with a dragon's head, holds three small lighted candles in its mouth. This *Serpentina* is held by an altar-boy, the Spanish 'Draconifer'. At the appropriate time, the Celebrant, holding aloft the lighted Paschal Candle, advances against the *Serpentina*. The Celebrant addresses the people:

Priest: 'Do you reject Satan?
People: 'I do'.
Priest: 'And all his works?'
People: 'I do'.
Priest: 'And all his empty promises?'
People: 'I do'.

After each 'I do' the Celebrant, using a candle extinguisher, quenches a candle in the snake's mouth and finally the 'Dragon' retires into the darkness, defeated.

The three candles in the serpent's mouth are mentioned in the Sacred Triduum Liturgy of St Mary's Abbey, York, as well as the kindling of the New Fire by means of a crystal held between the sun and some very combustible material (*de berillo exposito soli lucenti*). It seems surprising that the sun at Easter would be sufficiently strong to light a fire, considering that York is so far north. The alternative, if the sun were obscured by cloud, was to use the ordinary method of flint struck by steel as in the Tridentine Rite (*H. B. S.*, London, 1936, Vol LXXV, 274)

The quenching of the candle is reminiscent of Lugh Lámhfhada's putting out the Balor's evil eye in *Cath Maighe Tuireadh* and Percival's adventure in the 'Chapel Perilous' where a black hand emerges from behind the altar to extinguish the only candle lighting up the haunted edifice, as well as St Patrick's victory over the candle-bearing snake of Ballina.

From Liam de Paor's study of this Co Clare area, 'Saint Mac

Creiche of Liscannor' (*Ériu*, XXX, 1979, 93ff), it is clear that Kilmacrehy, Liscannor, Loch Ratha / Loch Broicsí, the Sandhills, Killinaboy (*Cill Iníon Bhaoí*) with its Síle-na-Gig, Kiltolagh, Slievecallan, Dubhloch – and the characters involved: Mac Creiche, Blathmac, Senán, Donn na Duimhche, Fionn Mac Cumhaill, Cathach, Brigid, Iníon Bhaoí – it is clear that this area was something of a huge 'landscape sanctuary' teeming with supernatural activity where the ordinary people were oppressed by plagues such as the Crom Chonaill and the depredations of dragons, and depended on great dragon-fighters such as Mac Creiche, Fionn Mac Cumhaill and St Senán to liberate them. It may be compared to the other 'landscape sanctuaries' we have seen – Maigh Sléacht, Lough Gur, Brú na Bóinne, Cnoc Fírinne and West Witton.

The dragon-fight or psychomachia can be seen at different levels:

1. In the heavens, Perseus fights Cetus the Dragon to rescue Andromeda.

2. In the biblical story, Moses overcomes the Pharaoh and leads the Israelites out of the slavery of Egypt into the freedom of the Promised Land.

3. Lugh Lámhfhada fights and overcomes Balar whose baleful fiery eye is causing destruction on a massive scale.

4. Fionn Mac Cumhaill fights a dragon who swallows him and 24 of the Fianna. Fionn takes his sword in with him and batters his way out. A similar story is told of St Patrick who was swallowed by a dragon at *Loch Dearg*. He hacked his way out, using his *Bachall* or bishop's staff. The lake was formerly known as *Fionnloch*, white lake, but is now *Loch Dearg* (red lake) from the dragon's blood. This is the great penitential site visited by thousands of pilgrims, especially at Lughnasa. This type of dragon-fight is reminiscent of the biblical story of Jonah being swallowed by a whale and subsequently coughed up. Of this episode Jesus said: 'For as Jonah was in the belly of the sea-monster for three days and three nights, so will the Son of Man be in the heart of the earth for three days and three nights' (Mt 12:40).

5. In Europe, and in Ireland in particular, local powerful saints such as Mac Creiche, St Finbarr, St Patrick, St Senán and many oth-

ers, engage in numerous dragon-fights to rescue the people from plagues, flooding, failure of crops and diseases associated with dragons.

6. The final level is the death and resurrection of Christ by which we enter into a new dimension of reality:

> We praise you with greater joy than ever on this Easter night (day) when Christ becomes our paschal sacrifice. He is the true Lamb who took away the sins of the world. By dying he destroyed our death; by rising he restored our life.
>
> He has made us children of the light, rising to new and everlasting life.
>
> He has opened the gates of heaven to receive his faithful people.
>
> His death is our ransom from death; his resurrection is our rising to life.
>
> In him a new age his dawned, the long reign of sin is ended, a broken world has been renewed, and man is once again made whole.
>
> As he offered his body on the cross, his perfect sacrifice fulfilled all others. As he gave himself into your hands for our salvation, he showed himself to be the priest, the altar, and the lamb of sacrifice.
>
> He is still our priest, our advocate who always pleads our cause.
>
> Christ is the victim who dies no more, the Lamb, once slain, who lives for ever.
>
> By his rising from the dead we rise to everlasting life; in his return to you in glory we enter into your heavenly kingdom.
>
> In his risen body he plainly showed himself to his disciples and was taken up to heaven in their sight to claim for us a share in his divine life.
>
> The joy of the resurrection and ascension renews the whole world, while the choirs of heaven sing for ever to your glory.
>
> Today you sent the Holy Spirit on those marked out to be your children by sharing the life of your only Son, and so you brought the paschal mystery to completion.

Here we have a collection of phrases gathered together for

convenience from the Prefaces to the Eucharistic Prayer in the *Roman Missal*. They proclaim the great mystery of our redemption through the death and resurrection of Christ from different points of view. Mankind was separated from God and in a state of deep alienation. A ranson had to be paid before a reconciliation was effected and God, once again, reunited with men. The ransom was not money but the surrender of a chosen victim to death. Christ was the ransom. To whom was the ransom paid? Was it to God who had been offended by the rebellion of mankind, or was it to Satan into whose possession man had given himself? Satan, the Dragon, may have felt that he should be compensated for depriving him of his possessions – or was it to both?

Death, in the sense of perpetual death, a state of being cut off, dis-connected from the sustaining life-flow of God himself, had been cancelled and life as a participation in the immortal life of God was restored: 'His resurrection is our rising to life'. 'He has opened the gates of heaven; he has made us children of light, rising to new and everlasting life.' In other words, a new and eternal destiny is provided for mankind, the world has moved into another dimension of reality through the death and resurrection of Christ.

From his new home in heaven, at the right hand of God, the Risen Christ sends down the Holy Spirit on mankind to inject into them his own glorified life, and this is already signified by the people lighting their candles from the great Paschal Candle at the Easter Vigil. Christ's death and resurrection was not for himself alone but was to spread out among the multitude of mankind. This extension throughout the centuries is shown in the archaic ritual of cutting the trace of the Cross and the numerals of the current year on the Paschal Candle with a knife, with the words:

> Christ yesterday and today, the beginning and the end, Alpha and Omega; all time belongs to him, and all the ages; to him be glory and power, through every age. Amen.

In the 'Sedro' prayer for Easter Sunday, in the Maronite Rite, while clouds of incense ascend, the priest summarises the doctrine of the Paschal Mystery:

On this day, O Lord, Maker of life,
your church glorifies you
and cries out to you with the fragrance of this incense;
as you saved us by your passion
and granted us life by your resurrection,
so now clothe our bodies with the power of your Spirit,
that we may all shine in the robe of glory
and be able to meet you, O Christ, the true Bridegroom.
In your grace, make us worthy to enter your heavenly
kingdom,
along with all our faithful departed,
that we may glorify you, your Father and your Holy Spirit,
now and for ever.' (Qurbono: *The Book of Offering, Season of the
Glorious Resurrection*, Brooklyn, 1994, 15)

A legend related in Jocelyn Kettle's great novel *The Athelsons*
(Coronet Books, London, 1974) throws a curious light on the
scenario of Christ's self-sacrifice for our redemption.

The book describes this old family estate in north-west
England which began with a Viking invader who came to plunder
the area, but instead fell in love with it and settled down in it. The
family, the Athelsons, prospered throughout the centuries and
preserved as best they could the laws and customs of their Viking
ancestors, helped, no doubt, by the isolation of the area, surrounded
by hills and sea which kept strangers at bay.

In the year 1349, the great plague, The Black Death, was raging
but because of its isolation Cler Athel managed to escape. Then,
one morning, the youngest son of the Great House, the fourteen-
year-old Godwin, was missing.

He was eventually seen in the middle of a great field of golden
ripe corn and when they came to the edge of the field, the boy
shouted at them to keep away. He told them that a stranger had
wandered into the field during the night. He had the plague and
had contaminated the whole field of corn. The boy said that what
was to be done was to set the field of corn on fire and so prevent
the plague spreading. All knew that this was the correct procedure, but it was a hard decision to make, for the loss of this vast field
of wheat would mean hunger. On the other hand, it was not un-

known for a whole community to be wiped out by the plague and no one left to bury the dead.

And so, a decision was reached and lighting torches were thrown into the dry corn which blazed voraciously in all directions.

The father shouted to the son to strip off his clothes and run out while there was still time. But the son, Godwin, shouted back that it was too late, for he himself had contracted the plague.

The father made a desperate attempt to rush in and drag his son out of the field. He was held back by the men of the village as they watched the conflagration devour the plague-infected corn, the plague-bringer, and Godwin the sacrificial victim.

CHAPTER FOURTEEN

The Defence Prayer Tradition

While theoretically the Celts were afraid of only three things – that the sky would fall down on them, the earth swallow them or the ocean drown them – in practice, and apart from these three great cosmological events, in ordinary life there was often a lot of fear from the ever-present divinities – the Tuatha Dé Danann and, especially in Brittany, the Unhappy Dead, as well as natural accidents, diseases, inimical attacks of humans and demons.

People lived in a dangerous world surrounded by inimical forces against which one needed protection. To supply this need, the Irish in particular developed a type of Protection Prayer called the *Lúireach* of which *Lúireach Phádraig* (St Patrick's Breastplate) is the best known, but there are several others. Some are also found in Wales and many in Gaelic Scotland. The word *Caim* is often used in Scottish Gaelic to describe this kind of protection prayer with its accompanying ritual. It is envisioned, for instance, that a person may become aware of some danger or disturbance or some inimical force attacking him. He calls on God, Mary, the angels and saints to form a protecting ring around him to prevent these from harming him.

He stands and stretches out his right arm and index finger, and makes a circle around himself, turning *deiseal* – sunwise, follow-ing the course of the sun – while reciting a formula such as:

Caim Dhé nan dúla,
Caim Chríosda chúmha,
Caim Spioraid Númha,
Dha m'chumhnadh, dha m'chomhnadh' (Carmichael, A., *Carmina Gadelica*, Edinburgh 1940, Vol.111, 106)
(May the protecting ring of the God of the Elements, of gentle Christ, of the Holy Spirit be protecting me, be protecting me.)

This spiritual rampart protects the person from his attackers.

When a large number of these *Lúireacha* are gathered together, it will be seen that this type of prayer-formula contains eight major divisions:

1 An invocation of the Trinity.
2 An invocation of Christ.
3 An invocation of Angels and Archangels.
4 An invocation of various categories of saints such as apostles, martyrs, confessors.
5 An invocation of the forces of nature, the elements.
6 A list of the various parts of the body needing protection.
7 A calling on God to surround the person by his protction in a general way and in the various states and conditions in which the person finds himself.
8 A list of the various evils and dangers against which the person needs to be protected. (cf Mac Eoin, G., *Studia Hibernica* 2, 1962, 212-217)

This may appear as a very complicated list of elements but in fact it may well have evolved from a simple type of formula such as the familiar *Dia idir sinn agus and t-olc* (God between us and all harm).

Now, in one of the most ancient of all the church's prayers – the Litany of the Saints sung at certain solemn occasions such as the Ordination of a Priest while the candidate lies prostrate on the ground – we find the equivalent of the Irish prayer: *Ab omni malo, libera nos, Domine* (From all evil, deliver us, O Lord.)

As the metal breastplate (*Lorica/Luireach*) or shield comes between the soldier and the swords, spears and arrows directed at him, so God comes between us and the evils and dangers which beset us. This is the basic meaning of the *Lúireach* and this type of prayer is characteristically Celtic. Once again, we see the importance of the 'psychomachia' or spiritual warfare in the ancient Irish journey to God. The person was surrounded by inimical forces eager to attack him and he had to call on God, the angels and saints, and the elements of earth, air, fire and water to rally round and defend him. In the Celtic Christian view, life was very dangerous but very exciting.

The Celtic Christians were doing no more than following the admonition of St Paul: 'Finally, grow strong in the Lord, with the strength of his power. Put God's armour on so as to be able to resist the devil's tactics' (Eph 6:10-11).

The Preface to St Patrick's Breastplate treats this matter in some detail:

> And this is a corslet of faith for the protection of body and soul against devils and men and vices.When anyone shall repeat it every day with diligent intentness on God, devils shall not dare to face him. It shall be a protection to him against every poison and envy, it shall be a defence to him against sudden death, it shall be a corslet to his soul after his death (Stokes, W., and Strachan, J., *Thesaurus Palaeohibernicus*, Cambridge, 1903, 354).

If we take the simple, basic, Irish formula, *Dia idir mé agus an t-olc*, we find that it contains three basic components: 1: *Dia* (God), 2: Mé (me/I) and 3: Olc (evil/danger), and the various *Lúireacha*, in different ways, elaborate on these three elements.

Under the first heading, *Dia*, we find the Trinity, Father, Son and Holy Spirit, Christ, and those closely associated with God, the angels, saints, and forces of nature.

Under the second heading, *Mé*, we have the soul and the body. As we know little about the soul, the *Lúireacha* tend to emphasise the body. The body consists of various parts such as the hands, the feet, chest, etc, and these parts stand in need of protection as they are easily harmed or used for sinful purposes. A fine example of this is provided by the *Lúireach* of Mael Ísu Ua Brolchán, 'A Choimdiu, nom-choimét', in which a particular part of the body is associated with a particular sense, which is then associated with a particular vice, as for instance in the case of the eyes which are associated with the sense of seeing which in turn is associated with the vice of covetousness:

Comét dam mo shúile,
A Ísu meic Máire,
Nacham-derna santach
Aicsin cruid neich aile.
(Murphy, G., *Early Irish Lyrics*, Oxford 1956, 24)

(Guard for me my eyes, O Jesus, Son of Mary, lest, seeing another person's wealth, I become covetous.)

In this way, Maol Ísu goes through the eight chief sins, corresponding more or less to our Seven Deadly Sins, showing how
each of them is connected to a particular part of the body.

Maol Ísu's treatment of this subject, in which he devotes a
verse to each part of the body and its associated vice, has a parallel
in the Anointing of the Sick in the older version of the *Rituale
Romanum*. Here, the priest anointed with oil the various parts of
the body, again mentioning the vice associated with each particular part:

'For the Eyes': 'Through this holy anointing and his own most
gracious mercy, may the Lord forgive you for any fault you
may have committed by seeing.'
'For the Ears': 'Through this holy anointing and his own most
gracious mercy, may the Lord forgive you for any fault you
may have committed by hearing.'
Similarly for the other senses of the body – smelling, tasting ,
touching.

As well as considering the person in relation to the parts of his
or her body, there is also the state in which the person is and the
circumstances in which he finds himself, and these situations are
covered by the *Lúireach* where the person asks for God's protection: 'In sleeping and in waking, in sitting down and in lying down,
in standing and in walking, in speech and in silence.'

A very simple, popular *Lúireach* of this kind occurs in Modern
Irish:

Éirím suas le Dia,
Go n-éirí Dia liom,
Lámh Dé i mo thimpeall
Ag suí is ag luí
Is ag éirí dhom.
(Ó Laoghaire, D., *Ár bPaidreacha Dúchais*, Baile Átha Cliath,
1975, 6)
(I rise up with God, may God rise up with me, may the hand of

God be around me when I am going about my business, when I
am going to bed and when I am getting up.)

As well as God accompanying the person in these three vital
actions of the day, the sun also performs the same three activities
each day – it rises in the east in the morning, it goes around the
world during the day giving light and heat to all, and at night it
sinks down to rest in the west, so that according to the *Lúireach*
God and myself and the sun are all united in the same three fundamental activities. Here theology and cosmology meet.

A person may also need God's protection in different geographical and spatial situations: 'Indoors and out, on sea and on
land, in storm and in rain, and in all weathers, by day and by
night.'

Of the three components of the formula *Dia idir mé agus an t-olc*
only *olc* (evil / harm) remains.

Category No 8 of the Lúireacha covers this and consists of a list
of the various evils and dangers which the person has to face and
for which he invokes God's protection.

By combining different texts we arrive at a long list of evils and
dangers:

1   Hostile forces originating in the human person: Death, sudden
    and unprovided death, pain.

2   Hostile forces associated with health: jaundice, swelling,
    fever, disease in general, hunger, plague.

3   Hostile forces of elemental nature: fire, sea, lakes, storm, thun-
    der and lightening, stones, trees, harbours, bad weather,
    flooding.

4   Hostile forces associated with warfare: spears, battles, mas-
    sacre, wounding.

5   Hostile forces having their origin in social life: envy, jealousy,
    reviling, satire, ill-will, cursing, contempt, poison, violence,
    theft, revenge, burning, bad laws.

6   Hostile forces of a psychological nature: shame, general em-
    barrassment, dishonour, urgings of pride, sensuality, ambition,

terrifying visions, bewilderment, weariness, depression.

7   Dangers from wild animals: bears, snakes, wolves.

8   Dangers from supernatural forces: hell, sin, druids, druidesses, blacksmiths, demons, spirits, spells, Slua Sí (Tuatha Dé Danann), spectres (scáthanna), the Evil Eye (Súil Bhalair), magic in general.

Because of this comprehensive list of dangers to which the person was conscious of being exposed, the 'putting on of God's armour', that is reciting the *Lúireach*, was essential if one were to engage in the great spiritual battle, the 'psychomachia' that was going on in the world between the forces of good and the forces of evil.

The *Lúireacha* formed a complex and highly sophisticated pattern of prayer operating within a vision of a world which saw the created, ordered cosmos as being under constant threat from dark forces intent on dragging it back into the watery chaos from which it had emerged.

Perhaps the Celts had a vague idea of an evolving Universe slowly and painfully emerging from chaos and always in danger of being dragged down into the watery depths once more. In that case each person, in his own way, was contributing to the continual creative process going on in the world. Did each person feel that he had a part to play in the building up of an ordered Universe? Did he consider himself to be a 'Cosmos Builder'?

Lúireach Phádraig is the best-known example of this type of protection prayer or incantation. In the opinion of the great Celtic scholars, Kuno Meyer and Gerard Murphy, its composition goes back to the eighth century and Professor Binchy accepts this, saying that:

> The hymn does not contain a single syntactical archaism (for the dative without a preposition is still found in a number of eighth-century texts), nor indeed any linguistic archaism whatever (*Ériu* 20, 1966, 235).

Nevertheless, the opening phrase, *Atomriug indiu*, which occurs before each of the first five sections of the poem, has caused considerable problems. The word *indiu* as in modern Irish (*inniu*) means 'today' but there are different views on *Atomriug*. One view is that it is the present indicative, first person singular, of the verb *Ad-rig* to 'bind' used with the first person singular of the in-fixed pronoun (cf Strachan, J., *Old Irish Paradigms*, Dublin 1949, 26-27), to give the meaning 'I bind myself / I gird myself / I buckle on myself'. The recurring *niurt* is the dative of *nert* (strength / power) and though a preposition is absent, the most obvious and satisfactory meaning is that supplied by Binchy: 'I bind myself / gird myself with strength / power.' This strength / power (*nert*, modern Irish *neart*) is the strength of the Trinity, the strength of the acts of Christ – his life, death, resurrection, etc, the power of angels, of saints, and of the forces of nature. These various sources of strength are, as it were, the various pieces of armour (cf Ephesians 6) which the Christian warrior buckles on himself when going forth in the morning to confront the forces of evil arrayed against him. There is an obvious analogy with getting up in the morning and putting on one's clothes. It is also reminiscent of the marvellous account of Cú Chulainn binding on himself his 27 battle tunics, his battle girdle and his various aprons as he embarks on the terrible massacre 'Brisleach Mhór Mhuirtheimhne (O'Rahilly, C., *Táin Bó Cuailgne*, Dublin 1967, ll. 2205-2323).

Another view of the word *Atomriug* is that its root could be *ess-reg* (to arise), so that used reflexively it could mean something like 'I raise myself up.' The phrasing then would be: 'I raise myself up with the strength of Christ's birth and baptism', and so forth. Both of these interpretations are legitimate, and in the end, probably the best solution has been given by Professor P. L. Henry in his book *Saoithiúlacht na Sean-Ghaeilge*, Baile Átha Cliath 1978, 136:

> *Is é an chiall chéanna atá leis an dá leagan seo ar deireadh thiar: achainí ar na cumhachtaí ósnádúrtha agus ar na dúile faoi mar atá i gcuid mhaith dánta eile, teacht i gcabhair ar an bpersona. De bhrí go mbaineann iltagairt le nósmhaireacht na luathlitríochta is cóir glacadh leis an dá dhearcadh seo i dteannta a chéile: tar éis an tsaoil, ní gan tuiscint ar an tSean-Ghaeilge a chum an file an dán* (In the last analysis, the two versions have the same meaning: a request that the supernatural powers, and the elements, come to

the help of the person – a theme that is found in many other poems. Because of the fact that multi-reference is a feature of the early literature, it is right to put these two views together; after all, it was not without understanding of Old Irish that the poet composed the poem)

In the light, then, of the suggestion of an 'Ongoing Creation Scenario', we can visualise the person putting on his spiritual protective armour in the morning and setting out to co-operate with God in the continuous construction of the world, unhindered by the forces of disintegration. In this way he is building on earth the 'City of God', a place of peace and harmony, a place of integration of a multitude of diverse elements, as surely as the medieval builder working on a great medieval cathedral whose archetype was the 'Heavenly Jerusalem', *Urbs Jerusalem Beata*.

This ancient tradition of the *Lúireach* or protection prayer has continued down to our own day in different forms.

In the traditional *Commendation Animae* recited over the dying by the priest, a great Jewish prayer was used in a slightly adapted form as, for instance in the invocations:

Save, O Lord, your servant, as you saved Noah from the flood;
Save, O Lord, your servant, as you saved Isaac from the hand of his father Abraham;
Save, O Lord, your servant, as you saved Daniel in the lion's den;
Save, O Lord, your servant, as you saved the three young men in the fiery furnace.

In all of these biblical cases, the subject was in grave danger, placed in an impossible position from which he had no hope of escape, and yet, at the last moment God intervened and saved him. The prayer asks that God will intervene and rescue the dying person here and now just as, long ago, he intervened to rescue Noah, Isaac and the others. This type of *Lúireach* is called 'paradigmatic', as it shows two different situations, widely separated from each other, brought together in a parallel position.

This same type of prayer formula is preserved in modern Irish in such folk-prayers as: '*Saor mé, a Thiarna, mar a shaor tú Noa ón díle; an triúr ón bhfoirnéis lasrach; Donall an fáidh ó fhala na leon'*, etc. (Ó Laoghaire, D., *Ár bPaidreacha Dúchais*, BÁC, 1975, 383). (Deliver me, O Lord, as you saved Noah from the flood, the three from the fiery furnace, Daniel, the prophet, from the fury of the lions.)

Subjects such as these 'belong to a very old set of represent-ations which occurs in the paintings of the catacombs of Rome' (Henry, F., *Irish High Crosses*, Dublin 1964, 35) and they are found again depicted on the Irish High Crosses of Arboe, Moone, Donaghmore, Monasterboice and others. It is suggested that the sculptures were once painted, which would cause the various scenes to stand out more prominently than they do today.

Sections of the *Lúireach* type of prayer, such as those in St Patrick's Breastplate, suggest the *Reacht aigeanta* or revelation of God in nature in addition to his revelation of himself in the Bible and in the incarnation. Striking and awesome pictures of nature are chosen, such as 'the light of the sun, the shining of the moon, the speed of lightening and the wind, the depth of the sea, the firmness of land and the stability of rock'. This is the language of the experience of exposure to nature in both its benevolent and terrifying forms and this experience portrayed something of the nature of God. One wonders if the authors were thinking of some places where nature expressed itself in a particularly dramatic and awesome way as in Sceilg Mhichíl (Skellig Rock) off the coast of Kerry. The extreme isolation and exposure to the elements, along with the well-preserved beehive huts and monastic chapels, speak of a different form of monasticism from that of the more urbanised type found elsewhere in the West.

Little is known of the history of Sceilg; if, for instance, it were occupied all the year round or only seasonally when the weather was less severe. As well has being a monastery, it remained a place of pilgrimage for ordinary people until relatively recently and it was believed that one could avoid the pains of purgatory by performing the extremely demanding and dangerous climb through the perilous rocks, past the 'Stone of Pain' and the 'Eye of the Needle' to the summit several hundred feet above the raging sea. This is somewhat similar to Cú Chulainn's journey to the Land of Scáthach, for the gods and goddesses of 'Shadow-Land' did not give away their gifts easily. They made Cú Chulainn earn them the hard way. From the summit, the terrifying 700 feet drop lurks below. The pilgrim knows that one tiny error in movement could hurl him or her into the sea.

When one contemplates the sheer physical danger of this exercise, it is easy to see the pilgrimage to Sceilg Mhichíl as a 'Threshold Experience' in which, having overcome the enormous difficulties of the way the pilgrim arrives at the final or catastrophic point, he stands on the threshold of life and death, of this world and the otherworld. One or the other is a real present possibility. One might even wonder if such an experience is more severe on the subject than it sometimes is in the case of a real death, as often the dying person seems to be only semi-conscious and not entirely aware of his position on the threshold. On Sceilg, however, the pilgrim is fully aware. He certainly wouldn't have negotiated the perilous climb to the summit without having all his wits about him. Here he is poised between time and eternity. This must have been the supreme mind-expanding experience. No rationalistic exercise here, no provision of a man-made sanctuary, no contrived ritual and props but an overwhelming happening provided by a spectacular natural arrangement of rock and sea, of sun and wind, of height and depth, the stark confrontation of two worlds. It was the great religious experience of the 'Eleusinian Mysteries' of ancient Greece without the urbanisation.

This type of religious experience, in which the person is brought into dramatic contact with a supernatural dimension, must have had an intense religious effect. Perhaps, in the pre-Celtic culture of Brú na Bóinne and other megalithic sites, as well as in other cultures, the same effect was brought about by means of intense ritual exercise, prolonged dancing and use of hallucinogenic herbs.

While the *clocháin* or beehive huts and chapels belong to the Christian era, possibly the ninth century, the Christian pilgrimage may well have been a continuation of a pre-Christian institution. Whether the stone huts were used by a monastic community or by pilgrims delayed on the island by bad weather, or by both groups, is unknown.

Some miles further south from Sceilg Mhichíl there is another

similar rock emerging from the sea. This is well-known in tradition as *Tech nDoinn*, the 'House of Donn'. Donn is the god of the
dead and to him all the dead come after their death. This is the
same Donn spoken of earlier in connection with Cnoc Fírinne in
Co Limerick. There he is known as 'Donn Fírinne'. He probably
corresponds to the *Dis Pater* mentioned by Caesar – the god of the
dead from whom the Celts claimed they were descended, so that
when they died they, as it were, returned to their father's house.
Fishermen on the Kerry coast maintained that they were aware of
the souls of the dead being transported to *Tech nDoinn*.

It is here that the suggested connection with St Michael occurs.
St Michael in the tradition of the Catholic Church is associated
with high places on the sea, places such as Monte Gargano, Mont
St Michel, St Michael's Mount in Cornwall and Sceilg Mhichíl. He
is usually depicted as a 'dragon-fighter' in recognition of his role
in driving Lucifer and his followers out of heaven in the rebellion
of the angels. But fighting dragons is not his only role.

He is equally well known as a 'psychopomp', that is the
archangel who leads the souls of the dead into paradise. After the
Old Testament saints had been released from their underworld
prison by the Risen Christ in the *Argain Ifrinn* or destruction of hell
episode, it is St Michael who leads them into heaven. He is intimately connected with the transportation of souls from this world
to paradise.

Now, Sceilg Mhichíl conforms to tradition as a dramatic rock formation jutting out of the sea. But its position relative to this other rock formation (*Tech nDoinn*) jutting out of the sea in proximity to it suggests that there
may have been another reason why the church set up a monastic foundation here. The church may have set up a religious centre in this inhospitable
situation and named it after St Michael as an act of rivalry to the pagan god
Donn. Donn and St Michael were both psychopomps, they were both, as it
were, engrossed in the same business – the conducting of souls to the
Otherworld. So, it may be that the Christians set up their own man on
Sceilg to counteract the influence of Donn who was intent on bringing
souls to his own paradise of *Tír na nÓg*, the Land of Youth, where the blacksmith god Goibniu distributed the magic drink which kept the drinkers
perpetually young.

Since the manuscripts, if they ever existed, have vanished, we have to fill up the blank spaces by considering the general tradition of the area. When one looks at those two stark rock formations jutting out of the turbulent sea, Sceilg to the west of Ballinskelligs and *Teach nDoinn* (Bull Rock) to the west of Dursey Island, it is easy, indeed, to imagine the two mighty warriors Michael and Donn engaged in single combat in the 'psychomachia' or war of souls, a battle that continues for ever as two great forces contend for the destiny of mankind. As the Easter Liturgy puts it: *Mors et vita duello, conflixere mirando*. (Together, death and life in a strange conflict strove). A person looking out at this violent area of sea separating the two sites can well imagine it as a great battlefield where St Michael still fights the dragon.

It may be no accident that from the Uíbh Rathach Peninsula looking out over this very area of the ocean, a quite remarkable and perhaps unique ritual of the dead and dying is recorded.

Nuair a bheadh duine a' fáil bháis do shocrófaí ar phláta dhá cheann déag do bhuaieasaí, déanta do (de) chuinnil chéarach bheannuithe, agus do lasfaí iad le hagha' an bháis, agus bheifí á leogaint timpal air. Thosnófaí le n-a cheann, agus leogfaí timpal an pláta nao n-uaire, agus fé mar a bheifí á leogaint timpal dearadh na haenne as béal a chéile: 'Dia 'gus Muire, agus Micheál Naofa, 'gus a' dá Aspol déag teacht i gcoinnibh t'anama (Béaloideas 11, Uimh IV, Nodlaig 1930, 395).*

(When a person was dying, they would fix twelve pieces of a wax candle which had been blessed on a plate and they would be lighted for the death rite, and they would be taken around the dying person nine times, beginning at his/her head. And while they were being taken around him/her everybody would say all together: 'May God and Mary and St Michael and the twelve apostles be coming to meet your soul').

The meaning of the rite is quite clear from the formula: it is an invitation to God, the Virgin Mary, St Michael the psychopomp and the twelves apostles to come and meet the departing soul and transport it to heaven.

The light-bearer, in all probability, went around *deiseal*, keeping the bed at his/her righthand side, following the course of the sun in the Celtic manner. By following the course of the sun one put one-self into harmony with the cosmos. That is the way things were done in the sky and that is how they should be done on earth. It is not unlike the prayer, 'Thy will be done on earth as it is in heaven.'

The ecclesiastical counterpart of this ritual is found in the funeral liturgy when the celebrant circumambulates the coffin while sprinkling it with holy water and then, going around it again while incensing it. In the ecclesiastical manner, he goes around *tuathal*, that is anticlockwise, against the sun, and this may be a 'banishing rite' or purification ritual to disperse any negative forces in the area. In the Coptic Rite, for instance, the celebrant re-cites the psalm 'Arise, O Lord, and let your enemies be scattered' as he scatters clouds of incense smoke around the altar.

Again, at the funeral, the coffin will be taken around the grave-yard, *deiseal* before burial.

CHAPTER FIFTEEN

Ancient Religions of Ireland

When we think of the vast period of time that has passed between us today and the megalithic builders of Brú an Bóinne and so many other sites, we realise that the religious vocabulary we use comes from a later period and may not express very clearly the religious mores of such ancient times.

In the Catholic and Orthodox churches the 'Creed' ('I believe in one God, the Father, the Almighty, maker of heaven and earth, of all that is, seen and unseen', etc.) is very important. It expresses, in short, clear, succinct form, the faith of the church. In the Greek Orthodox Church (Byzantine Rite) which I attend occasionally, during the Divine Liturgy (Mass) the Creed is first recited in Greek, and it is indeed a moving experience to hear the old theological terms in the language of the great Ecumenical Councils of the early church. Then somebody from the congregation recites the Creed in Slavonic, English, and one or two other languages while all listen attentively knowing that the same faith is being expressed by all even though they differ in language and culture.

It is estimated that the first inhabitants of Ireland arrived as early as about 9,000 BC from Scotland and began their lives in the north of Ireland, gradually spreading to other areas and leaving certain traces in the Dingle Peninsula, Lambey Island, and along the shores of Lough Voora and Lough Derraveragh. These first inhabitants must have been few in number and belonged to the 'hunter-gatherer' type of society who depended on the wild animals and wild fruits and berries for their food. Following the animals they moved from place to place without setting up permanent dwellings or religious buildings so that there are only scant remains of this prehistoric group (Malone, K., *Discovering Ancient Ireland*, Dublin, 2110, 17) Like some present day groups of gatherers, they may have developed a highly sophisticated knowledge of berries, roots and herbs rivalling in nutritional value the common foods of today.

Since so little remains, there is no real knowledge of their religious ideas or system. Nevertheless, from comparison with hunter-gatherer groups of today, and from hints in folkloric remains, it may be surmised, as has already been pointed out, that by the very character of their lifestyle, dependance on nature, reciprocal giving and receiving, a mentality which was intensely aware of receiving everything they had from nature and when they died, the exposure of the body to the forest to be devoured and returned to nature – paying one's dues to nature as we have already seen in discussing the archaic rite of hunting the wren. It is surmised that this absolutely basic religious concept in which nature was seen as the great universal Divinity who gave and took away was expressed at a late historical period in the death of King William Rufus of England and lasts on in Christianity as a fundamental principle. Strangely, in Irish, God is known as *Rí na nDúl* – King of the Elements (earth, air, fire and water).

One wonders if there is some connection here with the ancient tradition of the triple death – by wounding / strangling, burning and drowning, as in the case of King Muircheartach Mac Earca. The king was wounded by demons, the roof was on fire and falling down on him so that he jumped into a vat of wine and was drowned. Finally, the clerics buried what was left of him in the graveyard of Dulane near Kells, so that it might be argued that three became four and that nature expressed in its fourfold manifestation took him back to itself in a dramatic manner. In this case, of course, unlike that of William Rufus, the King was not a willing victim.

Some would argue that, in this climate of total recognition of nature as universal giver and universal receiver, religion was at its purest, devoid of assumptions of personal independence. Teamwork must have been vital for the hunting of wild deer and wild pigs and the general good of the group came before that of any individual person. Perhaps, as a simple image of this age, we could visualise a great stag with massive antlers standing among the trees of the forest challenging his pursuers.

This scenario began to change fundamentally with the arrival, five or six thousand years ago, of a new people with a new and very different culture. These were the people of the Neolithic or New Stone Age. With them came a new and very different way of life.

They were farmers, and they understood the process of clearing the land of trees and preparing it for the cultivation of basic crops such as wheat, oats and barley. They understood the domestication and herding of cattle, sheep, pigs and goats. They fenced off fields for grazing their stock and no doubt, in a smaller way, continued to hunt wild animals and collect wild fruits whenever possible. It is unlikely that a rigid division between two forms of living occurred abruptly. The many accounts of deer hunting in the *Fiannaíocht* of a much later date, and even the fox hunting of the present day, indicate that the tradition was never really forgotten. What a strange coincidence it is too that the great fox hunting occasion is St Stephen's Day (26 December), the Winter Solstice, the day of the hunting of the wren whose significance we have already discussed.

At any rate, the people of the New Stone Age changed the face of Ireland by the introduction of settled, stable farming communities, some living in individual farmsteads, as today, and some in what we would call villages giving easy access to the surrounding land. They introduced pottery and field systems. It was the beginning of agriculture as we know it today. They had the distinct advantage that the climate was much warmer and drier than it is now. Under the new economy, food could be stored for the winter months and some leisure time made available for the pursuance of non-food production activity.

For perhaps the first time in the history of the world, with the introduction of agriculture in the Neolithic Age, man achieved some kind of precarious independence, as food could be produced during many months of the year and stored for the 'hungry months'. He wasn't entirely at the mercy of the hunt which could be successful or unsuccessful. Perhaps the many images of a 'horned god', *Cernunos*, or 'The Green Man' or *Fear Coille* or *Dearg Corra* suggest a semi-animal-human god, with, for instance, a human body but a stag's antlers on his head, a supplier of food to animals and to men. Perhaps there was some kind of acknowledged relationship between the animals and man in which an animal allowed himself to be killed, on occasion, on the understanding that the hunter would also surrender himself, at the end, to the animal. If such a mystical relationship between the hunter and the hunted existed, so that they formed a partnership in the drama of existence, then that arrangement was largely shattered at the coming of the Neolithic Age. With his new control over food production and storage, he was no longer completely dependant on the animals and he proceeded to the taming and domestication of herds. By constructing enclosed pastures he excluded the animals except for those he had domesticated. But even as late as the early twentieth century, when herds were much smaller than today, individual cows were often treated affectionately and given names such as 'Daisy', 'Brownie', etc. When herds increased enormously and electric fences arrived, this type of relationship vanished and the herd became a product.

It would seem that at a very early period, at the introduction of the Neolithic, a new mindset appeared mirroring the new way of life with its greater control over nature. Some would say that the great Megalithic Age, with its mighty achievements in agriculture, astronomy and architecture, was still a period of religious decline because it was losing its feeling of dependency on nature and moving towards domination rather than partnership.

On the other hand, as we have seen, the Neolithic Age was a period of great expansion in agriculture and clearly defined territories, with a megalithic structure of some kind marking a specific territory. Moreover, some of the impressive remains from this period indicate a new orientation towards the sky rather than towards the wood as in the earlier hunting period.

Monuments from the Neolithic period (c. 4000-2000 BC) proliferate in Ireland. They are of various kinds such as Passage Tombs, in which a covered passage of standing stones leads to an inner chamber in which the cremated remains of the dead were laid. The whole is covered with a mound of earth and stone. Newgrange is a world-famous example of this kind of monument.

Another well-known type of tomb is the Court Tomb, very common in the northern part of the country. In this type of large stone monument, a semicircle of stones surrounds the entrance and this may have been the area where funeral rites were performed before interment.

The Portal Tomb is also well known. Here, a large capstone, often of enormous size and weight, is supported by smaller stones like the legs of a table. But very often the huge stone is not flat, as one would expect, but slopes upwards towards the entrance like the stance of a bird. The name *cromleac* – bent stone – is often appropriately given to this type of structure.

Another very prominent type of funerary monument is the so-called Wedge Tomb, as its shape resembles that of a wedge, wide at one end and tapering to a lower and narrower end. This type of tomb is common in the western half of the country.

Then there are the *Galláin* or mysterious individual standing stones, stone rows and stone circles which lead into the Bronze Age and the arrival of metals. J. H., Brennan's *A Guide to Megalithic Ireland* (London 1994) is most useful to anyone visiting the various sites.

As regards the interpretation of the monuments of the Megalithic period, while much remains obscure and uncertain, the *Banais Rí*, or wedding of the Sky-Father to Earth-Mother seems to stand out as a marker of man's effort to create a theatre in which a cosmic drama is enacted annually with the purpose of keeping the Universe in its accustomed motion and guaranteeing a fruitful earth. Death, re-birth, the cult of Ancestors, a journey of the dead to the region of the circumpolar stars hint at an incredible religious awareness of man's relation to the cosmos.

While Brú na Bóinne and Sliabh na Caillí (Loughcrew) are the great centres of the 'Sky-Earth Drama', the fact that this area is comprised of very rich agricultural land may have its own significance, and was perhaps instrumental in allowing large numbers of people to be free to undertake the construction of such massive monuments.

But what of less favoured areas throughout the country where megalithic monuments occur but on a much more modest scale?

Could it be that the 'Holy Well', of which there are more than a thousand known in the country, should be included as a possible, though not constructed, component of the megalithic liturgical cycle?

Could the Holy Well, with its female associations, be aligned with the sun, as in Newgrange, for the performance of the *Banais Rí*? Instead of the grandiose performance of the wealthy community of Brú na Bóinne, could not a more humble wedding of the Sky-Father and the Earth-Mother, of An Daghdha and Bóinn, take place for a small, struggling megalithic community lacking in resources, with the Well as the goddess of the land? Not every wedding is a Royal Wedding. This would give a central place to the Holy Well in a local megalithic landscape with features such as tombs and standing stones in close proximity. This line of enquiry opens up and enormous field of research. Why is it that some wells are 'Holy Wells' at which sacred rites are performed at a sacred day of the calendar, while other wells in the same locality are regarded as ordinary wells and used for ordinary domestic purposes? Other questions arise such folkloric traditions of the sun shining into the well at a certain time, a skull being thrown into the well, etc. Presumably, the stone covers and entrance walls which are common at Holy Wells today are modern constructions, but could they, in some instances, replace a primitive path of orientation? And what of the calendrical date on which the people gather to perform the *turas* or ritual pilgrimage? Is it a significant date such as Winter Solstice, Summer Solstice, Spring Equinox, Autumn Equinox; Samhain, Imbolc, Bealtaine and Lughnasa? Then, did the *Banais Rí* take place at the same date (eg the Winter Solstice as at Newgrange) or could it take place at a different date at a different site? Questions such as these show the enormous amount of research which still remains to be done. As it is, some Holy Wells are so deep that steps lead down to the water, so that if exposure to the sun took place, the sun would have to be high in the heavens. If only we had a few clearly marked sites where all or most of the elements were present – a Holy Well at which the ritual was performed annually; a significant calendrical date; a Megalithic Tomb; a Cursus; *Galláin*; Leylines; Orientations;

etc, then, the way of understanding and interpretation would be advanced.

Perhaps a unique case is that of the Stone Circles, Stone Rows and Cairns of Beaghmore in the Sperrin Mountains near Cookstown, Co Tyrone, in which a bog grew up and preserved the stones in their original shape and position so that this massive Neolithic Bronze Age and very mysterious site can be viewed today as it must have appeared to those who performed rituals there thousands of years ago. The site is brilliantly described by Cary Meehan in her invaluable book *Sacred Ireland* (Gothic Image, 2002).

How did this great megalithic civilisation, with its apparent cosmic awareness, cult of ancestors and rest for the souls of the dead among the circumpolar stars, come to an end so that only vestiges remain?

Some would say that a devastating earthquake occurred in Iceland which caused a blanket of opaque dust, obscuring the sun, to cover vast areas of the northern world, including Ireland, about 2000 BC.

The climate underwent a disasterous change for the worse, giving something of the cold wet weather we are so familiar with today. In this situation, the fertility of the land declined and with it the certainties of the old religion, to leave the sacred sites lonely and abandoned on the wind-swept landscape.

The superb megalithic monument of Brú na Bóinne, Newgrange, with its calendrical connection to the sky and the megalithic religion, leads on to the next religious layer, that of the Tuatha Dé Danann (peoples of the goddess Dana) or *Aos Sí* (people of the hollow hills). In English, these are often called 'fairies', though this term with its connotation of diminutive, gossamer-winged creatures, hardly corresponds to the powerful, immortal Tuatha whose mother is Dana whose breasts are outlined in *Dá Chíoch Dhanann* (the Paps) in the two adjacent hills near Killarney. Here, the great goddess of fertility is portrayed in the landscape for all to see. The Tuatha Dé Danann occupy a highly significant place in the religious lore of Ireland, in both literature and folklore, and traces of *An Creideamh Sí* (the faith of the hollow hills), or *Bunadh na gCnoc* (the people of the hills) last on until the present day. An important effect of this ancient and widespread religion is the preservation of ancient monuments intact which might otherwise be destroyed, as it was a firm belief that these sacred places belonged to the *Aos Sí* and any damage done to them by humans would be avenged. Archeologists and conservationists can look on the Tuatha Dé Danann as their greatest friends. The folklore of this area cites the case of a farmer who destroyed a fairy mound and was banished from house and home by the local *Bean Sí*, Gráinne Óg.

While the *Creideamh Sí* is generally associated with the later Celts, nevertheless the older monuments belonging to the megalithic people, and especially Brú na Bóinne, are filled with Celtic gods and goddesses: An Daghdha/Eochaidh Ollathair; Aonghus Óg; Manannán Mac Lir; Midhir; Fionnbharra; Eithne; Bóinn; Curcóg.

The magnificent and emotionally charged story, *Altram Tige dá Medar'* from the 15th-century 'Book of Fermoy' (*Ériu* X1 – Part 11; 1932; 184-225) tells of the descent of the Tuatha Dé Danann gods and goddesses into the *Síthe* or hollow hills and prehistoric monuments after their defeat by the Celts at the Battles of Tailltean and Drom Lighean.

Manannán Mac Lir, the god of the sea, seems to have had overall control of the Tuatha Dé Dannann and appointed each one of the nobles to his own particular Sí, underground. In the Sí, the TDD carried on their divine lives, invisible to humans, but they could make themselves visible whenever they wanted to. The *Bean Sí*, for instance, who can be heard lamenting the aristocratic dead, may also make herself visible as a red-haired woman combing her hair. This invisibility is called *Feth Fiadha*. Like the human Celts, the Tuatha Dé Danann feasted on bacon. The *Muca Mhanannáin*, or pigs of Manannán, which they killed today, would be alive again tomorrow to be re-killed and so there was an unending supply of food. The *Fleadh Ghoibhneann*, or distribution of magic mead by the blacksmith god Goibhne, kept the *Aos Sí* forever young.

Manannán appointed Bodhbh Dearg, King of the Tuatha Dé

Danann to Sí Bhoidhbh, Midhir to Sí Throim, Sighmhall to Sí Neannta, Fionnbharr to Sí Mheadha, Lir to Sí Fhionnachaidh, Dearg Dianscothaidh to Sí Chleitigh and so for several other high-ranking members. A similar list of nobles and *síthe* can be found in *Toraíocht Dhiarmada agus Ghráinne*. A multitude of *síthe* is known throughout the country – Sí Áine, Sí Úna, Sí ar Feimhin, Sí Rua, Sí an Bhrú, etc. These are the 'cathedrals' of the Old Religion, the *Creideamh Sí*, scattered all over the country, and each of these is a local version of *Tír na nÓg*, the land of youth.

Other accounts, such as *Eachtra Thaidhg Mhic Chéin* say that a diet of apples and berries and the scent of flowers and vegetation sufficed for the food of the Tuatha Dé Danann.

The basic consideration, then, is that in Ireland as elsewhere, in pre-Rationalism times, a 'bi-cosmic' philosophy prevailed. There were two worlds, two population-groups, one human, the other supernatural, living side by side and constantly interacting with each other.

With the 18th century 'Enlightenment' and the advance of science to show that certain effects, once attributed to supernatural agents such as angels or demons or spirits, could be shown to be caused by purely natural forces, everything could be explained on a rational basis without calling in a supernatural world. Since the Enlightenment, the prevailing mindset of the West has moved from being 'bi-cosmic' to 'mono-cosmic', from the vision of two worlds to that of one world. Over the centuries, unusual events were thought of as having been caused by demons or spirits or some kind of supernatural intervention, often demanding placation. Now they could be explained by a rational examination of the forces within nature itself without going any further. Churchmen haven't always appreciated the immense significance for religion of this intellectual upheaval in the thinking process of the Western World. Even up to Vatican II in the 1960s the prayer of Pope Leo XIII,(1884), was recited after Low Mass. This expressed very clearly indeed the traditional bi-cosmic view of the Catholic Church regarding the life of humans on earth being surrounded and attacked by invisible supernatural beings such as Satan and his demons and being protected by the Archangel

Michael and his army of angels in the 'psychomachia' or continual battle for souls: 'Holy Michael, the Archangel defend us in the conflict; be our protection against the malice and snares of Satan. May God restrain him, we humbly pray, and do thou, O prince of the heavenly host, by the divine power, thrust into hell Satan and the other evil spirits who go about in this world seeking the ruin of souls.'

Here the bi-cosmic thinking of traditional Christianity and beyond it, is shown plainly in two different groups of invisible spirits at war, as they try to gain possession of visible humans. It has been suggested that this battle is portrayed in the sea-location of Sceilg Mhichíl and *Tech nDoinn* off the coast of Kerry where Michael, the Christian psychopomp, battles eternally with the Pagan psychopomp Donn for the souls of the human dead.

Similarly, at the celebrated Battle of Moytura (*Cath Maighe Tuireadh*) two opposing groups of Spirits, the Tuatha Dé Danann, or gods of light and prosperity, battle it out with the Fomhóraigh, or dark gods of the northern seas, for the possession of Ireland.

A recent author on Africa shows how the traditional areas of Africa, which have not come under European influence, have preserved the bi-cosmic mentality once common to vast areas of the world, in their belief in an alternative world close to their own human world, in which spirits and demons abound. He makes an interesting case for the imagined return of three world-famous characters to this African world of spirits and shows that they would be completely at ease in this bi-cosmic environment, as it corresponded to the type of worldview prevalent in their time and place. The three people are the Greek poet Homer, who would find himself at ease with the spirits of pre-scientific Africa. Similarly with Jesus Christ and with Shakespeare. But if these three had come to Europeanised Africa, or to Europe of today, they would not feel at ease, for the mentality of the present day is so utterly different from the bi-cosmic vision of their time.

The author gives an interesting little incident which occurred to him. As he was walking close to a river, a woman shouted a warning at him: 'Keep away from the river or the river-god will drag you in.'

The incident reminded me of the river Sulán in Cúil Aodha and Baile Bhóirne in West Cork. Unlike most Irish rivers, the Sulán is masculine and calls for a drowning once every seven years as a reward for the amount of fish given. As the time draws near, the river can be heard murmuring:

Is mise an Sulán fuar fada fireann,
anois an t-am, cá bhfuil mo dhuine?
(I am the cold, long, masculine Sulán,
now is the time, where is my victim?)

These examples illustrate the bi-cosmic world of *An Creideamh Sí,* a world in which humans formed only part of the population. The unseen population was made up of a variety of spirits, some good, some bad, some indifferent, but always dangerous. One had to be on one's guard and know and respect their ways and customs. Surrounded by the somewhat unpredictable *Aos Sí,* human life was dangerous but very, very exciting.

The connection of the *Aos Sí* (Tuatha Dé Danann) to the human population was very close, so that while one tried to ignore them, this wasn't always possible.

CHAPTER SIXTEEN

A Guided Tour of the Otherworld

A very fine exposition of the world of the Tuatha Dé Danann or *Aos Sí* and its interaction with humans is given in the story *Echtra Thaidhg Mhic Chéin* from the *Book of Lismore* (14th-15th century) (O' Grady, S., *Silva Gadelica*, Dublin 1892, Vol 1, 343-359).

Tadhg, a descendant of Oileall Ólom king of Munster, is travelling in West Munster when he is attacked by Cathmann king of Freisean. Some forty of Tadhg's warriors, his wife Lí Ban and his two brothers are abducted. Tadhg, with his remaining followers and a hostage they have captured from the marauders, set out in pursuit to retrieve their losses.

After various adventures in different islands on the way to Freisean, they eventually arrive at what in effect is *Tír na nÓg* (Land of Youth) or paradise of the Tuatha Dé Danann.

It is an idyllic island with a beautiful climate, magnificent trees and vegetation which give off a scent which satisfies hunger so that the inhabitants do not need to eat, except that they may partake of the magic apples, acorns and hazel nuts which grow there.

Beautiful woodland and the music of multicoloured birds soothe the senses.

While it is winter in Ireland, it is summer here.

They come to a blissful plain covered with dew of honey and in the distance they see three hills with a *dún* or fortress at the side of each one.

Here, a ravishingly beautiful woman appears who introduces herself as the daughter of Goithniad and welcomes Tadhg by name. She takes them on a guided tour of the island.

The island is called Inis Locha (*Inis Locha a sídaib*) – showing its connection with the *Aos Sí*.

One of the fortresses is the home of the royalty of Ireland, from Éireamon son of Míle to Conn Céadchathach who is the last to come. This is the Otherworld Residence of the kings of Ireland, who, although dead as humans, are alive among the *Aos Sí* in Inis Locha or Tír na nÓg and provided with palatial residences as befitting their royal status. After their human death, then, the kings are transferred to the Otherworld where they are alive again but under a different form to that which they had on earth. In these ancient stories, it is heroes, kings, queens and princes who are considered; little or no attention is given to ordinary people and their fate is left undetermined. Even the Bean Sí will cry only for the aristocracy. It should be remembered, of course, that we had so many kings in Ireland and that they had so many wives and mistresses, that the aristocracy may be much more extensive than we think. Nevertheless, it does seem that the process of democratisation was going ahead, and in the later folklore the ordinary people were becoming involved.

In another *dún*, they meet Ceasair, the first woman to come to Ireland with 50 women and 3 men – Fionntan, Ladhra and Bith. They came from Egypt to Ireland to escape the Flood but were eventually drowned and now they too are in Inis Locha. The story of this first invasion is told in *Leabhar Gabhála Éireann* (The Book of Invasions). The saints of Ireland are also accommodated in an island (*Inis Dearglocha*) within the island of Inis Locha. These are so holy and so close to God that the ordinary Tuatha Dé Danann cannot see them, just as ordinary humans cannot see the *Aos Sí*. It does seem that there is a hierarchical system of etherialisation in which the Tuatha Dé Danann recognise that the Irish saints are more spiritual than themselves. In the story *Altram Tige dá Medar* also, Manannán Mac Lir, the god of the sea, recognises that the God of the Christians is more powerful than the gods of the *Aos Sí*.

Another fortress contained the early invaders of Ireland: Parthalon, Neimheadh, Fir Bholg, Tuatha Dé Danann themselves and Clann Mhíle, as discussed in *Leabhar Ghabhála Éireann* also.

Inis Locha, the Tír na nÓg of the Tuatha Dé Danann, is a very comprehensive place able to embrace the Cristian heaven and the great sweep of the history of Éire from its most ancient times. What an extraordinary vision is contained here, in which the great figures of myth and history are gathered together in one place, and are all alive and able to discuss their varied past. Another royal residence awaits the future kings of Ireland who accept the Christian Faith. This includes Tadhg himself.

Then a famous pair of lovers appear, Connla, son of Conn Céadchathach, and Veniúsa. Veniúsa, in the ancient story, appears to Connla and persuades him to accompany her to Tír na nÓg. Connla, however, though passionately in love with the woman, is reluctant to leave his friends. She gives him one of the magic apples of Avalon (Tír na nÓg) and departs. The apple never diminishes and Connla finds that he is losing interest in the affairs of this world of humans. The woman returns after a month and this time Connla has no further hesitation. He steps into her crystal boat, a magic mist descends and they sail away to Avalon out of human sight. This pair appear to Tadhg who knows the Connla story of the *Leannán Sí* or fairy lover already. Connla is still eating his apple and it is explained that they derive all their happiness from gazing rapturously at each other without ever having sex – something which Tadhg finds difficult to understand: *'Is ait sin,' ar Tadhg'* (that's odd, said Tadhg). This and the fact that food is not necessary raises interesting questions about the nature of the etherial body after death.

Then the beautiful goddess Clíona appears, well-known in Co Cork from the place-names Tonn Chlíona and Carraig Chlíona and as Bean Sí of the MacCarthys, O'Callaghans and O'Keefes.

Clíona gives three beautiful birds to Tadhg whose singing will cure all sorrow and depression. She also gives him a magic cup which turns water into wine. When he loses this cup he will die. His death will come about by an attack by a deer followed by an onslaught by a foreigner, in a glen near Brú na Bóinne. It is there that his body will be buried.

Tadhg's soul, however, will come with Clíona to this place (Inis Locha) (*'ticfa th' anam lemsa conicce so.'*) And Tadhg will receive a light, aerial body around him after that, and they will be here until the day of judgement (*'ocus geba corp etrom aierda umat iar sin, ocus beimit sunna co la in mhesraigte.'*)

Now, this short passage is of significance as it comes to grips with the great mystery of life and death which is not only of historical but of personal importance to each of our individual selves: what happens after the heart has given its final beat?

The goddess Clíona assumes a position of enormous import- ance here as somehow being the arbiter of life and death. We have already seen that she is the Bean Sí of some of the royal families of Cork who wails at their deaths, so that she is intimately involved in the process of transition from one form of life to another.

In this account, the obvious distinction between soul and body is expressed. The soul (*anam*) keeps the body alive. When the soul departs the body dies. Only the inert bodily shell remains which soon begins to disintegrate. In this story, Clíona predicts that Tadhg's soul will leave his body after the attacks of the deer and the foreigner – in other words he will die – and this is perfectly clear as his lifeless body will be buried in a glen at Brú na Bóinne and a little hill will arise over his grave. So far, this is all perfectly clear from ordinary funeral practice today.

Tadhg's body goes into the grave to become dust. This is the end of the human body he had during his lifetime on earth. This site of his human experience is gone for ever, it is all over.

But the second factor involved in Tadhg's death is his soul, and this has not come to an end like his body. It has, however, depart- ed from Tadhg leaving his body inert, lifeless.

Now, where does the departing soul go? According to Clíona, she herself takes Tadhg's soul with her to Inis Locha or Tír na nÓg (*ocus ticfa th'anam lemsa*).

This is not unlike the rite of assisting the dying (*In Exspiratione*) in the *Rituale Romanum* – the book used by a Catholic Priest in ad- ministrating the sacraments.

Such was the sanctity and awe of this occasion, when the soul was taking its leave of the body, that the ancient church recom- mended that, where it was the custom, the bells of the parish church should be rung so that the faithful outside would join in prayer with those inside the death-chamber.

> *Egressa anima de corpore, statim dicatur hoc:*
> *Subvenite, Sancti Dei, occurite, Angeli Domini, Suscipentes ani- mam eius, Offerentes eam in conspectu Altissimi.*
> (When the soul has gone out of the body, immediately the fol-

lowing is said: Come to his/her aid, O saints of God. Hasten to meet him/her, O angels of the Lord. Take up his/her soul and present it in the sight of the Most High.)

In this intense drama, the angels and the saints are summoned to take charge of the departing soul and present it to God.

In *Eachtra Thaidhg Mhic Chéin*, however, it is Clíona, the Earth Spirit, of Spirit of Nature, who takes possession of the soul and carries it to Tír na nÓg.

It is then, apparently, that Tadhg's soul is clothed or covered with a light, ethereal body, so that, in Tír na nÓg, Tadhg's soul, which is immortal, now enlivens, gives life to a new and more spiritual type of body. Tadhg is alive and well again, in Tír na nÓg, and delighting in his new light, angelic type of body so different from his former heavy, vulnerable, awkward one. Whether this new spiritual body is Clíona's gift to Tadhg is uncertain.

The word *umat* (on you/around you) may indicate that Clíona puts the new etherial body around Tadhg's soul, wrapping his soul in it, so that his unchanged soul is now the life principle, or engine, driving a new, lighter and less material body.

Again, one may notice a similar scenario in the beautiful poetic expressions of the Preface for the Mass for the Dead in the *Missale Romanum*:

> *Tuis enim fidelibus, Domine, vita mutatur, non tollitur, et dissoluta terrestris hujus incolatus domo, aeterna in caelis habitatio comparatur.* (For, in the case of your faithful people, O Lord, life is changed, not taken away, and when this temporary, earthly, house is destroyed, an everlasting dwelling place is prepared for them in heaven.)

In the *Rituale Romanum* it is the saints, the spiritual ancestors of the Christians, along with the angels, who transport the soul of the dead person to heaven to deliver it into the hands of God: 'Into your hands, O God, I commit my spirit.' The spiritual ancestors act as psychopomps, conductors of souls, of whom St Michael the Archangel is the prime example in Catholic tradition.

In *Eachra Thaidhg* it is Clíona, the ancestral goddess of the kings of Munster, who acts as psychopomp, to bring the souls of the southern aristocracy to the special *Dún* or fortress of the Kings of Ireland in Inis Locha or Tír na nÓg, there to be fitted out, like Tadhg, with a light, ethereal body and so continue living in a new way, in a new environment.

The story expresses clearly the eschatological or otherworldly aspect of the ancestral goddess who takes care of her tribe both in this material world and in the world after death. After human death, her people are transferred to a new state where they live among the gods.

At last, Tadhg and his companions decide that it is time for them to leave the magic land of Inis Locha and be on their way to rescue Tadhg's wife and his followers from Cathmann, King of Freisean.

Clíona informs them that a year has passed, though they thought that it was only a single day. The abducted party must have given up all hope of rescue at this stage.

During this long period in Inis Locha Tadhg and his companions have had nothing to eat or drink, but have felt no hunger as they have been sustained by the scent of the various flowers growing in the island. They are sad to say goodbye to Clíona but the singing of the magic birds dissipates their sorrow. They sail away on the open sea and a magic mist descends behind them to hide Tír na nÓg from view.

Eventually, they arrive at the island of Freisean and attack Cathmann and his forces. After fierce fighting, Cathmann is killed. Tadhg and his followers win a great victory and appoint a new ruler. With his wife, Lí Ban, and followers, Tadhg Mac Céin returns victoriously to Ireland.

Bibliography

Abrahams, R., 'Folk Arts; Folk Drama', in; Dorson, R. (ed), *Folklore and Folklife: An Introduction* (Chicago 1972)

Bell, L., *Temples of Ancient Egypt* (London 2005)
Bord, J. and C., *Sacred Waters* (London 1985)
Brennan, M., *The Stones of Time* (Vermont 1994)
Brennan, J., *A Guide to Megalithic Ireland* (London 1994)

Campbell, J., *Primitive Mythology* (Penguin 1976)
Carney, J. (ed), *The Poems of Blathmac Son of Cu Brettan* (Dublin 1964)
Carroll, K., *Yoruba Religious Carving* (London 1967)
Carmichael, A., *Carmina Gadelica* (Edinburgh 1940)
Chevalier, J., *Symbols* (London 1996)
Colgan, J., *Triadis Thaumaturgae* (Lovanii 1947)
Collins, A., *The Cygnus Mystery* (London 2008)
Concannon, M., *The Sacred Whore: Sheela Goddess of the Celts* (Cork 2004)
Cooper, Q. and Sullivan, P., *Maypoles, Martyrs and Mayhem* (London 1994)

Dalton, J.P., *Cromm Cruaich of Magh Sléacht* (PRIA 1922, Sect C, 23-67)
Dames, M., *Mythic Ireland* (London 1992)
Dames, M., *The Avebury Cycle* (London 1977)
Danaher, K., *The Year in Ireland* (Cork 1972)
De Bhaldraithe, T., *Cín Lae Amhlaoidh* (Baile Átha Cliath 1976)
Devereux, P. and Thompson, I., *The Ley Hunters Companion* (London 1979)
Dineen, P., *Foclóir Gaedhilge agus Béarla* (Dublin 1927)

Eliade, M. (ed), *The Encyclopedia of Religion* (New York 1987)

Frazer, J., *The Golden Bough* (London 1923)

Gimbutas, M., *The Goddesses and Gods of Old Europe* (London 1989)
Green, M., *Symbol and Image in Celtic Religious Art* (London 1992)
Grey, E., *Cath Maige Tuired* (Dublin 1982)

Hazlitt, W., *Dictionary of Faiths and Folklore* (London 1905 / 1995)
Henry, *Irish High Crosses* (Dublin 1964)
Heselton, P., *Leylines* (London 1999)

James, E., *Seasonal Feasts and Festivals* (London 1961)
James, E., *The Beginnings of Religion* (London 1958)
Jones, C., *Temples of Stone* (Cork 2007)

Kennedy, P., *Folksongs of Britain and Ireland* (London 1975)
Kettle, J., *The Athelsons* (London 1974)
Killip, M., *The Folklore of the Isle of Man* (London 1986)
King, A., *Liturgies of the Primatial Sees* (London 1957)
Krupp, E., *Skywatchers, Shamans and Kings* (New York 1997)

Layard, J., *Stone Men of Malekula* (London 1942)
Lefebvre,G., *St Andrew's Daily Missal* (Bruges 1945)
Logan, P., *The Holy Wells of Ireland* (Gerrards Cross 1980)

Macalister, R., *Lebor Gabála Érenn/The Book of the Taking of Ireland* (Dublin 1938)
MacCana, P., *Celtic Mythology* (London 1970)
MacDonagh, S., *Green and Gold: The Wren Boys of Dingle* (Brandon Press 1983)
Mackenzie, W., *Gaelic Incantations: Charms and Blessings of the Hebrides* (Inverness 1895)
MacNeill, M., *The Festival of Lughnasa* (Dublin 1982)
Maier, B., *Dictionary of Celtic Religion and Culture* (Woodbridge 2000)
Malone, K., *Discovering Ancient Ireland* (Dublin 2010)
Meehan, C., *The Traveller's Guide to Ancient Ireland* (Gothic Image 2002)

Moynihan, *Sliabh Luachra Milestones* (Crede: Sliabh Luachra

Heritage Group 2003)

Murphy, A. and Moore, R., *Island of the Setting Sun* (Dublin 2006)

Murphy, G., *Early Irish Lyrics* (Oxford 1956)

Ní Chleirigh, M. (eag), *Eachtra na gCuradh* (Baile Átha Cliath 1941)

Ní Shé, N., *Toraíocht Dhiarmada agus Ghráinne* (Baile Átha Cliath 1971)

Ó Baoill, S. agus M., *Ceolta Gael* (Baile Átha Cliath 1975 / 1986)

O'Connor, P., *Beyond the Mist* (London 2000)

Ó Crualaioch, G., *The Book of the Cailleach* (Cork 2003)

Ó Duinn, S., *Orthaí Cosanta sa Chráifeacht Cheilteach* (Maigh Nuad 1990)

Ó Duinn, S., *Forbhais Droma Dámhgháire: The seige of Knocklong* (Cork 1992)

O'Flaherty, W., *The Rig Veda* (Penguin 1981)

Ogilvie, R., *The Romans and their Gods* (London 1986)

O'Grady, S., *Silva Gadelica* (Dublin 1892)

Ó Laoghaire, D., *Ár bPaidreacha Dúchais* (Baile Átha Cliath 1975)

Ó Loinsigh, E., *An Táin* (Baile Átha Cliath 1989)

O Kelly, C., *Illustrated Guide to Newgrange* (1971)

Ó hÓgáin, D., *Myth, Legend and Romance* (New York 1991)

O'Rahilly, C. (ed), *Táin Bó Cualgne* (Dublin 1967)

O'Rahilly, C., *Five Seventeenth Century Political Poems* (Dublin 1977)

Plummer, C., *Miscellanea Hagiograpgica Hibernica* (Bruxelles 1925)

Pollack, R., *The Body of the Goddess* (London 2003)

Purcell, D. and Blake, L., *Lough Derg* (Dublin 1988)

Radford, E., *The Encyclopedia of Superstitions* (Oxford 1995)

Raya, J., *Byzantine Missal* (Birmingham, Alabama 1958)

Roberts, J., *Exploring West Cork* (Clonakilty 1989)

Rundle Clark, R., *Myths and Symbols in Ancient Egypt* (London 1959)

Smith, H., *The World's Religions* (San Francisco 1991)

Smyth, D., *A Guide to Mythology* (Dublin 1988)
Stokes, W., *Three Irish Glossaries* (London 1862)
Stokes, W. and Strachan, J., *Thesaurus Paleohibernicus*, Vol 2 (Cambridge 1903)
Strachan, J., *Old Irish Paradigms* (Dublin 1949)
Stout, G., *Newgrange and the Bend of the Boyne* (Cork 2002)

Taylor, I., *The Giant of Penhill* (York 1987)
Thurian, M. and Wainsright, G., *Baptism and Eucharist: Ecumenical Convergence in Celebration* (Geneva 1983)
Tierney, J., *The Celtic Ethnography of Posidonius* (Dublin 1960)
Tolhurst, J. (ed), *The Ordinale and Customary of the Benedictine Nuns of Barking Abbey* (London 1927)

Vendreyes, J. (ed), *Airne Fíngein* (Dublin 1953)
Vilebsky, P. and Humphrey, C., *Sacred Architecture* (London 1997)
Villianey, C., *Immortality* (London 1926)

Wallace-Murphy, T., *Cracking the Symbol Code* (London 2005)
Wilde, W., *Irish Popular Superstitions* (Dublin 1853)
Williams, C. agus Ní Mhuiríosa, M., *Traidisiún Liteartha na nGael* (Baile Átha Cliath 1979)

Index